Travel and Tourism

for BTEC National Award, Certificate & Diploma

Book Two

Ray Youell

t and t
publishing
.co.uk

Published by Travel and Tourism Publishing Limited.

www.tandtpublishing.co.uk
info@tandtpublishing.co.uk

First published 2005

British Library Cataloguing in Publication Data is available from the British Library on request.
ISBN 0 9550190 1 X

Designed and typeset by Jenks at Cambrian Printers
Cover design image courtesy of Airtours plc
Printed in the UK by Cambrian Printers, Aberystwyth

Table of Contents

Note: Unit numbers exactly follow the Edexcel specifications

Acknowledgements

I am grateful for the help and support of many individuals and organisations in completing this book. Thanks to Arabella Stewart for help with researching photos and Jenks and the team at Cambrian Printers who handled the typescript very professionally. But, as always, the biggest thanks go to Sue, Megan and Owen.

The publishers extend thanks to the following for granting permission to reproduce images throughout the book:

Arabella Stewart

Association of British Travel Agents (ABTA)

Association of Train Operating Companies (ATOC)

Boeing Corporation

British Airports Authority (BAA)

British Museum

Canvas Holidays

Carlson Wagonlit Travel

Cunard Line

Delta Airlines

Eden Project

Exodus Travel

Glasgow Airport

Henley Regatta

Himalayan Kingdoms (www.himalayankingdoms.com)

Hull Trains

InterContinental Hotels Group

Jorvik Viking Centre in York

Keycamp

Legoland Windsor

Manchester United plc

National Express

Norwegian Cruise Line (NCL)

Ocean Village

Outward Bound Trust

P&O Cruises

Sampson Lloyd/St Paul's Cathedral

SSPL/Science Museum

St David's Hotel and Spa, Cardiff

Stagecoach

Sustrans

Thomas Cook

Travelsphere

Virgin Balloons

VisitBritain

Warwick Castle

World Tourism Organisation

Introduction

Exactly matched to the BTEC National specifications, this book builds on the units included in Book 1 (ISBN 0955019001), giving you a range of specialist option units needed to complete the BTEC National Certificate or BTEC National Diploma in Travel and Tourism.

How to use this book

Each unit includes:

1. An introductory page – giving details of the content and assessment for the unit;
2. Clearly-labelled sections – exactly covering the specification content for the unit;
3. Activities – based on the assessment criteria to help you learn more;
4. Focus on industry – short practical statements of how the travel and tourism industry implement key topics in the unit;
5. Weblinks – Internet links to organisations and topics in the unit;
6. Case studies – longer examples of organisations and topics included in the unit, with questions to expand your knowledge;
7. Unit summary – concise overview of key topics covered in the unit;
8. Test questions at the end – to build your knowledge of what's been covered in the unit;
9. A sample assignment – covering all the grading criteria for the unit.

About tandtONLine

Everybody who buys this book can register for free access to tandtONLine, a brand new web resource for travel and tourism students and staff. It gives you a host of extra features that are regularly updated by academic staff and industry experts, including:

- Latest news from the travel and tourism industry;
- Key statistics on UK, European and global tourism;
- Glossary of common terms and key definitions;
- Links to useful websites;
- Top tips for students on completing assignments;
- Extra staff teaching resources linked to textbooks (PowerPoint slides, worksheets, links to websites featured in the book, suggestions for extra reading, etc.).

Register by going to www.tandtonline.co.uk and completing the online registration form using the unique book code found on the inside back cover of this book.

I hope you find this book a useful companion for your BTEC course and wish you well in your studies.

Ray Youell
Aberystwyth
July 2005

Unit 8
Business Travel Operations

INTRODUCTION TO THE UNIT

Business travel is one of the most dynamic sectors of the travel and tourism industry. It includes travel for business meetings, staging conferences and conventions, trade fairs and exhibitions, as well as incentive travel. Worldwide business travel was badly affected by the events of 9th September 2001 and today faces many other challenges, not least the dramatic growth in Internet travel bookings and the decision by airlines to reduce or eliminate commission payments to agents.

This unit gives you the opportunity to learn more about the business travel environment, examining the role of different types of agents and key issues affecting business travel today. You will investigate a range of working practices in business travel and explore the role of a number of trade and regulatory bodies, including IATA, ABTA and the CAA. The unit gives you the opportunity of developing your practical business travel skills by producing a multi-sector business travel itinerary to meet client needs, including information on additional travel products and services.

WHAT YOU WILL STUDY

During the course of this unit you will:

1. Examine the **business travel environment;**
2. Investigate business travel **working practices;**
3. Produce **multi-sector business travel itineraries** in accordance with client needs and working practices;
4. Provide information on a range of **additional products, services and information** relating to multi-sector business travel itineraries.

You will be guided through the main topics in this unit with the help of the latest statistics, examples and industry case studies. You should also check out the weblinks throughout the unit for extra information on particular organisations or topic areas and use the activities to help you learn more.

ASSESSMENT FOR THIS UNIT

This unit is internally assessed, meaning that you will be given an assignment (or series of assignments) to complete by your tutor(s) to show that you have fully understood the content of the unit. A grading scale of pass, merit or distinction is used for all internally assessed units, with higher grades awarded to students who show greater depth in analysis and evaluation in their assignments. An assignment for this unit, which covers all the grading criteria, can be found on page 27. Don't forget to visit www.tandtONLine.co.uk for all the latest industry news, developments, statistics and tips to help you with your assignments.

Unit 8

SECTION 1: BUSINESS TRAVEL ENVIRONMENT

Business travel is a sector of the travel and tourism industry that provides products and services for business people travelling to meetings, attending conferences and conventions, and taking part in trade fairs and exhibitions. It also includes 'incentive travel', where holidays, short breaks and other travel services are offered to members of staff as an incentive to reach work targets. Some people use the term 'business tourism' rather than 'business travel' when talking about this sector of the travel and tourism industry. Business tourism tends to be a more all-embracing term that includes all aspects of a business traveller's experience, whereas business travel focuses on getting the business traveller from point A to point B.

In the first section of the unit we investigate the business travel environment, the different types of business travel agents and the key issues currently affecting the sector.

Environment

Business travel is an increasingly important sector of the UK travel and tourism industry, since it is often 'high value tourism', earning hoteliers, caterers, transport providers, travel agents and a host of other service providers significant income. Business travel is considered a high value sector since:

- Clients often have to travel at short notice, meaning that they are not able to take advantage of discounted advance purchase rates;
- Business people often use high quality accommodation;
- Business travel invariably includes an element of entertaining business colleagues;
- Travel is often in upgraded seating, e.g. business class or first class.

The business travel sector can be divided into four distinct elements:

1. General business travel (GBT);
2. Corporate hospitality;
3. Conferences, exhibitions and meetings;
4. Incentive travel.

Each element has its own particular characteristics and products, as the next sections of this unit demonstrate.

General business travel

This part of the business travel sector consists of travel agents making a variety of travel arrangements on behalf of business clients. The agent may deal only with business customers or may be an agent that sells to both leisure and business clients. Many larger business travel agencies prefer to call themselves travel management companies (TMCs), reflecting the wide range of services they offer to their clients. Organisations of all sizes and in all sectors of the economy often need their staff to travel on business. Sole traders, members of partnerships, company directors, public sector staff, junior and senior managers, all travel from time to time on business. This could be in their local area, elsewhere in the UK, to countries in continental Europe or further afield in the world. General business travel operates across all types of industry sectors, from manufacturing, mining and construction to banking, insurance, financial services and even the travel industry itself! Many of the UK's largest business travel agents are members of the Guild of Travel Management Companies (GTMC).

WEBLINK

www.gtmc.org

Check out this website for more information on the work of the Guild of Travel Management Companies.

FOCUS ON INDUSTRY – The Guild of Travel Management Companies (GTMC)

Formed as the Guild of Business Travel Agents (GBTA) in 1968, GTMC changed its name in 2005 to reflect the changes in the business travel sector. The Guild is a trade association representing a broad spread of business travel agents in the UK, from major travel companies such as American Express and Carlson Wagonlit Travel to specialist, independent agents including Bath Travel and Fleet Street Travel. GTMC's members dominate the business travel market, with some 80 per cent of the share of agents' business air travel bookings, and a combined turnover of £6.9 billion in 2000. The Guild is also active in promoting business travel as a career and has developed its own professional qualification, the Certificate in Business Travel.

Corporate hospitality

Corporate hospitality is a specialist sector of travel and tourism that focuses on providing hospitality and entertainment to business clients. It may be offered as a reward to a customer for placing business with a company or to encourage businesses that are not yet customers to deal with the company. It is also seen as a good way for a company to make new business contacts. Corporate hospitality events take many forms, ranging from lavish events at Wimbledon or the Henley Regatta to the owner of a business inviting his or her bank manager for a meal in a local restaurant. Many corporate hospitality functions are centred around sports events, such as motor racing Grands Prix, golf championships, cricket, rugby and football matches. There are many specialist companies that handle all the arrangements for corporate events, from sending our invitations and 'meet and greet' services to providing catering and entertainment.

Unit 8

Corporate hospitality facilities at Manchester United FC

Conferences, exhibitions and meetings

Attending conferences, exhibitions and meetings is an important part of trade and commercial activity throughout the world. Companies need to keep up to date with the latest developments in their field and meet customers and suppliers to generate new business. Staff who work for public sector organisations also travel extensively for meetings and conferences. Figure 8.1 gives an indication of the many types of public and trade meetings that take place.

The UK government is keen to promote Britain as a place to hold domestic and international meetings, exhibitions and conferences of all kinds, to reap economic and political benefits. It has developed a website (www.ukexhibitions.co.uk) as a 'one stop shop' for the UK exhibition and trade show industry. The website is sponsored by UK Trade & Investment, the government organisation responsible for all British trade promotion and development work, and by VisitBritain, which promotes tourism to Britain and

Category	Definition
Day meeting	A whole day, or part of day, where overnight accommodation is not usually required by delegates
Multi-day meeting	Where some delegates may use overnight accommodation in the venue or nearby
National meeting	Majority of delegates are from within the home country
International meeting	High proportion of visitors from overseas
Exhibition	An event that brings together suppliers and buyers to generate new business activity
Trade exhibition	Specific industry gathering where attendance is by invitation only to the business community
Public exhibition	Event that is open to the general public
Conference	Event where businesses and academics convene to discuss key issues of interest in their particular specialist sector

Fig. 8.1 Different types of meetings

encourages travel to this country for exhibitions, conferences, meetings and incentive travel. The UK Exhibitions Calendar on the website lists forthcoming trade, industrial, consumer and public events due to held across the UK.

Unit 8

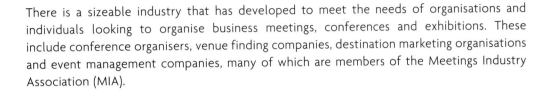

There is a sizeable industry that has developed to meet the needs of organisations and individuals looking to organise business meetings, conferences and exhibitions. These include conference organisers, venue finding companies, destination marketing organisations and event management companies, many of which are members of the Meetings Industry Association (MIA).

WEBLINK

www.mia-uk.org

Check out this website for more information on the Meetings Industry Association.

FOCUS ON INDUSTRY – The Meetings Industry Association (MIA)

The Meetings Industry Association is the recognised professional trade organisation for the conference industry in Great Britain and Ireland. Its main aims are to help position its members at the forefront of a highly competitive business environment and to raise the profile of the country as an international business travel destination. Moving the industry forward, the MIA pursues the best interests of members and meetings buyers alike, encouraging both excellence and ethical standards. It has also initiated the development of professional services for the meetings industry, including training, research, codes of conduct and the promotion of recommended contractual practices.

ACTIVITY

Choose three members of the Meetings Industry Association and carry out some research into the products and services they offer to clients. Produce three illustrated fact sheets that contain all the relevant details that a client would need to know about the company.

This activity is designed to provide evidence for P1.

Incentive travel

'Incentive travel' is defined by the Society of Incentive and Travel Executives (SITE) as:

'A global management tool that uses exceptional travel experience to motivate and/or recognise participants for increased levels of performance in support of organisational goals'.

Typically, incentive travel comprises a luxury holiday or short break offered to an employee as a reward for meeting a specific work target or goal. It also refers to the industry that supplies, develops, markets and operates incentive travel programmes. Companies

Unit 8

WEBLINK

www.site-intl.org

Check out this website for more information on the Society of Incentive and Travel Executives (SITE)

implement incentive travel programmes to drive sales, increase profits, improve service, enhance staff morale, retain staff or provide high-profile recognition. Being a recipient of an incentive travel award conveys status and prestige on the winner. Many participants are multiple award winners and are highly experienced and discerning travellers. A high proportion of incentive travel programmes include partners to increase the motivational value of the incentive. The appreciation of travel incentives as a business tool has continued to increase in recent years. More and more businesses now recognise the value of incentives and design performance plans for employees, with specific objectives and measures of success related to incentive travel rewards.

Characteristics of the business travel environment

Before we consider the different types of agents found in the business travel sector, it is important to highlight some of the key characteristics of the business travel sector, for example:

Incentive travel often focuses on luxury experiences (courtesy St Davids Hotel and Spa, Cardiff)

- The importance placed on price, value for money and effective use of time – as we saw earlier in this unit, business travel can be 'high value' travel, since business people often have to make journeys at short notice and generally use high quality accommodation. However, this does not mean that they are not concerned about the prices they pay for travel. Just like leisure travellers, business people expect to get good value for money when they travel. In order to make their travel budgets stretch as far as possible, UK business travellers are increasingly making use of low-cost airlines, such as easyJet and Ryanair, when they travel. Organisations that have a large budget for business travel can negotiate better rates for accommodation and travel when compared to companies with small travel budgets. Many business travellers are prepared to pay extra for travel if the arrangements mean that they can make better use of their scare time;

- Credit arrangements for travel payments – business travel is generally offered on a credit account basis, with the travel company making the travel arrangements setting up credit terms with its business clients. Smaller businesses may well pay for their travel arrangements by business credit or debit card;

- The need to be able to make reservations or changes to bookings at short notice – travel agents making arrangements for businesses must be able to respond quickly to

Unit 8

clients' needs, which may change quickly due to unforeseen circumstances such as a cancelled conference or hastily-arranged meeting;

- Making bookings out of normal office hours – in today's global 24-hour society businesses expect to be able to make their travel arrangements out of normal office hours. Business travel agents are responding by extending their office hours and/or allocating specific members of staff to handle out-of-hours enquiries;
- The particular needs of business travellers – people travelling on business look for speed, convenience, flexibility and quality when choosing their travel suppliers. Today, there are far more women travelling on business than in the past, meaning that travel companies must strive to meet their particular need for safety and security;
- Type and class of travel and accommodation – business people tend to use higher quality accommodation and upgraded travel, particularly when entertaining important clients. However, there is an important sector of the business travel market that uses budget hotel accommodation and the new, budget airlines in order to keep travel and accommodation costs to a minimum;
- Management information reports – large business travel management companies, such as BTI UK, Thomas Cook, American Express and Carlson Wagonlit Travel, offer their clients regular management information reports detailing the extent of travel by members of staff and expenditure incurred;
- Direct reservations via the Internet – the dramatic growth in the use of the Internet is having an impact on the work of business travel agents. The Internet gives business travellers the opportunity of searching for particular travel products and making their own bookings direct with travel companies. However, this can be a very time-consuming process and many companies still prefer to use the services of a business travel agent with their experience, industry knowledge and buying power.

Types of agent

Figure 8.2 indicates the main types of business travel agents found in the UK – transnationals, nationals, independents, implants and e-agents.

Transnational business travel companies

These are large corporations that operate their business travel services on a global scale. Often referred to as travel management companies (TMCs), they include American Express Travel, Carlson Wagonlit and Business Travel International –

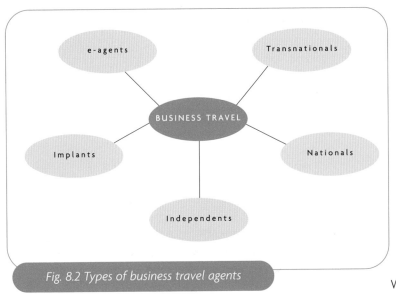

Fig. 8.2 Types of business travel agents

Unit 8

Carlson Wagonlit is a major player in the business travel sector

part of Hogg Robinson plc (see case study below). By operating high-volume businesses across continents, transnationals aim to benefit from economies of scale and can negotiate favourable discounted rates with suppliers, for example airlines, hotel companies and car hire firms. They offer a wide range of services to their clients, as the following case study demonstrates.

CASE STUDY – British Travel International (BTI) UK

Introduction

BTI UK is one of the top business travel management companies (TMCs) in Britain, providing travel services to more than 6,000 companies through a national network of business travel centres, implant and outplant operations. Around 40 per cent of the FTSE top 100 companies use BTI UK to organise their business travel needs. BTI UK was the founding partner and is a major shareholder in Business Travel International (BTI), one of the world's leading business travel management companies, with more than 30,000 employees and 3,000 offices worldwide. BTI UK is a wholly owned subsidiary of Hogg Robinson plc, the international corporate travel services company.

BTI's goal

BTI UK's goal, as stated on its website is as follows.

'Our goal is always to be whatever our customers want us to be. Responsive, helpful and expert. Comprehensive, innovative and down to earth. Able to get up close and provide outstanding value and service to our clients. And that goes for everyone. From sole traders to the biggest multinationals'.

Unit 8

Products and services

BTI UK's core activity is providing business travel arrangements to its corporate clients, for example booking UK and worldwide flights, hotels, car hire, rail travel, ferry reservations, etc. In addition, the company offers a variety of additional services for clients, including:

- Passport and visa service;
- Travel insurance;
- VAT reclaim;
- Foreign exchange;
- Airport assistance;
- Executive transfers;
- Airport chauffeur parking;
- 'Meet and greet' service;
- 24-hour traveller assistance.

BTI UK can also provide group travel services, conference and incentive travel arrangements, leisure travel services and tickets for theatres and special events.

BTI UK Direct

This is BTI UK's Internet-based booking service that gives its clients access to 49,000 hotels and some 750,000 airfares worldwide, including exclusive BTI UK special fares and services offered by the low-cost airlines. It is designed to meet the needs of business travellers and corporate travel bookers, allowing users to compare prices and make informed decisions about their travel needs. It also allows secure access to a company's own negotiated air fares and hotel rates.

WEBLINK

www.bti.co.uk

Check out this website to help answer the questions in this case study and for more information on BTI UK.

CASE STUDY QUESTIONS

1. What are the key challenges facing BTI UK in its bid to remain one of the UK's foremost business travel management companies?
2. How does BTI UK generate its revenue?
3. How does being a part of Hogg Robinson plc help BTI UK?
4. What is the difference between an 'implant' and an 'outplant'?

Unit 8

National business travel companies

These are UK-based companies that are part of a national chain of travel agencies, such as Thomas Cook, Thomson/TUI, Going Places and First Choice, which are themselves part of large, vertically-integrated travel groups. These agencies deal primarily with holidays and other leisure travel products, but can meet the needs of business travellers as well. Agencies that are located in parts of the country with high concentrations of companies and a large business community often generate a sizeable proportion of their turnover from business clients.

Independent business travel agents

Across the UK, there are many independent travel agents that specialise in business travel arrangements. They are not part of a national chain and are often managed by the owner and a small team of staff. Independent business travel agents trade on their ability to offer their clients a wide range of travel products backed up with a very personal service. As well as being members of ABTA (the Association of British Travel Agents), many independent agents join consortia such as Advantage Travel or Worldchoice in order to benefit from supplier discounts, make useful business contacts and to have their voices heard.

ACTIVITY

Research and write a case study on an independent business travel agent of your choice. Include details about its aims, structure, products and services, staffing, membership of trade organisations, etc.

This activity is designed to provide evidence for P1.

Business travel implants

This is when a travel agency is invited by a business client to manage all its travel arrangements from within the company's own premises. Depending on the volume of business, this could be just one member of staff from the agency working full or part-time in the company's offices or a team of agents moving into the company and setting up a travel agency function. The staff who take up the positions are known as 'implants'. The company benefits from having travel expertise close to hand, while the travel agency gains extra business and hence extra commission and fees.

e-agents

The growth in the use of the Internet has led to the development of e-agents specialising in business travel arrangements (where e stands for electronic). These are a kind of 'virtual travel agent' as they have no branches and usually operate from a single base with the latest IT systems and equipment. Examples of e-agents include lastminute.com, ebookers, Travelocity and Expedia. E-agents benefit from the speed and flexibility of the Internet, but must generate high sales volumes to remain profitable. E-agents are also tour operators since their websites allow the packaging of accommodation and flights. In fact, Civil Aviation Authority (CAA) figures for 2004 show that e-agents were the fastest-growing sector carrying passengers under ATOLs (Air Travel Organisers' Licences), with Expedia growing by 169 per cent on 2003 and the Destination Group (part of lastminute.com) showing a 120 per cent rise in customers carried.

Issues in business travel

Business travel is a very dynamic sector of the travel and tourism industry, always having to react to internal and external pressures to remain competitive. A combination of the Internet, cheaper fares, disappearing airline commission and increasing cost-consciousness on the part of businesses generally, mean that business travel companies have to work hard to 'add value' to the travel services they provide to their clients. At the time of writing, the high price of oil on the world market is forcing airlines and other transport providers to increase their travel prices, raising costs for businesses and putting even greater pressure on business travel agents to find cost savings for their clients.

Low-cost airlines

There is little doubt that the introduction of low-cost airlines has revolutionised travel attitudes and habits. Helped by the growth of Internet use, research from Mintel estimated that the low-cost airline sector in Europe carried around 80 million passengers in 2004, of which over 60 million started or ended their journey at a UK airport. There are approximately 60 low-cost carriers operating within Europe, although the UK market is dominated by Ryanair and easyJet, which carried over 55 million passengers during 2004. Interestingly, the same research showed that the number of British people booking their low-cost flight through a travel agent rose from 14 per cent in 2002 to 21 per cent in 2004.

Low-cost airlines are also proving to be a big challenge to the business travel sector. Research carried out for Carlson Wagonlit Travel in 2003 showed that low-cost carriers have 8 per cent maximum coverage of the European business travel market by sales and offer typical savings of 56 per cent on the routes they operate when compared to full service airlines. It is no wonder that there is growing pressure in companies for their employees to use low-cost carriers for business trips whenever possible. Many business travel agents now book low-cost flights for their clients as part of the overall service they provide, even though the airlines don't pay commission to agents. Carlson Wagonlit Travel has introduced a booking tool that gives its clients access to the widest range of air fares, including those offered by the low-cost carriers. The biggest impact of low-cost airlines on the business travel sector may well be in how they influence traditional carriers to change their ways. This is already happening, with full service airlines cutting their fares and promoting the high quality of the products and service they offer.

Internet distribution

The growth of the Internet has empowered people in many ways, not least in how they now find travel information and make bookings for holidays and other travel products. Business travellers can now work out their own itineraries and make their own reservations without ever having to consult an agent. In reality, most companies still prefer to deal with a business travel agent or travel management company, valuing their expertise and ability to keep costs to a minimum.

Transaction fees

With commission on the sale of airline tickets all but disappeared, business travel agents are having to rethink the financial relationship they have with their clients. One way they do this is by charging fees for the services they deliver. This has introduced greater competition between agents to see who can offer the best value for a given fee. Charging fees is becoming the norm in travel agencies; only one respondent to the 2004 Price Waterhouse Coopers/ABTA Travel Agents' Benchmarking Survey did not charge service fees. This is a marked change from 2002 when 70 per cent of those interviewed charged fees and a further 18 per cent were considering charging fees. The 2004 survey showed that smaller travel agents, who in 2002 were unsure about fees, were now charging them to clients. The most common types of service fees were levied on low-cost airline flights, credit card use and flights on scheduled airlines. The majority of agents charging fees were taking between £5 and £20, with a small number charging over £20.

Airline alliances

Airline alliances are groupings of airlines that work in partnership in order to raise their profile, make cost savings and ultimately increase their profitability, while each airline still retains its own identity. Partner airlines share passengers on certain routes to reduce costs and offer travellers 'interlining' across all members, i.e. the ability to use the same ticket regardless of which airline they are using. The airlines also benefit from 'economies of scale' in purchasing, management information systems and administration. For the business traveller, airline alliances can help to reduce travel costs and simplify booking procedures. The Star Alliance offers a programme for corporations and travel management companies called Corporate Plus, which allows the corporate to set up one deal with the Star Alliance rather than having to negotiate with each of its 15 member airlines separately. The Oneworld Alliance has two well-established programmes for business travellers, Businessflyer and Eventflyer. The former gives small and medium-sized businesses in certain markets the same level of discounts as large companies receive on travel within Europe, to the Americas, Africa, Australia or Asia. Eventflyer eases conference and event booking for corporate clients and travel management companies by offering bookers a simpler and cheaper fare structure tailor-made for each event.

WEBLINK

www.oneworld.com;
www.staralliance.com;
www.skyteam.com

Check out these websites for more information on the Oneworld Alliance, Star Alliance and Skyteam.

FOCUS ON INDUSTRY – The Oneworld Alliance

Founded in 1999, this alliance has eight member airlines – Aer Lingus, American Airlines, British Airways, Cathay Pacific, Finnair, Iberia, Lan and Qantas. Oneworld Alliance members serve approximately 600 destinations in 135 countries, handling 223 million passengers in a typical year.

Delta is a member of the Skyteam Alliance

Unit 8

SECTION 2: WORKING PRACTICES IN BUSINESS TRAVEL

Business travel agencies differ in the way that they manage their business activities and develop their business procedures. This is influenced by a number of factors, such as whether the agency is an independent or part of a larger organisation, how many people it employs and the type of IT systems used in the company. Whatever working practices and business systems are used, the key requirement is to provide clients and their companies with an efficient and effective service. More information on working practices and business documentation can be found in another unit that is part of your course – Unit 2 The Business of Travel and Tourism.

Account management

Sound financial and account management systems are an essential ingredient of a successful business travel agency. Senior managers must ensure that procedures and documentation are in place to ensure effective account management, especially in relation to:

1. Service level agreements – these are the contracts between agents and clients, giving details of agreed levels of business, rates and payment schedules;
2. Management information – regular and accurate data is needed on sales volumes and costs in order to be able to make informed business decisions;
3. Payment and accounts procedures – must ensure that payments are made and received in line with agreed credit periods so as to control cash flow;
4. Client profiles – whether held manually or on a computer database system, these are essential for staff to be able to provide the best standards of service to customers;
5. Frequent flyer programmes – clients who travel extensively like to take advantage of the offers available from airlines in these schemes.

ACTIVITY

Compare and contrast the frequent flyer programmes offered by three different airlines. Present the information you find as a comparative chart.

This activity is designed to provide evidence for P2.

Unit 8

Front and back office

It is common for travel and tourism businesses to divide their business functions into 'front office' and 'back office', developing systems and procedures in support of each. In simple terms, the 'front office' (sometimes referred to as 'front of house') refers to the reception area of any travel and tourism facility, the point at which the customer first makes contact with the organisation. The 'back office' (also known as 'back of house') refers to the organisation's functions that take place behind the scenes, for example accounting, maintenance, training and stock control. Common front and back office procedures include:

- Reservation procedures;
- Production of tickets and travel documentation;
- Commission and non-commission structures agreed with suppliers;
- Payment timelines for clients and suppliers;
- Transaction fees, e.g. for credit card payments, booking non-commissionable products, etc.

The concept of front and back office is widespread in the business travel sector. The division into front and back office allows management to focus resources on particular functions and train staff in these areas. The selection and training of staff to work in the 'front office' is particularly important, since it provides the visitor with his or her first impressions of the organisation. Staff with an understanding of the particular needs of business travellers and a commitment to providing excellence in customer service should be chosen to work in this high profile area. The environment in which the 'front office' is positioned also needs to be carefully planned, and should provide a clean, warm, efficient, welcoming and friendly atmosphere.

Examples of the different functions carried out by front and back office staff in the business travel environment are shown in Figure 8.3.

FRONT OFFICE FUNCTIONS	BACK OFFICE FUNCTIONS
Welcoming customers	Cash and credit control
Taking bookings	Accounting
Selling services	Client databases
Providing information	Brochure stock control
Handling cash, cheques and cards	Maintenance
Controlling entry	Marketing and publicity
Promoting products and services	Analysis of management data
Answering enquiries	Staff training
Maintaining records	Personnel/human resources
Passing information to back office	Health and safety

Fig. 8.3 Front and back office functions in business travel

There must always be good co-ordination between front and back office functions. In large business travel management companies the job of making sure that everything runs smoothly between front and back office falls to an account manager, who is responsible for handling a number of clients' accounts and acting as their first point of contact.

Unit 8

FOCUS ON INDUSTRY – American Express Travel

American Express offers business travellers and agents the opportunity to research itineraries and make reservations 24 hours a day using its PowerRez Internet-based facility. Using Galileo technology, PowerRez allows users to:

- Make any airline, hotel or car reservation online;
- Keep a personal profile of particular travel needs and preferences;
- Search for up-to-date travel information;
- Investigate health, passport and visa requirements;
- Gather information on weather and destinations around the world.

Trade and regulatory bodies

Companies in the business travel sector can join a number of different trade associations that represent their interests and offer a range of member benefits. The work of business travel companies is also controlled by a variety of regulatory bodies to ensure that standards of safety, security, consumer protection and other measures are in place and regularly monitored.

Trade associations

Trade associations are set up to represent the interests of companies in a particular industry sector. Many trade associations draw up codes of conduct that lay down the minimum standards under which member companies of the association are expected to conduct their business with customers and suppliers. The Guild of Travel Management Companies (GTMC) is a specific trade body representing the business travel sector in the UK (see page 3). ABTA (the Association of British Travel Agents) is the main trade association for all retail and business travel agents in the UK.

Companies that are granted membership of ABTA are required to adhere to strict rules governing their business practice. These are contained in ABTA's Code of Conduct, which regulates all aspects of tour operators' and travel agents' relationships with their customers and which have been drawn up in conjunction with the Office of Fair Trading (OFT). The Code of Conduct is designed to regulate the activities of:

- Members dealing with customers;
- Members dealing with other ABTA members;
- Members dealing with principals and agents who are not members of ABTA.

Unit 8

The aims of the Code of Conduct are to:

- Ensure that the public receive the best possible service from ABTA members;
- Maintain and enhance the reputation, standing and good name of the Association and its membership;
- Encourage initiative and enterprise in the belief that properly regulated competitive trading by and between members will best serve the public interest and the wellbeing of the travel industry.

The Travel Agents' Code of Conduct regulates all aspects of travel agents' relationships with their customers, covering their responsibility with regard to the standard of service they provide and the information they give to clients. It also lays down rules concerning travel agents' trading relationships with tour operators. In addition, members of ABTA are required to adhere to precise financial specifications, overseen by ABTA's Financial Services Department, which checks all members' accounts at least once a year.

WEBLINK

www.abta.com

Check out this website for more information on ABTA.

FOCUS ON INDUSTRY – Association of British Travel Agents (ABTA)

ABTA is the UK's premier trade association for travel agents and tour operators. Its current number of 1052 tour operator and 6310 travel agency offices are responsible for the sale of some 85 per cent of all holidays sold in the UK. ABTA members had a combined sales turnover of £26 billion in 2004. It represents the interests of both leisure and business travel agents, as well as those that combine both functions. The Association is a self-regulatory body run by its membership. A network of Councils and Committees, appointed by member travel agents and tour operators, make up the policy-making and enforcing machinery of the Association and help to ensure that ABTA remains in close contact with the whole of its membership. Members of ABTA are required to provide bonds to protect their customers in the event of financial failure. ABTA currently holds bonds valued at £201 million for travel agents and £170 million for tour operators. The bond can take a number of forms, but is often an insurance policy for the amount required by ABTA, or a bank guarantee.

Business travel agents can choose to become members of a variety of trade consortia to help generate extra business. Often these are groupings of independent travel agents that work together to increase their influence and buying power with the airlines, hotel groups and other travel suppliers. Being a member of a consortium allows a travel agency to retain its independence while at the same time reaping the benefits of the extra negotiating power that a consortium can offer. There are a number of consortia operating in the travel agency sector, including:

Unit 8

- Freedom Travel Group;
- Global Travel Group;
- Worldchoice;
- Travel Trust Association;
- Travelsavers;
- Advantage Travel;
- Midconsort.

Advantage Travel, also known as the National Association of Independent Travel Agents (NAITA), is the biggest travel agency consortium in the UK representing some 860 independent agents across leisure and business travel. Worldchoice has more than 600 member companies.

WEBLINK

www.worldchoice.co.uk

Check out this website for more information on Worldchoice.

FOCUS ON INDUSTRY – Worldchoice

Established in 1976, Worldchoice was one of the first travel agents' consortia. Today, it has over 600 travel agency members, making it one of the largest travel groups in the UK. The group considers its independence to be its biggest asset and its combined strength gives the consortium the negotiating power to command the best possible products and prices in leisure and business travel. Members of the consortium are independent agents who are not tied to any of the multiple chains, thereby having the flexibility to offer business customers a wide range of travel products. Worldchoice offers its members a range of services, including the best commercial rates of any travel consortium in the UK (according to data from Price Waterhouse Coopers). The consortium negotiates commercial terms with over 140 business partners every year on behalf of its members. The combined strength of over 600 agencies with an annual turnover in excess of £1 billion helps ensure attractive discounts to members. Worldchoice has its own automatic credit accounting system (ACAS), which can help members reduce administrative costs and bank charges, as well as improving cash flow.

ACTIVITY

Carry out some research into the Worldchoice and Advantage travel agents' consortia. Write a short report comparing and contrasting the aims of each consortium, the benefits they offer their members and the particular services they offer to business travel agents.

This activity is designed to provide evidence for P3.

Unit 8

WEBLINK

www.caa.co.uk

Check out this website for more information on the work of the Civil Aviation Authority (CAA).

Regulatory bodies

The major regulatory bodies that affect the operation of the business travel sector are the Civil Aviation Authority (CAA) and the International Air Transport Association (IATA). The CAA is the UK's independent aviation regulator, with all civil aviation regulatory functions – economic regulation, policy on airspace, regulation of safety and consumer protection for air travellers.

CASE STUDY – International Air Transport Association (IATA)

Introduction

IATA is an international trade body representing the interests of the world's major airlines. It was founded in Havana, Cuba in 1945 and is the principal vehicle for inter-airline co-operation in promoting safe, reliable, secure and economical global air services. When it was founded IATA had 57 members from 31 nations, mostly in Europe and North America. Today it brings together approximately 265 airlines, including the world's largest carriers, from more than 140 countries in every corner of the world. Flights by IATA-member airlines comprise 94 per cent of all international scheduled air traffic. UK-based members of IATA include British Airways, bmi, GB Airways, Virgin Atlantic Airways and flybe (British European). The modern IATA is the successor to the International Air Traffic Association founded in the Hague in 1919 – the year of the world's first international scheduled air services.

What does IATA do?

IATA's work covers many important areas concerning air travel, including:

1. Aircraft operations – e.g. resolving flight operation issues, quality assurance, reliable supplies of aircraft fuel at airports, etc;
2. Safety and security – co-ordinated efforts to improve installations, communications, route organisation, air traffic control and staff training to reduce accident rates;
3. Finance – IATA offers a range of financial services to airlines to help them contain their costs, improve their cash flow and maximise revenues;
4. Consumer issues – IATA works with the airline industry to simplify the travel experience, minimising hassle for passengers and giving them more control, e.g. IATA is committed to 100 per cent e-ticketing across all airlines by the end of 2007;
5. Environment – the Association is committed to developing an airline industry that balances social, economic and environmental impacts and responsibilities.

Unit 8

Who benefits?

- Consumers – by helping control airline costs, IATA contributes to cheaper tickets for passengers. It co-ordinates all 'interline' activity, i.e. the use of tickets across different airlines;
- Airlines – IATA allows airlines to work more efficiently, working in partnership to exploit new opportunities, reduce costs and solve problems. Airlines knit their individual networks into a worldwide system through IATA, despite differences in languages, currencies, laws and national customs;
- Third parties – IATA has a collective link between a range of third parties and the airlines, e.g. passenger agents, equipment manufacturers, service prviders, etc;
- Governments – governments can use IATA as an effective way of working with airlines, drawing on the Association's experience and expertise.

IATA travel agents

Business and leisure travel agents in the UK, in common with agents worldwide, can apply for an IATA licence to sell airline tickets and other services of IATA member airlines. Since these airlines only pay commission to approved IATA sales agents, an IATA licence is a much sought after commodity. Applying for an IATA licence has similarities to an application for ABTA membership, in that the applicant has to meet certain minimum criteria and will be subject to an inspection and interview by an IATA representative. The criteria for approval are concerned with a number of factors, including:

- Nature of the premises - the agency must be open for business on a regular basis and clearly identified as a travel agency;
- Security of premises - premises must be adequately protected and a safe installed for the storage of airline tickets and other valuables;
- Staff qualifications - staff selling the IATA tickets and services must be permanent employees and have relevant experience and qualifications, e.g. British Airways Fares and Ticketing Courses;
- Finances - applicants must submit a full set of audited accounts for scrutiny by IATA personnel and meet certain minimum share capital/capital account amounts. Additionally, approved agents are required to submit a copy of their annual report and accounts within 6 months of the financial year end;
- Bonding - a bank or insurance company bond will be required, based on a percentage of annual turnover.

On payment of a non-refundable application fee and an entry fee, the successful applicant will be granted an IATA licence to sell airline tickets and the services of IATA member airlines.

Unit 8

CASE STUDY QUESTIONS

1. Carry out some further research to find out how the IATA Clearing House (ICH) works.
2. What activities does IATA carry out as part of its environmental responsibilities?
3. How does IATA's work help business travellers?
4. Looking to the future, what are the key political, economic, social and technological issues that are likely to affect the Association and its member airlines?

Corporate policies

Business travel agencies of all sizes, but particularly the larger travel management companies (TMCs) such as BTI UK, American Express and Carlson Wagonlit Travel, develop a variety of company policies to comply with relevant laws and regulations, as well as concerning their business relationships with clients and other companies. These include policies covering:

- Health and safety;
- Environmental and social responsibility;
- Data protection;
- Financial propriety.

Details of the policies are including in company publications and on their websites.

ACTIVITY

Carry out some research into the environmental or corporate social responsibility policies of a business travel agency or travel management company. Present your findings as a short report.

This activity is designed to provide evidence for P3.

Unit 8

SECTION 3: MULTI-SECTOR BUSINESS TRAVEL ITINERARIES

A multi-sector itinerary is one that involves more than one 'leg' of a journey, i.e. a trip that consists of a flight from Birmingham to Brussels followed by a train journey from Brussels to Cologne is considered multi-sector as it is made up of two legs. Similarly, a business trip from London to Shanghai, with a stopover on the way out in Bangkok and one on the way back in Hong Kong, is multi-sector since it consists of four separate legs.

Sources of information for planning itineraries

Business travel agents and travel management companies (TMCs) need to be able to access and process a great deal of information when planning itineraries for clients, particularly multi-sector itineraries. An essential skill for a business travel agent is to know where to source a wide variety of information quickly and reliably, e.g. flight times and costs, details of hotel accommodation, car hire charges and surface transport arrangements.

WEBLINK

www.galileo.com;
www.sabre.com;
www.worldspan.com

Check out these websites for more information on Galileo, Sabre and Worldspan.

Much of the information needed for producing business travel itineraries is sourced from computer systems, increasingly using Internet-based technology. Depending on the size of the business travel agency or travel management company, staff may have access to sophisticated global distribution systems (GDS) such as Galileo, Sabre and Worldspan. As well as having details of available flights, these systems hold a great deal of information on other travel products and services, such as hotel accommodation, car hire and rail services. Many other Internet-based travel companies, for example lastminute.com, ebookers, Expedia and Travelocity, have websites with sophisticated search facilities covering a wide range of business travel products and services. In addition, airlines, rail companies, car hire firms, coach companies, hotels, etc. have their own websites that can be used by business travel agents.

WEBLINK

www.oag.com

Check out this website to see the full range of OAG Guides for the travel and tourism industry.

Manuals are aimed at people working in travel and tourism (the 'travel trade') rather than the general public. They provide very detailed information on, for example, destinations, airlines, hotels and rail companies. *The World Travel Guide* from Columbus Press has country-by-country information, including transport to and within areas, passport, visa and health requirements. OAG (formerly Overseas Airways Guides) publishes a range of guides for air and rail services, including the *OAG Rail Guide* and the *OAG Flight Guide*. Trade Associations, e.g. ABTA, the Passenger Shipping Association (PSA), AITO (the Association of Independent Tour Operators) and IATA (the International Air Transport Association) produce specific manuals for the travel trade.

Individual airlines, ferry operators, cruise companies, tour operators, rail companies and coach/bus operators produce their own timetables to help travel agents and members of the public plan journeys. Timetables are available in printed form and many are published on the Internet, e.g. the UK National Rail Timetable. Rail travellers wishing to go further afield can consult the *Thomas Cook European Timetable* and *Thomas Cook Overseas Timetable* to plan their journeys. Rail Europe provides details of train journeys in Europe on its website.

Content and format of itineraries

Itineraries produced by business travel agents and travel management companies must contain all the information a business client needs to make informed decisions when travelling. The precise content and layout of an itinerary will vary between companies, but a typical itinerary will include:

- Client details;
- Check-in details;
- Transport type, e.g. aircraft, train;
- Flight or service numbers;
- Transport operator, e.g. which airline, train company;
- Class of travel;
- Departure and arrival date/time (in local time);
- Intermediate stops;
- Reconfirmation of flight or service details;
- Transfer details;
- Additional services, e.g. car hire, event tickets;
- Notes section covering passport, visa and health requirements;
- Additional information and procedure for alterations to booking.

The format of an itinerary must be clear, logical and presented to a professional standard. Figure 8.4 gives an example of a multi-sector business travel itinerary (you may find this useful when completing the assignment for this unit).

Unit 8

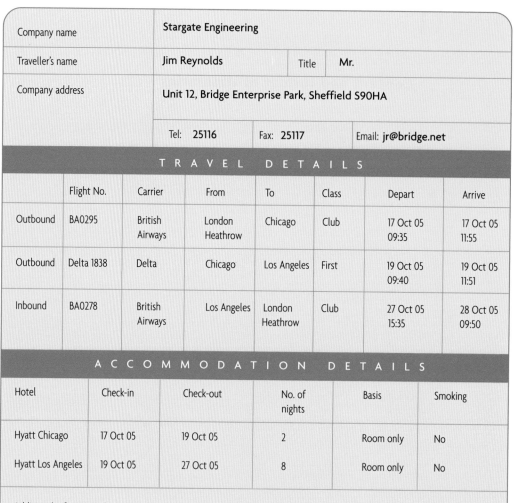

Company name	Stargate Engineering		
Traveller's name	Jim Reynolds	Title	Mr.
Company address	Unit 12, Bridge Enterprise Park, Sheffield S90HA		
	Tel: 25116	Fax: 25117	Email: jr@bridge.net

T R A V E L   D E T A I L S

	Flight No.	Carrier	From	To	Class	Depart	Arrive
Outbound	BA0295	British Airways	London Heathrow	Chicago	Club	17 Oct 05 09:35	17 Oct 05 11:55
Outbound	Delta 1838	Delta	Chicago	Los Angeles	First	19 Oct 05 09:40	19 Oct 05 11:51
Inbound	BA0278	British Airways	Los Angeles	London Heathrow	Club	27 Oct 05 15:35	28 Oct 05 09:50

A C C O M M O D A T I O N   D E T A I L S

Hotel	Check-in	Check-out	No. of nights	Basis	Smoking
Hyatt Chicago	17 Oct 05	19 Oct 05	2	Room only	No
Hyatt Los Angeles	19 Oct 05	27 Oct 05	8	Room only	No

Additional information (passport, visas, health, currency, insurance, etc.)

Fig. 8.4 Multi-sector business travel itinerary

Unit 8

This section outlines the many different products that business travel agents can recommend to their clients in order to ensure that their journey is as trouble-free as possible.

Products and services

As profit margins in business travel become squeezed, agents and travel management companies are always keen to give clients the chance of buying add-ons and ancillary products and services, such as travellers' cheques and foreign currency, airport car parking, passport and visa services, travel insurance and car hire. Percentage commission on these products is often much higher than for arranging flights and other transport services, so staff are encouraged to offer them to clients.

ACTIVITY

Make a list of the add-ons and ancillary products and services that could be offered to the following business clients by their travel agent:

- A sales manager on a week-long tour of customers in Belgium;
- A law firm arranging a seminar for 50 delegates in London;
- A group of UK business people going a two-week long fact-finding tour of China;

This activity is designed to provide evidence for P5.

Information

Business travel can be very complicated, particularly if a trip involves crossing many borders and continents. It is the job of business travel agents to make sure that their clients are provided with all the necessary information for a successful trip. The precise information needed will differ depending on individual client circumstances, but may include advice on:

- Different payment methods available in destinations – e.g. credit cards are not always universally accepted in some countries;
- Currency conversion rates – it is good practice for business agents to supply their clients with a conversion calculator for use on their travels and to give advice on the most cost-effective way of paying for goods and services in foreign countries;
- Visa and passport restrictions – e.g. whether a visa is needed for a particular trip, how long it will take to arrive, how much it will cost, etc;

Unit 8

- Health regulations – business agents must know where to get up-to-date advice on health issues for their business clients;
- Local customs, events and activities – knowledge of different customs when visiting a country on business, plus details of social events and activities, are part of the service a business travel agency or travel management company offers to its clients;
- Insurance policy terms and booking conditions – sometimes referred to as 'the small print', these are the important points that business travellers need to be made aware of in case they run into difficulties while travelling abroad.

WEBLINK

www.americanexpress.com

Check out this website for more details of the American Express Travellers Cheque Card.

FOCUS ON INDUSTRY – American Express Travellers' Cheque Card

American Express has recently launched a travellers' cheque card that can be pre-loaded with either US Dollars, Euros or Pounds Sterling. The card combines the convenience of a payment card with the security of travellers' cheques. The card can be used in shops, restaurants and ATMs worldwide where American Express cards are accepted. If the card is lost or stolen, the card holder's balance can be returned, usually within 24 hours.

UNIT SUMMARY

This unit has investigated the business travel environment and found it to be a very dynamic and competitive sector that is facing many challenges in the 21st century. You have explored the various categories of business travel, examined different types of business travel agents and learned about the key issues facing the business travel sector today, including the impact of low-cost airlines, the growth in use of the Internet, reduced commission payments and airline alliances. You have been introduced to working practices in business travel and have investigated the roles of trade associations and regulatory bodies in business travel. The assignment for the unit gives you the opportunity of developing your practical business travel skills by producing three multi-sector business travel itineraries, which include details of the additional products, services and information you have covered in the unit. Throughout the unit you have been shown many industry examples, while the case studies on BTI UK and the International Air Transport Association (IATA), highlight key issues in the operation and regulation of the business travel sector.

If you have worked methodically, by the end of this unit you should have:

- Examined the business travel environment;
- Investigated business travel working practices;
- Produced multi-sector business travel itineraries in accordance with client needs and working practices;
- Provided information on a range of additional products, services and information relating to multi-sector business travel itineraries.

Unit 8

You are now in a position to complete the assignment for the unit, under the direction of your tutor. Before you tackle the assignment you may like to have a go at the following questions to help build your knowledge of business travel operations.

Test your knowledge

1. How was worldwide business travel affected by the events of September 11th 2001?
2. What is 'incentive travel'?
3. Describe the aims and structure of the Guild of Travel Management Companies (GTMC) and list five of its member companies.
4. What is a transnational business travel company?
5. What is an 'implant' in business travel?
6. Describe the impacts that the growth of low-cost airlines is having on the business travel sector.
7. Name three airline alliances, giving five member airlines of each alliance.
8. What is a 'service level agreement' in business travel?
9. What is the difference between the 'front office' and 'back office' in a business travel agency?
10. Describe the function of trade associations in business travel.
11. How does ABTA help business travel agents in their work?
12. Name three activities undertaken by IATA.
13. What is a 'multi-sector business itinerary?
14. What information can be found on a global distribution system (GDS) such as Galileo?
15. Name two good sources of information for planning itineraries involving train travel.

UNIT 8 ASSIGNMENT: Business travel operations

Introduction

This assignment is made up of a number of tasks which, when successfully completed, are designed to give you sufficient evidence to meet the Pass (P), Merit (M) and Distinction (D) grading criteria for the unit. If you have carried out the activities and read the case studies throughout this unit, you will already have done a lot of work towards completing the tasks for this assignment.

Unit 8

Scenario

You are working for Excel Business Travel Ltd, a single branch independent agency situated in the north of England. The company is a family business run by John and Glenda Newman, with three other members of staff – two full-time consultants and one part-time book-keeper. You have joined them on a trail basis after finishing your course to see if business travel is a career that you would like to follow. The idea is that you will get involved in as many different aspects of the business as possible to find out what's involved with working in the business travel sector. John and Glenda have three specific tasks that they would like you to tackle, which are concerned with:

1. The structure of the business travel environment and current issues affecting it;
2. Trade and regulatory bodies in business travel and how they affect the business travel environment and working practices;
3. Producing multi-sector business travel itineraries.

Task 1

Glenda is the chair of the local chamber of trade and has been asked to give a talk on business travel at the chamber's next monthly meeting. She would like you to produce a PowerPoint presentation that she could use at the meeting, in which you should:

(a) Describe the business travel environment;

(b) Describe current issues affecting the business travel working environment;

(c) Analyse how two particular current issues are likely to affect the business travel environment;

(d) Evaluate the future potential of the business travel sector to respond to the two issues analysed in task 1 (c).

These tasks are designed to produce evidence for P1, P2, M1 and D1.

Task 2

John is going to an ABTA regional meeting at the end of the month to discuss key issues affecting business travel agents. One of the items on the agenda is the role of trade and regulatory bodies in the business travel sector. John's knowledge in this area is a little rusty and he has asked you to prepare a short written report in which you should:

Unit 8

(a) Describe the role of trade and regulatory bodies that affect working practices of business travel operations;

(b) Explain how trade and regulatory bodies affect the working practices of business travel operations.

These tasks are designed to produce evidence for P3 and M2.

Task 3

To give you some experience in preparing itineraries for business clients, John would like you to:

(a) Produce three multi-sector (four or more flight/surface sectors) business travel itineraries in accordance with client needs and working practices;

(b) Provide information on additional products, services and information for the customer relating to each of the multi-sector itineraries produced in task 3 (a).

These tasks are designed to produce evidence for P4 and P5. Producing three logical and coherent multi-sector business travel itineraries to business standard, explaining how additional information provided will benefit both the customer and the organisation, will provide evidence for M3. If you undertake independent and sustained research using a range of techniques to present information clearly, logically and coherently, this will provide evidence for D2.

The following three scenarios should be used as the basis for task 3 (a) and 3 (b).

Scenario 1

Jenny Smith has asked Excel Business Travel to produce an itinerary for her next sales trip to Europe. She is the Sales Director for JSE Design, a specialist Internet design company based in Leicester. Her travel requirements are as follows:

1. Depart from a Midlands or London airport on the first Monday of next month (morning departure);
2. Fly to Geneva in business class;
3. Spend 2 nights in hotel accommodation in Geneva;
4. Pick up a hire car (medium size with air conditioning) from Geneva and drive to Lausanne;
5. Spend 3 nights in hotel accommodation in Lausanne (keeping the hire car);
6. Drive to Lyon and drop off the hire car;
7. Spend 4 nights in hotel accommodation in Lyon;

Unit 8

8. Travel by train to Paris;

9. Spend 1 night in hotel accommodation in Paris;

10. Return by air to the same airport as departure (business class).

Your itinerary should include all timings and a breakdown of costs. For hotel accommodation, you should budget for approximately £90 per night. Jenny will pay for fuel for the hire car using her credit card, so there is no need to include this in your cost breakdown. Your itinerary should also include information on additional products, services and information for the customer, e.g. foreign currency requirements in destinations, passport and visa information, health advice and requirements, insurance, local customs, events and activities.

Scenario 2

Geoff Brown, the owner of a newly-established manufacturing company GB Engineering, has been in touch with Glenda about a business trip he will be making to the Far East in a couple of months time. His travel requirements are as follows:

1. Depart from a Midlands or London airport on the first Tuesday of the month after next (morning departure);

2. Fly to Bangkok for a two-night stopover in hotel accommodation;

3. Depart Bangkok and fly to Shanghai;

4. Spend 5 nights in hotel accommodation in Shanghai;

5. Depart Shanghai and fly to Hong Kong;

6. Spend three nights in hotel accommodation in Hong Kong;

7. Depart Hong Kong and return to the same UK airport as departure.

Your itinerary should include all timings and a breakdown of costs. For hotel accommodation, you should budget for approximately £110 per night. All flights should be in business class. Geoff would like you to include the cost of half-day guided tours of Shanghai and Hong Kong in the itinerary. Your itinerary should also include information on additional products, services and information for the customer, e.g. foreign currency requirements in destinations, passport and visa information, health advice and requirements, insurance, local customs, events and activities.

Scenario 3

An up and coming local four-piece rock band called Arrowhead have contacted the agency to help arrange a short promotional tour of Ireland (Northern Ireland and Eire). Their travel requirements are as follows:

1. Pick up a hired minibus from their home city of Manchester on the second Friday of next month early in the morning;
2. Drive to Liverpool to board a ferry for Dublin;
3. Spend 3 nights in hotel accommodation in Dublin;
4. Depart Dublin and drive to Belfast in the hired minibus;
5. Stay for 2 nights in a Belfast hotel;
6. Depart Belfast and drive to Sligo;
7. Spend 2 nights in a hotel in Sligo;
8. Depart Sligo and drive to Dublin;
9. Spend 2 nights in a Dublin hotel;
10. Depart Dublin, returning by ferry to Liverpool;
11. Return the hired minibus to the depot in Manchester later the same day.

Your itinerary should include all timings and a breakdown of costs. They are looking for two rooms in reasonably-priced 3-star hotel accommodation throughout the tour. They will cover fuel costs themselves, so these need not be included in your costing. Your itinerary should also include information on additional products, services and information for the customer, e.g. foreign currency requirements in destinations, passport and visa information, health advice and requirements, insurance, local customs, events and activities.

Unit 8

Unit 9
The Cruise Sector

INTRODUCTION TO THE UNIT

Cruising is one of the most vibrant sectors of the travel and tourism industry, offering a wide variety of job opportunities to people from all backgrounds who want to see the world while they work. Cruising has a very glamorous image and has long been considered an expensive way to travel and explore destinations. However, the cruise sector is changing rapidly – new companies have entered the market and offer cruises at package holiday prices. Also, cruising is no longer just the preserve of the rich and famous. People from all walks of life go on cruises, tempted by the lower prices and the informality offered by some of the new cruise operators.

In this unit you will learn about the development of cruising and the structure of the sector. You will also have the opportunity to investigate the major cruise areas and ports in the world. The unit also examines different types of cruises on offer to customers, the facilities they can expect on board and the target markets of the cruise companies. Finally, you will look in detail at the many employment opportunities offered by the cruise sector, both on board and on shore, and consider the advantages and disadvantages of taking a job in cruising.

WHAT YOU WILL STUDY

During the course of this unit you will:

1. Examine the development of the **cruise sector** of the travel and tourism industry;
2. Investigate **cruise areas** of the world;
3. Explore the **types of cruises** and how they appeal to different markets;
4. Investigate **employment** opportunities within the cruise sector.

You will be guided through the main topics in this unit with the help of the latest statistics, examples and industry case studies. You should also check out the weblinks throughout the unit for extra information on particular organisations or topic areas and use the activities to help you learn more.

ASSESSMENT FOR THIS UNIT

This unit is internally assessed, meaning that you will be given an assignment (or series of assignments) to complete by your tutor(s) to show that you have fully understood the content of the unit. A grading scale of pass, merit or distinction is used for all internally assessed units, with higher grades awarded to students who show greater depth in analysis and evaluation in their assignments. An assignment for this unit, which covers all the grading criteria, can be found on page 71. Don't forget to visit www.tandtONLine.co.uk for all the latest industry news, developments, statistics and tips to help you with your assignments.

t and t ONLine

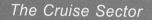
Unit 9

SECTION 1: THE CRUISE SECTOR

The cruise sector of the travel and tourism industry is going through a period of rapid growth and change. In the past, cruising was seen as the preserve of the elderly, rich and famous. Today the number of cruise passengers is growing steadily and the sector has introduced products geared to a wide range of customers, including families, young people and groups. Prices for some cruise products have fallen as the major tour operators have entered the market. For the first time in 2003, more than one million British people took a cruise of one sort or another, according to figures from the Passenger Shipping Association (PSA), the trade body representing passenger shipping interests in the UK (see case study on page 46). Before looking in more detail at the present-day cruising industry, we begin this section with an overview of the historical development of cruising.

Cruising is growing in popularity

Key milestones in the history and development of cruising

The early days of cruising

Although several theories have been put forward to explain the beginnings of the concept of cruising, the most widely-accepted story concerns a fantasy article in the *Shetland Journal* in 1835, in which Arthur Anderson proposed the idea of sailing for pleasure as a passenger on an ocean-going vessel. He suggested trips between Scotland and Iceland in the summer and as far as the Mediterranean in the winter. Two years later his dream moved closer to reality when he co-founded the Peninsular and Oriental Steam Navigation Company, later shortened to P & O.

Long-distance international travel by sea dates back to the mid-19th century, when Cunard Line's *RMS Britannia* (RMS stands for Royal Mail Ship) became the first ship to take passengers on regularly-scheduled, trans-Atlantic crossings. This came about because of the need to introduce a dependable mail service between Britain and America, which prompted Queen Victoria's government to invite interested parties to bid for the contract. Samuel Cunard of Halifax, Nova Scotia in Canada was the successful bidder and his contract to deliver the mail across the Atlantic from Britain to North America was signed on 4th May

1839. Cunard was a highly successful and enterprising Canadian businessman and one of a group of 12 individuals who directed the affairs of Nova Scotia. In order to carry out the trans-Atlantic contract successfully, he worked with the engineer Robert Napier and three other businessmen who provided financial backing for the project. These five men founded the British and North American Royal Mail Steam Packet Company, later to become known as the Cunard Line.

In the 1880s, the Orient Line and North of Scotland Company, both later to be taken over by P & O, pioneered modern-style cruises and in 1904 P & O offered its first cruise holiday programme, arranged by Thomas Cook. The tour used the liner *Rome*, renaming her *Vectis* in her new role as a 'cruising yacht'.

Cruising in the 20th century

The first half of the 20th century was the heyday for large cruise liners, which were built to serve the increasing numbers of passengers travelling between Europe and North America. The largest passenger steamship of the time, the *Titanic* was launched in 1912, but tragically sank on its maiden voyage on the night of 14th April, with the loss of nearly 1,500 lives. The sinking of the *Titanic* led to safety and communications improvements on board passenger ships to reduce the likelihood of such an event ever happening again. By the end of the 1930s, Cunard operated trans-Atlantic crossings every 10 weeks. Bigger and better ships were introduced and they competed to make the fastest crossing of the Atlantic. Many raced for the 'Blue Riband' trophy awarded to the ship making the fastest trans-Atlantic crossing, most notably the *Queen Mary* and *Queen Elizabeth*, launched in 1934 and 1938 respectively. Other important ships of the time included the *Mauretania*, the *Aquitania* and the *Windsor Castle*. Cruising in these ships was a luxurious experience, only available to the rich and famous.

By the 1930s, cruise-orientated amenities and facilities began to feature more prominently in passenger ship design. American ocean liners introduced air conditioning, a majority of cabins with private facilities and some with private verandas. Grace Line's Santa liners even had retractable roofs over their dining rooms to allow passengers to dine under the tropical stars.

The majority of ships in cruise service after World War Two (1939-1945) were liners whose sources of income gradually began to diminish. The number of people emigrating began to decrease (emigrants were an important market for many ship companies). Also, the development of the jet engine and long-haul passenger aircraft, such as the Boeing 707 in 1958, led to a dramatic reduction in the number of passengers using cruise ships from the mid-20th century onwards. The decline began in the late 1950s and resulted in ships like the *Queen Elizabeth* becoming redundant. By the 1970s, the advent of the Boeing 747 'jumbo jet' really saw the end of the golden period of trans-Atlantic cruise liners. With no regular mail contracts for the shipping companies after 1945, cruising became even more important to the shipping industry. P & O's last ship built for scheduled voyages, the *Canberra*, was

Unit 9

launched in 1961, but in little more than a decade jet aircraft had taken many of the company's regular passengers and freight was transferred onto purpose-built cargo ships.

In the late 20th century the true ocean liners declined and diminished in number, being succeeded by cruise liners such as the *Oriana, Aurora, Royal Princess, Voyager of the Seas, Monarch of the Seas* and many others. Between 1964 and 1972, four companies that came to be known as the 'big four' were founded – Carnival Cruises, Royal Caribbean Cruise Line, Princess Cruises and the Norwegian Caribbean Line.

P & O Cruises launched the Oriana in 1995

21st century cruising

The cruise boom of the 1980s continued into the 21st century despite a brief blip in the early 1990s when fewer cruise ships were built due to concern about a possible slowdown in the cruise sector. Today, bigger and brasher cruise ships are being built to service a growing demand from travellers. Despite there being considerable integration and standardisation in the sector, with just three big players – Carnival, Royal Caribbean International and Star/Norwegian Cruise Line – plus other independent operators, there is still a great deal of variety in terms of ships and the products they offer their passengers, whether it be mass-market, small-ship, luxury, family-orientated, adventure of luxury cruising. The cruise ships of the early 21st century tend to be floating hotels or resorts and destinations in their own right.

In 2000, P&O Cruises introduced the *Aurora* as the UK's second superliner to follow the *Oriana*. In the same year a notable development took place in the cruising world, with the introduction of the world's first timeshare residential cruise ship called *The World*, which is the first step at turning the cruise ship into a floating city. In 2004, Cunard launched the *Queen Mary 2*, the first trans-Atlantic liner to be built for a generation and a year later P & O Cruises introduced the *Arcadia*. Based on the Vista class ships of the Holland America Line, *Arcadia* shows how cruise ships have become more standardised in terms of design, but can still show their individualism by brand and company heritage.

Unit 9

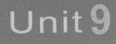

The Queen Mary 2 was launched in 2004 *(courtesy of Cunard)*

ACTIVITY

Write a 1,000-word newspaper article on key milestones in the development of cruising.

This activity is designed to provide evidence for P1.

Consumer demands/needs and the influence on cruising trends

The changing demands and expectations of passengers are a constant challenge for cruise operators, which must offer new products and services to a wide variety of customers, in order to remain competitive. This has resulted in a number of recent trends in the cruise sector, including:

1. Growth in the market;
2. New, larger ships;
3. Changing popularity of cruise areas;
4. Changes in customer profiles;
5. More informal cruising;
6. Growth in ex-UK cruises;
7. Demand for ultra-luxury cruising.

Growth in the cruise market

In 2004, worldwide cruise passenger numbers grew by 8.4 per cent to 13.4 million, according to figures published in the *Annual Cruise Review*. With just four new ships being delivered in 2005, compared with 10-12 ships in each of the last four years, bookings are not expected to grow quite as much this year. However, the number of new ships begins to accelerate from 2006, making it likely that passenger numbers will reach 15 million worldwide in 2006 and an estimated 20 million by 2012.

Unit 9

The UK cruise market, including river and ocean cruises, grew more than 8 per cent in 2004 to another record total of 1.14 million passengers. In the largest source market, North America, bookings for 2004 were up 8.5 per cent to 8.9 million.

New, larger ships

There are currently 23 new cruise ships to be introduced over the next four years. Almost all are large 'mega-ships', with a much wider range of dining and entertainment facilities to appeal to families and a much broader age group generally.

This trend towards building larger ships not only makes good financial sense on account of the economies of scale, it also allows the companies to offer ever more elaborate facilities for guests on board ship, e.g. large show rooms with state-of-the-art lighting and sound equipment, shopping malls, ice skating rinks, fitness suites and even rock climbing walls! More restaurants on board have led to the introduction of new dining concepts where passengers are free to choose where and with whom they want to dine. Entertainment on board has developed from shows performed by talented crew members in the 1970s to full scale Hollywood and Las Vegas production shows on today's mega liners. Last but not least, cabins (often referred to now as staterooms) with balconies, Internet access, the latest movies on television and even butler service or 24-hour room service, have been introduced on the new breed of cruise ships.

Cruise ships now have excellent fitness suites on board (courtesy of Cunard)

It is not just new ships that are being designed to appeal first-time cruisers, families and younger passengers. Cruise lines are now starting to revitalise their existing ships, adding more cabins with balconies, internet cafés and family entertainment areas. Some, like RCI with the *Enchantment of the Seas*, are even 'stretching' ships by having them cut in half and adding a new central section with more cabins, restaurants, bars and entertainment venues.

Changing popularity of cruise areas

Data from the *Annual Cruise Review* indicates that the Mediterranean remained the most popular cruise destination with the British in 2004, followed by the Caribbean,

Scandinavia/the Baltic and the Atlantic Isles. Destinations showing the biggest rise in demand between 2003 and 2004 with British cruise passengers were Alaska (+ 69 per cent), round-the-world (+ 47 per cent) and the Caribbean (+ 25 per cent). During the same time period demand for cruises in the Far East/Australia fell by 63 per cent, due to SARS and other recent events, and short cruises out of Cyprus were down by 27 per cent, a reflection of political troubles in Israel and Egypt.

Changes in customer profiles

Although the UK population is ageing, with an increasing proportion of over-50s compared to under-30s, the average age of cruise passengers continues to fall. This is partly due to the increased numbers of families with children now being attracted to cruising. It is also a reflection of the younger people being attracted to the sector by the new, informal and activity-orientated brands, such as Ocean Village, Island Cruises and easyCruise, all of which are planning to expand their operations over the next two years. All of these factors combine to paint a picture of a changing profile of customers that are attracted to cruising. In short, cruise passengers are:

- Younger than in the past;
- Interested in activities while on board ship and on shore;
- Looking for short cruises as well as extended journeys;
- Interested in travelling with families and friends;
- Looking for adventure.

Cruise companies are increasingly 'segmenting the market', i.e. developing cruise products and services to meet the needs of individual segments of the market, for example families, singles and younger passengers.

More informal cruising

A success story in recent years has been the introduction of more informal cruises, led by companies like Ocean Village, Island Cruises and easyCruise. These fashionable cruises are aimed at younger, and particularly first-time, cruisers. Formality is at a minimum, with no formal dress code, no fixed meal times, lots of activities on board and ashore, plus coffee shops and alternative entertainment.

Unit 9

WEBLINK

www.oceanvillage
holidays.co.uk

*Check out this website
for more information on
Ocean Village.*

FOCUS ON INDUSTRY – Ocean Village

Ocean Village is to introduce a second ship following the successful performance of the informal cruise operator, launched in 2003. The 1,690 passenger Regal Princess will transfer from its sister company Princess Cruises to begin Caribbean fly/cruise itineraries in the winter of 2006-2007, moving to the Mediterranean in May 2007 for summer sailings. The original Ocean Village ship, which is marketed as 'the cruise for people who don't do cruises', has to date taken more than 150,000 bookings, 60 per cent of which are from first-time cruise passengers. Facilities on board both ships include two pools, eight bars, four restaurants, a theatre, cinema, spa and nightclub.

ACTIVITY

Carry out some research on easyCruise and make an information sheet containing relevant information on the company and its products, e.g. destinations visited, facilities on board, prices, target markets, etc.

This activity is designed to provide evidence for P1.

Growth in ex-UK cruises

More people than ever are choosing to start their cruise holiday from a UK port, thereby saving the time and inconvenience of travelling abroad to a departure port. In 2004, passengers cruising to the Mediterranean from UK ports increased by 33 per cent over 2003. A 13 per cent increase in UK to UK cruise bookings in 2004, compared with just four per cent for fly/cruises, means that three passengers in every ten now take this option compared with just two in 10 as recently as 2000. In 2005, ex-UK port passenger numbers to the Mediterranean are expected to rise sharply again as there are more UK to UK ships operating (for RCI, Princess, P & O Cruises and Thomson) and more regional departures too.

Demand for ultra-luxury cruising

The growth in the popularity of mass-market cruising, aimed at a wide variety of passengers travelling on a budget, has led some wealthy customers to seek out small, exclusive cruises that offer exceptional personal service and attention to detail. To meet this demand, seven of the world's top cruising operators have joined forces to offer a variety of experiences, as the next example explains.

Unit 9

FOCUS ON INDUSTRY – Ultra-luxury cruising

www.exclusive-
collection.co.uk

*Check out this website
for more information on
The Exclusive Collection.*

Seven of the Passenger Shipping Association's ultra-luxury cruise line members have come together to form a new alliance, the Exclusive Collection. The alliance is aimed at attracting discerning holidaymakers seeking a sophisticated, bespoke holiday experience, but who may currently not consider a holiday afloat. Members of the Exclusive Collection are Crystal Cruises, Hebridean Island Cruises, Peter Deilmann River & Ocean Cruises, Radisson Seven Seas Cruises, Seabourn Cruise Line, Sea Line, SeaDream Yacht Club and Windstar Cruises. All seven cruise lines offer a crew to passenger ratio of at least one to two, thereby ensuring personal service and attention to detail.

Structure of the cruise sector

Cruising is a global industry, not just in terms of the worldwide destinations visited, but also from an ownership perspective, with just three companies dominating world cruising – Carnival, Royal Caribbean International and Star/Norwegian Cruise Line. In the following sections of this unit we will examine the range of cruise operators in more detail and explore how cruising links with other sectors of the travel and tourism industry.

Cruise operators

There are many different cruise operators across the world, but three companies dominate the sector and account for over 80 per cent of all cruise bookings worldwide (see Figure 9.1).

As Figure 9.1 demonstrates, Carnival is by far the biggest cruise company in the world, followed by Royal Caribbean International (RCI) and Star Cruises. Together, these three operators control 82 per cent of the global cruise market, according to data in the *Cruise Industry News Annual Report*, leaving a variety of smaller, independent cruise companies to make up the rest. There is a detailed case study on Carnival on page 42.

Founded in 1969, RCI has a fleet of 29 ships, branded as Royal Caribbean and Celebrity Cruises. Royal Caribbean has nine ships and appeals particularly to families and middle-market customers with its combination of value for money and quality. Since May 2005, RCI's *Legend of the Seas* has been based in

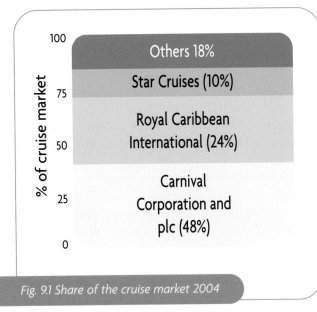

Fig. 9.1 Share of the cruise market 2004

Source: Adapted from Cruise Industry News data

Southampton operating an ex-UK cruise schedule for British passengers. Celebrity Cruises operates at the top end of the mainstream, large cruise ship lines. Renowned for good service, high quality catering and on board facilities, Celebrity has a fleet of ten ships, with capacities ranging between 1,300 and 2,000.

WEBLINK

www.islandcruises.com

Check out this website for more information on Island Cruises.

FOCUS ON INDUSTRY – Island Cruises

This single-ship *(Island Escape)* cruise line was launched in 2002 as a joint venture between RCI and First Choice. With flexible dining and familiar 'brands' on board, like Costa Coffee, Oddbins wines and Holmes Place gyms, Island was aimed firmly at younger passengers who may have been put off by the formal, 'stuffy' image of traditional cruise lines. For the 2004-2005 season, the company changed it approach to attract more first-time cruisers and families, operating Mediterranean cruises during the summer and cruises from Brazil in the winter. A second ship, *Island Star*, is due to join the fleet in the spring of 2006, with a capacity of 1,700 passengers.

Star Cruises was founded in 1995 and is already the world's third largest cruise operator. It tapped into the cruise potential of the Asia Pacific region and has since acquired Norwegian Cruise Line (NCL) and Orient Lines. Star has eight ships operating in Asia Pacific, two of which – *Superstar Virgo* and *Superstar Leo* – are available through UK tour operators and agencies. The NCL group operates a fleet of 16 ships in service or due to be delivered.

CASE STUDY – Carnival Corporation and plc

Introduction

Carnival Corporation and plc (public limited company) is the world's biggest cruise operator, accounting for nearly half of all cruises booked in the world. Many of the best-known names in the cruising sector are wholly or partly-owned by Carnival, including Cunard, Swan Hellenic and Ocean Village. In 2003, Carnival Corporation and P & O Princess Cruises plc formally merged, the latter now adopting the Carnival name. Carnival's mission is:

'To deliver exceptional vacation experiences through the world's best-known cruise brands that cater to a variety of different lifestyles and budgets, all at an outstanding value unrivalled on land or at sea'.

With its headquarters in Miami, Florida, Carnival has more than 650,000 employees worldwide and operates a fleet of 75 ships, with 9 new ships scheduled for delivery by mid-2006. With 123,000 berths and almost 55,000 crew members, there are roughly 175,000

Unit 9

people at sea with Carnival at any given time. The company also owns two tour businesses that complement its cruise operations – Holland America Tours and Princess Tours in Alaska and the Canadian Yukon. Carnival's combined holiday companies cater for around 5.4 million customers every year.

Carnival brands

Carnival has 12 distinct cruising brands aimed at particular market segments, made up of the leading cruise operators in North America, Europe and Australia:

1. Carnival Cruise Lines (www.carnival.com) – reputed to be the most profitable cruise line in the world, this brand operates 20 'fun ships', aimed primarily at the North American market. Destinations include the Bahamas, Canada, the Mexican Riviera and Alaska, with most cruises ranging from 3 to 7 days;
2. Holland America Line (www.hollandamerica.com) – a 12-strong fleet of five-star, premium ships sailing from 15 North American home ports, including Baltimore and Boston;
3. Princess Cruises (www.princesscruises.com) – there are 11 ships in the Princess fleet aimed mostly at the mid to upper market. The ships are deployed all around the globe, calling at more than 200 ports worldwide;
4. Seabourn Cruise Line (www.seabourn.com) – a three-ship fleet of luxury all-suite ships carrying just over 200 passengers each (*Seabourn Legend, Seabourn Pride* and *Seabourn Spirit*). Seabourn operates a passenger/crew ratio of close to 1/1;
5. Windstar Cruises (www.windstarcruises.com) – a fleet of three luxury sailing ships operating Caribbean and European itineraries in winter and summer;
6. AIDA Cruises (www.aida.de) – this is the best-known cruise brand in the fast-growing German cruise industry. The company's four ships cruise to the Mediterranean, Baltic, Norwegian fjords, Canary Islands and the Caribbean;
7. Costa Cruises (www.costacruises.com) – a ten- ship fleet ranging from the 800-passenger Costa Allegra to their latest three 2,200-passenger ships – *Costa Atlantica, Costa Mediterranea* and *Costa Fortuna*);
8. Cunard Line (www.cunard.com) – a fleet of three ships comprising the 700-passenger *Caronia, the QE2* and *the Queen Mary 2*, which made its maiden voyage in January 2004. A fourth ship, *Queen Victoria*, is due to join the Cunard fleet in summer 2007;
9. P & O Cruises (www.pocruises.com) – is the largest cruise operator in the UK, with six ships around the 2,000-passenger mark – the *Arcadia, Oceana, Adonia, Aurora, Oriana* and *Artemis*. In 2006, P & O will be offering 130 different cruise holidays to 181 ports in 72 countries, ranging from two to 25 nights in duration, plus one 80-night world cruise;
10. Ocean Village (www.oceanvillageholidays.co.uk) – this is a new cruise brand in the UK, which has been established to provide informal, contemporary and affordable holidays at sea for younger people. The single Ocean Village ship cruises in the Mediterranean in the summer and the Caribbean in the winter;
11. Swan Hellenic (www.swanhellenic.com) – offer 'discovery cruises' on board the *Minerva II*, focusing on the arts, culture and history of destinations from the Arctic Circle to South America, backed up with expert lecturers and excursions;

Unit 9

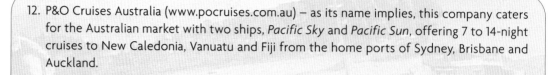

12. P&O Cruises Australia (www.pocruises.com.au) – as its name implies, this company caters for the Australian market with two ships, *Pacific Sky* and *Pacific Sun*, offering 7 to 14-night cruises to New Caledonia, Vanuatu and Fiji from the home ports of Sydney, Brisbane and Auckland.

Carnival cruise destinations

With such a huge range of cruise companies under its wing, Carnival operates in a wide range of cruise destinations around the world, including Alaska, the Caribbean, Canada, Eastern USA, the Mediterranean, the Pacific, Western USA and Mexico, plus trans-Atlantic and round-the-world cruises.

WEBLINK

www.carnival.com

Check out this website to help answer the questions in this case study and for more information on cruising with Carnival.

CASE STUDY QUESTIONS

1. Explain how Carnival Corporation and plc is a vertically-integrated company.
2. Why has Carnival chosen to enter into mergers and takeovers with other cruise lines?
3. Choose one of the Carnival 'brands' and carry out some further research on the company, so that you could advise somebody who wants to take a cruise with that operator.
4. What other sectors of the travel and tourism industry do Carnival's cruise companies work with on a regular basis?

Links with other sectors of travel and tourism

Like most sectors of the travel and tourism industry the cruise sector works in partnership with many companies and organisations in the course of its work. These 'partners' include:

- Travel agents – are the retail arm of the industry, advising and selling cruise holidays to customers. The vast majority of UK cruise bookings are made through travel agents; 86 per cent overall in 2004 and 90 per cent for fly/cruises, according to data included in the *World Cruise Review*. A cruise is often an expensive purchase, so many customers prefer the personal contact and reassurance of dealing with an agent. Agents benefit as well, since cruise companies pay good commission on sales;
- Hotels and other accommodation – cruise lines use a variety of accommodation for 'cruise and stay' holiday passengers;
- Attractions – cruise passengers often visit attractions as part of an excursion on shore;
- Transport operators – coach companies provide transfers to and from destination ports, as well as excursions on shore; some up-market cruise lines even offer chauffeur-drive and helicopter transfers as options;

Airlines – cruise lines contract with either scheduled or charter airlines when arranging fly/cruises for passengers.

WEBLINK

www.thomson.co.uk

Check out this website for more information on Thomson Cruises.

FOCUS ON INDUSTRY – Thomson Cruises and Leger Holidays

Thomson offers its cruise passengers a return coach service from a variety of UK departure points to one of their cruise terminals – Southampton, Harwich or Newcastle. Current fares range from £39 return for an adult travelling from, for example, Sheffield to Newcastle, up to £69 return for a journey from Glasgow to Southampton. The service is operated by Leger Holidays, but does not form part of the holiday arrangement that customers make with Thomson for their cruise. This arrangement makes good sense for both companies – Thomson gains by offering its passengers a useful extra service, while both companies make revenue from additional sales.

Horizontal and vertical integration

You have learned in other units on your course that there are many links between different companies and sectors of the travel and tourism industry; this is sometimes referred to as 'integration'. Horizontal integration occurs when a company owns or controls other businesses at the same level of the distribution chain or in the same sector, e.g. TUI owns a wide range of tour operating companies, including Thomson Holidays, Something Special, Simply Travel and OSL. Vertical integration is when a company owns or controls more then one level of the distribution chain, e.g. TUI not only owns a variety of tour operating companies, but also the chain of Thomson travel agencies and its own airline Thomsonfly. Companies get involved in integration via mergers and takeovers as a way of increasing their sales and gaining an advantage over their competitors.

Integration also occurs in the cruise sector. The three major cruise lines – Carnival, Royal Caribbean International (RCI) and Star/Norwegian Cruise Line – are all vertically-integrated companies, i.e. they own other shipping lines that operate under different names. For example, we saw earlier in the case study on Carnival (see page 42) that it owns 12 different cruise companies under different brand names, including Cunard, Ocean Village and P & O Cruises. RCI owns Celebrity Cruises, while Star Cruises own Norwegian Cruise Line and Orient Lines.

Trade and regulatory bodies

In the UK, the Passenger Shipping Association (PSA) is the principal trade body representing the cruise sector (see case study below). In the USA, there are a number of trade organisations that claim to represent the interests of the cruise sector, e.g. the International Council of Cruise Lines (ICCL) and the Cruise Line International Association (CLIA). Both organisations include the majority of cruise lines in their membership and are actively involved in training, marketing, research, safety and security in the cruising industry. The newly-formed European Cruise Council (ECC) held its first board meeting in Brussels in April 2004, with representatives from ten cruise lines in attendance. The ECC was formed to promote and defend the interests of the cruise sector within Euopean Union institutions, collate industry statistics to demonstrate the scale and breadth of the cruise industry, and provide a resource for the promotion of cruises in Europe. The 15 founder cruise company members of the ECC include Fred. Olsen Cruise Line, RCI, Saga Shipping, Thomson Cruises and Costa Cruises.

CASE STUDY – The Passenger Shipping Association (PSA)

Introduction

The Passenger Shipping Association (PSA) is a trade organisation that represents the interests of the leading UK-based cruise and ferry operators. The PSA was originally set up as Ocean Travel Development (OTD) in 1958 by a group of passenger ship owners. They had seen, for the first time in 1957, the number of passengers travelling across the Atlantic by air exceeding those travelling by sea on the great liners. OTD's main objective was to focus public attention, and that of the travel trade, on sea travel as a holiday and leisure pursuit, and as a modern alternative to transportation from A to B. The shipping lines conceded that they could no longer compete with the developing airlines, both on travel times and cost, and recognised that their future lay in full-time cruising. In 1976, it was agreed by the shipping lines that OTD's name should be changed to the Passenger Shipping Association, to reflect more accurately the aims of the association.

Mission statement and objectives

PSA's mission statement is:

'To provide a service of excellence to the Members and Associate Members of the PSA. To ensure that the PSA is the recognised industry body for the cruise and ferry sectors. To act as a forum for discussion on areas of mutual interest'.

Its objectives are:

1. The promotion of travel by sea by the public;
2. To encourage expansion in the volume of passenger travel, by sea and river;

3. To work towards the removal or prevention of the imposition of restrictions or taxes on passenger travel by sea;
4. To advise member lines to ensure that passengers travel in a safe, healthy and secure environment.

What does the PSA do?

In order to meet its objectives, the Association has a very wide-ranging work programme, including:

- Lobbying the government and officials in the European Union;
- Working with, and through other bodies, notable ABTA (the Association of British Travel Agents), the Chamber of Shipping and the European Community Shipowners' Association (ECSA);
- Providing a forum for the training and education of travel agents through its subsidiary company PSARA (see below);
- Acting as a spokesperson for the industry;
- Co-ordinating activities of its member shipping lines;
- Acting as an information centre for member lines and associate members;
- Acting as a statutory bonding authority for member lines as required;
- Promoting market growth in the passenger shipping industry through public relations campaigns;
- Ensuring that member companies are aware of the best practice and the statutory regulations on safety, the protection of the environment, health, hygiene and security.

Membership of the PSA

Currently, the PSA has 29 cruise line members, including Cunard, Norwegian Cruise Line, Thomson and Royal Caribbean Cruise Lines. Its 19 ferry company members include Brittany Ferries, Stena Line, Sea France and Hoverspeed. Associate members of the PSA, who work closely with the cruise and ferry sectors, include the Port of London Authority, Eurolines and the Port of Dover.

PSARA

In 1987, the PSA formed a subsidiary company – the Passenger Shipping Association Retail Agents Scheme (PSARA) – which was entrusted with fulfilling the Association's travel agency educational role. The scheme is self-funding, based on contributions from the cruise industry and retail travel agents. Cruise manuals, newsletters, product information and an extensive programme of training seminars, are the basis of the benefits to members. The PSARA Scheme is an important factor in the growth of cruising traffic in the UK and is steadily increasing its membership in the travel agency world.

Unit 9

WEBLINK

www.the-psa.co.uk

Check out this website to help answer the questions in this case study and for more information on the Passenger Shipping Association.

CASE STUDY QUESTIONS

1. What are the benefits of being a member of the PSA to an individual shipping company?
2. Over what sort of matters and concerns do you think that the PSA lobbies members of the government and the European Union?
3. Carry out some further research on the PSARA Scheme and make a list of the benefits of membership for travel agents;
4. Log on to the PSA's website and write a summary of two recent press releases concerned with cruising issues.

Unit 9

Cruise areas of the world

In this section we investigate a selection of cruise areas of the world that are popular with the British. According to figures quoted in the *Annual Cruise Review*, the ten most popular cruise destinations for British passengers in 2004 were:

1. The Mediterranean;
2. The Caribbean;
3. The Baltic/Scandinavia;
4. Atlantic Isles (Madeira and the Canary Islands);
5. Hawaii;
6. Alaska;
7. Short cruises ex-Cyprus;
8. Round-the-world;
9. South America/Antarctica;
10. Far East/Australia.

The Mediterranean

The Mediterranean Sea stretches for more than 2,200 miles, from the 22-mile wide straits of Gibraltar to the Black Sea in the east and the Suez Canal in the south east. It offers cruise passengers a mixture of ancient and modern, with many different cultures, geography and history all set in a beautiful climate. The Greeks, Romans and Egyptians all built their empires around the Mediterranean and have left behind some of the world's best-known tourist attractions, including the Pyramids, the Acropolis and the Coliseum. Most Mediterranean cruise itineraries include a short flight from the UK to Genoa, Palma or Athens, thereby avoiding the sometimes rough waters of the Bay of Biscay and offering instant sunshine. Alternatively passengers can take a coach, train or drive to their Mediterranean departure port. Others may opt for a cruise that starts and finishes in a UK port. All of the major shipping lines offer Mediterranean cruises, including Thomson, Costa Cruises, Cunard, P & O Cruises, Celebrity Cruises, Swan Hellenic, Island Cruises and Ocean Village.

Ports of call that might be visited on a Mediterranean cruise include:

- Spanish mainland ports such as Barcelona, Cadiz, Malaga and Valencia;
- Balearic Islands of Ibiza, Majorca and Minorca;
- Canary Islands such as Tenerife, Gran Canaria, La Palma, La Gomera and El Hierro;
- French ports of Cannes, Monte Carlo, St Tropez and Ajaccio (Corsica);
- Italian ports such as Genoa, Civitavecchia, Livorno, Venice, Sardinia, Amalfi and Catania;

Unit 9

- Valetta (Malta's main port);
- Cyprus ports of Limassol, Paphos and Larnaca;
- Piraeus, Corfu, Rhodes, Heraklion, Mykonos and Skiathos in Greece;
- Turkish ports of Izmir, Kusadasi, Bodrum and Antalya;
- Israel ports of Haifa, Tel Aviv and Ashdod;
- Ports in Egypt, including Alexandria, Port Said and Safaga;
- Black Sea ports of Varna and Nesebur in Bulgaria, Yalta and Odessa in the Ukraine, and Constanta in Romania;
- North African ports of Sidi Bou Said in Tunisia and Tangier, Agadir and Casablanca in Morocco.

ACTIVITY

Plot the above list of Mediterranean cruise ports on a blank map of Europe that can be downloaded from www.tandtONLine.co.uk

Figure 9.2 shows an example of a 14-night Mediterranean cruise offered by P & O Cruises on board the *Oriana*, starting and ending in Southampton. Highlights of the cruise include time to explore the history and culture of a variety of Mediterranean cities, including Barcelona, Florence, Pisa, Palma and Naples.

ACTIVITY

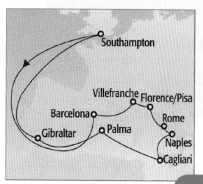

Study the itinerary shown in Figure 9.2 and make notes on the type of passengers that you think the cruise would appeal to. You may like to do some further research in brochures and on websites to help you with this task.

This activity is designed to provide evidence for P3.

Fig. 9.2 Mediterranean cruise itinerary

Unit 9

The Caribbean

There are 7,000 islands in the Caribbean Sea, lying between the southern tip of the eastern USA and the north coast of South America. The area stretches for more than 2,500 miles, so cruising is an excellent way to experience as much as possible of this part of the world. The area has a rich culture and heritage, with many languages spoken and varied geographical features. Nearly all UK passengers opt for a fly/cruise arrangement when buying their Caribbean cruise, allowing them to fit a cruise to a long-haul destination into a normal holiday period. All of the major shipping lines offer Caribbean cruises, including Royal Caribbean International, Carnival, Costa Cruises, Cunard, P & O Cruises, Celebrity Cruises, Orient Lines and Ocean Village.

Caribbean cruises can last anything from three days for a short holiday between Florida and the Bahamas to holidays lasting a month and covering the whole area. Examples of countries that could be visited on a Caribbean cruise include:

- Western Caribbean – Cozumel or Playa del Carmen in Mexico, the Cayman Islands and Jamaica;
- Eastern Caribbean – Puerto Rico, the US Virgin Islands (St Thomas and St Croix), St Martin, Dominica, Barbados, St Kitts and Martinique;
- Southern Caribbean – Puerto Rico, US Virgin Islands, Guadeloupe, Grenada, Barbados, Antigua, St Lucia, Martinique, Venezuela and Aruba.

ACTIVITY

Using an atlas for reference, draw a map of the Caribbean and include the above list of cruise ports found in the area.

The Panama Canal can also be combined with a Caribbean cruise. Passengers can choose to take a one-way or 'line journey' from Fort Lauderdale, Miami or Puerto Rico through to Acapulco or Los Angeles. Alternatively they can take a cruise that travels half way along the canal before returning.

Figure 9.3 shows an example of a 9-night Caribbean fly/cruise offered by Norwegian Cruise Line (NCL) on board the *Norwegian Majesty*, starting and finishing in Charleston, South Carolina. Highlights of the cruise include time to visit historic Charleston, the Mayan ruins in the Yucatan, Ernest Hemingway's home in Key West and the fashionable resort of Cozumel.

Unit 9

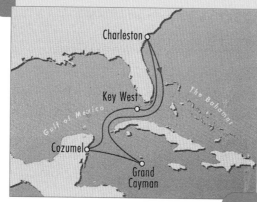

ACTIVITY

Study the itinerary shown in Figure 9.3 and make notes on the type of passengers that you think the cruise would appeal to. You may like to do some further research in brochures and on websites to help you with this task.

This activity is designed to provide evidence for P3.

Fig. 9.3 Caribbean cruise itinerary

The Baltic

Cruises in the Baltic Sea and Scandinavia appeal to people with an interest in history and culture, rather than beaches and hot weather. Baltic cruise itineraries include the great cities of Northern Europe, and the majority of cruises include a visit to the historic port of St Petersburg. Scandinavia offers cruise visitors tranquil fjords and breathtaking scenery. Cruise companies that feature the Baltic include Norwegian Cruise Line, Costa Cruises, Cunard, P & O Cruises, Celebrity Cruises and Voyages of Discovery.

Cities that are often included in Baltic cruise itineraries include:

* Amsterdam;
* Copenhagen;
* Helsinki;
* Stockholm;
* Oslo;
* Tallinn;
* Riga;
* St Petersburg.

Cruises that take in the Norwegian fjords and coastline can include the following ports of call:

* Bergen;
* Trondheim;
* Alesund;
* Tromso;
* Hammerfest;
* The North Cape.

Unit 9

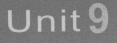

ACTIVITY

t and t ONLine

Plot the above list of Baltic cruise ports on a blank map of Europe that can be downloaded from www.tandtONLine.co.uk

Figure 9.4 shows an example of a 14-night Baltic cruise offered by P & O Cruises on board the *Arcadia*, starting and ending in Southampton. Highlights of the cruise include visits to many historic cities, museums, palaces and cultural sites.

ACTIVITY

Study the itinerary shown in Figure 9.4 and make notes on the type of passengers that you think the cruise would appeal to. You may like to do some further research in brochures and on websites to help you with this task.

This activity is designed to provide evidence for P3.

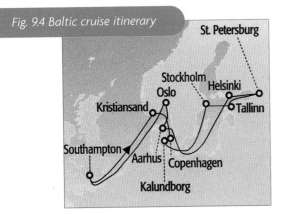

Fig. 9.4 Baltic cruise itinerary

Alaska

Alaska attracts cruise passengers, from May to October, to see its vast and unspoilt landscape of mountains, forests, glaciers and fjords. Its scenery and wildlife are the main attractions of the area, which covers more than 580,000 miles. There are two basic Alaska cruise itineraries:

1. The classic 'inside passage' – this is a round-trip, one-week cruise, beginning and ending in Vancouver, named because it lies within a long chain of coastal islands that act as a buffer to the open waters of the North Pacific. This type of cruise usually includes visits to tidewater glaciers, such as those at the head of narrow, cliff-sided Tracy Arm, or those found in the many inlets of Glacier Bay;
2. The 'glacier route' itinerary – this includes the Gulf of Alaska in a one-way route between Vancouver and Anchorage. These cruises include some of Alaska's most impressive tidewater glaciers, such as Hubbard Glacier in Yakutat Bay and Columbia Glacier in Prince William Sound.

Unit 9

Cruise companies that feature Alaska include Norwegian Cruise Line, Royal Caribbean International, Crystal Cruises, Holland America Line and Celebrity Cruises.

Figure 9.5 shows an example of a 9-night Alaska fly/cruise offered by Norwegian Cruise Lines on board the Norwegian Sun, starting and ending in Vancouver. Highlights of the cruise include time to explore Vancouver's historic Gastown and cosmopolitan Yaletown, plus cruising by the Sawyer Glacier and viewing all kinds of wildlife.

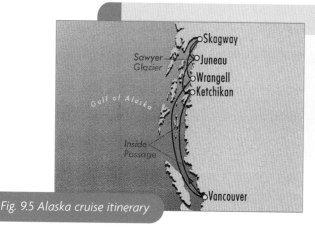

Fig. 9.5 Alaska cruise itinerary

ACTIVITY

Study the itinerary shown in Figure 9.5 and make notes on the type of passengers that you think the cruise would appeal to. You may like to do some further research in brochures and on websites to help you with this task.

This activity is designed to provide evidence for P3.

The Nile (river cruising)

The River Nile is the second most popular river cruise destination with British people, after the Rhine, but its popularity is growing much more quickly than that of the German river; the number of British passengers on the Nile rose by 43 per cent between 2003 and 2004, whereas the number of Rhine cruisers increased by just two per cent over the same period. Cruisers are attracted by the thousands of years of history in the region, inspiring monuments such as the Pyramids and Sphinx at Gizeh, the temples at Karnak, Philea and the Valley of the Kings. The majority of British visitors to Egypt include a short cruise on the Nile between Luxor and Aswan during their stay. Cruises of the 140-mile stretch of the Upper Nile typically last for four of five days. A number of Nile cruise operators combine a stay in Cairo with their cruises, giving passengers the chance to visit the Tutankhamun treasures in the Museum of the Antiquities.

Unit 9

Cruise ports

Cruise ports can be divided into three main types:

1. Ports of call – the destinations that a cruise ship visits as part of its itinerary;
2. Ports of embarkation – the ports where passengers begin (and sometimes end) their cruise;
3. Home ports – the ports where a ship has its operating base;
4. Gateway ports – these are major entry, exit and transit points for passengers and freight.

Florida is the cruising capital of the world, with the top three busiest embarkation ports – Miami, Port Everglades and Port Canaveral. The world's top five ports of call for cruise passengers are Cozumel (Mexico), Grand Cayman (Caribbean), Nassau (Bahamas), St Thomas (US Virgin Islands) and St Maarten (Caribbean).

Impacts of cruising

As with all sectors of the travel and tourism industry, cruising has both negative and positive impacts, particularly on the ports and cruise destinations visited by cruise passengers. As we have discussed earlier in this unit, the cruise sector is growing rapidly. This can have serious implications for ports of call on cruise itineraries that have to accommodate increased numbers of tourists and provide them with facilities and services.

Positive economic impacts on cruise ports and destinations include:

- Increased revenue – cruise passengers tend to visit ports in groups on organised excursions. While in port they spend money in shops, restaurants, attractions and on entertainment, thereby adding to the local economy. Taxi firms and coach companies also benefit financially from cruise passengers;
- Employment – cruising not only provides jobs for people working for the cruise lines, but also for travel and tourism businesses in ports, e.g. in hotels, restaurants, tourist attractions, tour operators and travel guides. Cruising also contributes towards 'indirect employment', i.e. jobs in non-tourism sectors that nonetheless benefit from influxes of cruise passengers, including construction, banking and craft industries.

The sheer scale of the cruise sector, as well as the numbers of passengers carried on each ship, can cause environmental, social and cultural problems, as the following case study on the impact of cruise tourism in Belize explains.

Unit 9

CASE STUDY – The impact of cruise tourism in Belize

Introduction

Belize is a small country situated at the base of the Yucatan in Central America. It borders Mexico and Guatemala, with the Caribbean Sea to the east. The country's area includes many small islands, known as cayes, which straddle a coral reef second only in size to the Great Barrier Reef in Australia. Belize has been developing its tourist industry in recent years based on its natural beauty and ruins associated with the ancient Mayan civilisation. Belize is included in the itineraries of cruise operators in the Western Caribbean, including Carnival Cruises.

The Belize Ecotourism Association (BEA)

The potential harmful impacts of cruise tourism on Belize have been brought to light by the Belize Ecotourism Association (BEA), a body set up in 1993 to:

'Promote environmentally responsible tourism, to be sensitive to the impact of tourism, to promote pollution prevention and environmental concerns, to continually observe the effects of all the above and to promote education for locals and visitors'.

The organisation is particularly concerned about the way that the type of 'mass tourism' associated with cruises may harm the country's economy in the long term, by alienating visitors to the country's small-sale tourism developments that have been nurtured over the last 20 years, based on ecotourism principles. The BEA wants to see a long-term plan for the sustainable development of all forms of tourism to Belize, including cruises.

Environmental concerns

BEA highlights a number of issues concerned with the environmental impacts of cruise tourism, including:

- Ancient Mayan ruins are under pressure from the large, and growing, number of cruise passengers;
- There is evidence of environmental deterioration on the cayes and coral reefs;
- Riverside erosion is increasing due to wash from the high-speed launches taking cruise passengers on adventure trips;
- Road systems are under pressure from the extra volume of traffic generated by cruise tourism;
- Solid waste from cruise passengers is increasing the burden on the area's sanitary infrastructure.

Cultural impacts

BEA believes that tourism should always contribute to cultural exchange between visitors and the people of Belize. Visitors attracted to Belize by the small-scale tourism developments, with the opportunity to learn about the local people and their traditions, are rewarded with warmth and kindness. With mass tourism associated with cruising there is a danger that these experiences may well be reversed. Expectations by street sellers of big sales are often disappointed. Passengers are hustled and their reactions may be seen to be hostile. The interaction, instead of being one of pleasure, can become one of distaste and an unwillingness to return to the country or recommend it to others.

The future

Tourism in Belize is estimated to be worth BZ$270 million to the country's economy, with cruise tourism accounting for some BZ$40 million. The Belize Ecotourism Association would like to see the burden of tourist taxes being spread more evenly amongst all visitors to the country – at present, tourists who stay overnight pay a higher tax than those just visiting for the day, including cruise passengers. They believe this is unfair, since the environmental impacts caused by cruise tourists are greater than long-stay visitors. A rise in the tourist tax for day visitors would give the government extra funds to allow proper monitoring of the impacts of cruise ship tourism. Also, it may attract higher-spending tourists to Belize, thereby benefiting the economy even more. The BEA would also like to see improvements in the country's infrastructure before any future plans for cruise tourism developments are considered and measures are in place to monitor developments for their environmental and cultural impacts.

CASE STUDY QUESTIONS

1. Why is it important for the government of Belize to monitor cruise tourism?
2. What measures could be introduced to reduce the pressure from tourists at the ancient Mayan ruins?
3. How can the government of Belize maximise the benefits from cruise tourism while at the same time minimising its negative impacts?
4. Carry out some further research to find examples of how cruise lines try to reduce their harmful environmental and cultural impacts.

WEBLINK

www.bzecotourism.org

Check out this website to help answer the questions in this case study and for more information on the Belize Ecotourism Association.

Unit 9

SECTION 3: TYPES OF CRUISES

We saw earlier in this unit that cruising now caters for a diverse range of customers, with the industry offering a wider than ever variety of products to suit all budgets. As a consequence, there are many different types of cruises on offer, geared to different segments of the market.

Types of cruises

The cruise sector has responded to the changing demands of travellers by developing different types of cruises to suit all tastes, including:

- Fly/cruise;
- Round-the-world;
- Mini-cruise;
- River cruise;
- Luxury cruise;
- Soft adventure;
- Sail ship;
- Cruise and stay;
- Special interest;
- All inclusive.

Fly/cruise

Fly/cruise is a popular arrangement that allows cruise passengers to combine their time at sea with a flight to or from the home port of their cruise, thereby beginning their cruise as soon as possible. All major cruise operators offer fly/cruise holidays for an all-inclusive package price. Cruise companies use charter airlines and scheduled services, depending on the destination and type of cruise. Scheduled services with major airlines tend to be offered on the more expensive cruises, for example Cunard has an arrangement with British Airways to transport its cruise passengers, offering upgrades on payment of a supplement. Wherever possible, passengers on Thomson cruises fly to their cruise home port with Thomsonfly (formerly Britannia Airways), which is part of the same company TUI. This is an example of vertical integration that we discussed in the first section of this unit.

Round-the-world

A round-the-world trip is most people's idea of the ultimate cruising experience – but you need the money and time to do it! Cunard's 2006 world cruise on the *Queen Elizabeth 2* lasts for 109 days and full brochure prices start at £18,999. Not surprisingly, therefore, these types of cruises tend to appeal to retired people with time to spare and a good income or savings. UK passengers wanting a round-the-world cruise can leave from Southampton or fly straight to the sun and start their circumnavigation at a port such as Miami or Los Angeles. Another option is to start the cruise from New York. Passengers who can't spare the time for a full world cruise can sample part of the experience – all world cruises are broken down into fly/cruise segments to allow passengers to select the time periods and destinations that are most convenient for them. One of the most popular options is a semi-circumnavigation from the UK to Australia or back.

The QE2's world cruise lasts for 109 days (courtesy of Cunard)

ACTIVITY

Plot the route of a round-the-world cruise on an outline map of the world, marking the embarkation port and all ports of call on the journey. You can download a blank world map from www.tandtONLine.co.uk

This activity is designed to provide evidence for P4.

Mini-cruise

Busy, modern lifestyles have created a growing demand for short trips or mini-cruises on board ship, giving passengers the chance to relax and unwind. Nearly one in five cruises booked by British people is of five days' duration or less. Typically, a mini-cruise (a trip of less than seven nights at sea) gives passengers the chance to visit two or three destinations in a short period of time. Short cruises starting and ending in UK ports are growing in popularity, although short trips from Mediterranean ports continue to be in greatest demand.

River cruise

River cruising offers passengers the opportunity of exploring an area at close quarters in a cosy, intimate environment. River ships typically carry up to 200 passengers and can make up to three stops a day, allowing plenty of time for sightseeing and shopping. The ships travel by day and moor up at night, the opposite of a typical ocean cruise. The River Rhine is the most popular river cruise destination for British people, closely followed by the Nile.

Unit 9

ACTIVITY

Carry out some research into three river cruise operators – one operating in the UK, one in Europe and one in the USA. Produce three fact sheets that include information about each operator for use by prospective river cruise passengers, e.g. company history, products on offer, prices, duration of trips, destinations visited, etc.

This activity is designed to provide evidence for P4.

Luxury cruise

Most cruise lines offer an element of luxury – indeed the very concept of cruising is closely tied up with luxury and opulence. However, there are only a handful of cruise operators that offer the ultimate luxury cruise experience. Passengers who book a luxury cruise can expect to be greeted on arrival with a complimentary bottle of champagne; to have a spacious cabin with walk-in wardrobe, an elegant bathroom, a well-stocked mini bar and 24-hour room service, with full in-suite dining available during restaurant hours. Passengers never have to queue for food and drink, and never have to wait to use equipment in the gym or to be seated in the dining room, because true luxury ships have more than enough space to accommodate everybody on board in comfort. The small, luxury ships owned by Seabourn Cruise Line and Radisson Seven Seas Cruises are the most exclusive in the world purely in terms of their size.

Soft adventure

'Soft adventure' is the name given to any type of tourist activity that gives people the chance to try out a new experience, but nothing too dangerous! Cruise lines now offer more adventurous shore excursions and have been developing new products geared specifically at those who like to get active on holiday. A prime 'adventure' destination is Alaska, where a number of cruise operators, including Princess Cruises, Norwegian Cruise Line and Holland America Line, have been updating shore tour programmes to include more unusual options like dog sledding, whale watching, hiking in the forest, go-karting, mountain biking and rock climbing. Passengers on Caribbean cruises can try their hand at diving or snorkelling, while Mediterranean cruise activities include abseiling, roller-blading, water rafting and cycling expeditions. Ocean Village is a good example of a cruise brand that appeals to younger, first-time cruisers who are keen to take part in activities while on holiday.

Unit 9

Ocean Village offers a variety of activities for passengers

Sail ship

Cruising in a sailing ship is a 'niche' product that appeals to a small number of people who are looking for a more authentic and traditional cruising experience. There are many companies that offer sail cruising, including Monaco-based Star Clippers, Windjammer Barefoot Cruises (the largest operator of tall ships in the world) operating in the Caribbean out of Miami and Windstar Cruises.

Cruise and stay

This is an arrangement that allows passengers to combine a fly/cruise holiday with a period of time in a hotel or other type of accommodation. For example, a passenger could fly to Florida and spend a week visiting the area and its many attractions, then join a cruise from Miami to the Caribbean for a second week. Cruise and stay is popular with people who are new to cruising and want to try it out before committing to a longer holiday.

Special interest

Realising that the interests of potential cruise passengers are very varied, cruise operators try to offer as wide a variety of special interests or 'themes' as possible in their programmes. These cruises give passengers the chance to enjoy a favourite hobby in a different setting, learn new skills or just increase their knowledge. They can choose from a wide variety of subjects – gourmet cuisine, gardening and music to culture, art appreciation and sculpture. Many special interest cruise operators feature well-known guest speakers, performances by noted entertainers or related shore excursions and the chance to mingle with leading figures in a particular field. Orient Lines is an award-winning ship line operating the *Marco Polo*, which offers special interest, destination-focused cruises. *Celebrity Xpedition*, part of the Celebrity Cruises' fleet, carries just 100 passengers and is designed for exclusive, expeditionary cruises to the Galapagos Islands.

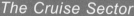

Unit 9

WEBLINK

www.swanhellenic.com

*Check out this website
for more information on
Swan Hellenic.*

FOCUS ON INDUSTRY – Swan Hellenic Cruises

Swan Hellenic has been offering 'discovery cruises' for more than 50 years to a variety of lesser-known locations throughout the world. The itineraries on board its ship *Minerva II* include diverse landscapes, cultures and historical settings; from the mysterious temples and pyramids of the Maya at Chichen Itza, the glacial landscapes of Arctic Norway to the tropical environment of the Amazon interior.

Cruise facilities

Spending so much time at sea makes the quality, availability and type of facilities on board ship very important to passengers. Cruises vary from very small, intimate experiences with a small number of fellow passengers to the mega-cruises with thousands of passengers aboard and a variety of facilities such as shops, bars, restaurants, entertainment venues, Internet cafés, currency exchange facilities and children's play areas. The facilities on offer must reflect the number of passengers, type of cruise, target market and the price paid by the passengers.

Perhaps the most important facility on board is the cabin (often referred to as the stateroom). Cabins vary in size and price according to where they are located on the ship. Inside cabins on lower decks tend to be the cheapest, while upper deck cabins and suites with sea views command the highest prices. Cruise brochures and websites include colour-coded deck plans indicating the location and prices of cabins with different facilites.

ACTIVITY

Choose a particular cruise and gather some information on the prices charged for the cruise based on different types of cabin (stateroom) booked. Make notes on the facilities and amenities offered in each of the cabin types on offer.

This activity is designed to provide evidence for P4.

Target markets

'Target market' refers to the customers that a company is trying to encourage to buy its products or services. We have seen earlier in this unit that the market for cruising has changed dramatically in recent years – cruising still appeals to the traditional market that

Choice of cabin is important with passengers

has always enjoyed the product, but there are now many new types of customers attracted to the sector, including younger, first-time cruisers and families. Figure 9.6 gives an indication of the many target markets in cruising today. Cruise operators develop products and itineraries to appeal to one of more of these markets and use a variety of marketing techniques to persuade them to book with their company, e.g. advertising, direct mail, sales promotions and public relations activities.

ACTIVITY

Gather information on cruise companies that offer products to satisfy the five target markets shown in Figure 9.6 (find one example of each).

This activity is designed to provide evidence for P4.

Factors influencing cruising

Fig. 9.6 Target markets in cruising

Like many other sectors of the travel and tourism industry, cruising is influenced by many factors. These factors can be 'external', i.e. not related to one particular company, but part of global events and decisions. There are also 'internal' factors, i.e. those that influence an individual passenger's choice of company or cruise destination.

Unit 9

Current external influences on the cruise sector include:

- Social – factors such as increased wealth in western countries, an ageing population and more educational opportunities all have an influence on how cruising develops;
- Geopolitical – world events such as terrorist attacks and political instability in certain countries affect the cruise sector;
- Climate – longer-term changes in climate and the 'greenhouse effect' will influence, for example, the choice of cruise destinations;
- Cost – fluctuations in exchange rates and the price of commodities such as oil and food influence the profitability of cruise operators.

Many of these factors are outside the control of the cruise companies themselves, but they try to influence decision-making through trade organisations such as the Passenger Shipping Association (PSA).

Internal influences on cruising include:

- Development of facilities, products and services – shipping companies are actively developing their on board and on shore facilities in order to capitalise on the overall growth in the cruise sector and to satisfy the new customers who have been attracted to cruising;
- Passenger/crew ratio (PCR) – the lower the PCR, i.e. the more crew available per passenger, the better the level of service provided and the overall passenger experience;
- Passenger/space ratio (PSR) – the lower the PSR, i.e. the more space available per passenger, the greater the feeling of space on board and less queuing for facilities;
- Itineraries – factors such as the number and type of on shore excursions, ports of call and cruise areas visited, influence a passenger's choice of cruise line and itinerary;
- Cruise etiquette – issues such as dress code and tipping policy can influence passenger choice, e.g. a person may prefer a more informal type of cruise with few formalities on an all-inclusive basis to a traditional cruising experience with formal dress code.

SECTION 4: EMPLOYMENT IN CRUISING

The rise in popularity of cruising worldwide means that there are many job opportunities in the sector for people with the right qualifications, skills and personal qualities. In this section we investigate key facts about working in cruising and examine the many job opportunities available on board and ashore.

Working in cruising – some basic facts

Entertainers on board the QE2 (courtesy of Cunard)

Working on board a cruise ship can be an exciting and rewarding experience, visiting exotic ports of call, working with people from all parts of the world, earning a good living, and having your room and board provided for free. However, like in other sectors of the travel and tourism industry, life on board ship is also demanding and challenging, working long hours (often 7 days a week), sharing accommodation with work colleagues and following the ship's rules and regulations.

Most cruise lines offer an average contract of six months, but depending on the position and the company, it could be as short as four months or as long as ten. Staff are paid only while on contract – holidays are unpaid and usually last two months. Once you've completed a contract you are not obliged to return to the same ship or company, but if you have enjoyed your work and have received a good reference, you are likely to be offered another period of work.

Details of jobs in cruising are available direct from individual cruise lines or through agencies, some of which charge applicants a fee for their services. The cruise sector has a relatively high staff turnover, so companies need to fill vacancies all year round with suitable people. Staff leave for new jobs on different ships, companies or countries. Others leave mid-journey for various reasons, including personal or family circumstances.

Qualifications, experience and skills required

Not all jobs in the cruise sector require formal qualifications. However, ambitious people who wish to develop their careers in the sector will generally find that their progression will be quicker if they have qualifications that are relevant to their job. Experience counts for a lot in the cruise sector – people who have on shore experience of, for example, retail, entertainment, hospitality and catering, will be more attractive to the cruise lines than applicants with no experience at all.

Personal skills and qualities, such as good appearance and grooming, a positive attitude, enthusiasm and reliability, are of paramount importance in the cruise industry, which is all about meeting and even exceeding passengers' expectations. In general, cruise lines look for people who:

- Are highly-motivated and enthusiastic;
- Are keen to take on a challenge;
- Have a strong desire to work on a cruise ship;
- Get on well with other people;
- Are happy to be away from home for long periods;
- Have a helpful and patient customer service manner;
- Are well-presented.

Job opportunities

There are literally hundreds of different jobs on offer with cruise lines, most on board ship but some based on shore. Jobs are offered in different departments on board ship, for example:

- Galley (kitchen);
- Engineering;
- Beauty and hairdressing;
- Hotel (reception);
- Housekeeping;
- Casino;
- Deck;
- Entertainment;
- Medical;
- Food and beverage;
- Tours and excursions;
- Photography;
- Sports, pool and gym.

Some jobs are more technical than others and require specialist qualifications, for example posts in medical, deck, engineering and gym work.

Unit 9

Bartender on the QE2 (courtesy of Cunard)

Job opportunities with cruise lines on shore include:

- Marketing;
- Reservations and sales (including call centre work);
- Finance;
- Administration;
- Human resources;
- IT;
- Operations;
- Customer service;
- Baggage handling;
- Catering.

There are many websites that offer advice on getting a job in the cruise sector and some have lists of posts available, for example www.cruiseworking.com and www.cruiseplacement.com

ACTIVITY

Log on to either of these cruise employment websites (www.cruiseworking.com; www.cruiseplacement.com) and find details of two jobs in cruising that interest you. Make a note of job roles and responsibilities, salary, contract period, location, etc.

This activity is designed to provide evidence for P5.

Figures 9.7 and 9.8 give details of two jobs on board a cruise ship, an Entertainments Officer and an Assistant Bartender.

SUMMER CRUISES PLC

Job description

Title of post:	Entertainments Officer
Post no:	SC/08/05
Location:	On board
Responsible to:	Cruise Director

Job summary

The Entertainments Officer is responsible for assisting the Cruise Director and his/her Deputy in the smooth running of all aspects of the Entertainments Division of the Hotel Services and Entertainments Department. The Entertainments Division is responsible for providing a diverse range of entertainment and leisure opportunities during both the day and evening for passengers in order to enhance their cruise experience. This includes production shows, guest lecturers' activities, quizzes, bingo, cabaret, musical programmes, karaoke and deck activities such as quoits, golf, tennis, cricket, football, etc.

Requirements

1. You must possess a warm, outgoing personality to ensure that passengers always have a friendly and understanding person to talk to;
2. Experience in hosting/introducing professional cabaret entertainment;
3. Effective communication skills, both written and oral;
4. You need to be available and visible to passengers at all times and to be easily identifiable as one of the public faces of the on board entertainment product;
5. You will undertake a pro-active role in the various activities delivered by the Entertainments Division.

Salary and benefits

- Competitive salary and benefits package is offered;
- Training and development is delivered mainly through in-house workshops, courses and programmes;
- Contract period of a minimum of 4 months to a maximum of 6 months with a 6-8 week unpaid leave period;
- Concessionary travel after a qualifying period of service.

Application procedure

To apply in the first instance, send a photo and CV to HR Division, Summer Cruises plc, Southampton.

Dated: 1st September 2005

Fig. 9.7 Job description for the post of Entertainments Officer

Unit 9

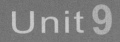

SUMMER CRUISES PLC

Job description

Title of post: Assistant Bartender
Post no: SC/09/05
Location: Fleet
Responsible to: Bartender

Job summary

- To ensure the smooth and efficient operation of the bar, under the direction of the bartender, in order to achieve passenger satisfaction;
- To generate and maximise revenue opportunities both individually and as a team;
- To portray a positive and professional image to all outside consultants, agencies, suppliers, passengers, officers and crew;
- To contribute to the creation and maintenance of an enthusiastic, motivated working environment;
- To maintain prescribed systems for the monitoring and control of stock and relevant costs in accordance with company procedures;
- To ensure all revenue is correctly posted to on board accounts;
- To assist with stock takes as required by the Finance Manager.

Requirements

1. Applicants should have attended catering college and obtained a City & Guilds pass in Food and Beverage Service 707;
2. Alternatively, applicants should have had experience in a superior class hotel, club or restaurant ;
3. Applicants should have experience of mixing and serving cocktails, and have a thorough knowledge of wines and liquors.

Salary and benefits

- Competitive salary and benefits package is offered;
- Training and development is delivered mainly through in-house workshops, courses and programmes;
- Contract period of a minimum of 4 months to a maximum of 6 months with a 6-8 week unpaid leave period;
- Concessionary travel after a qualifying period of service.

Salary and benefits

To apply in the first instance, send a photo and CV to HR Division, Summer Cruises plc, Southampton.

Dated: 1st September 2005

Fig. 9.8 Job description for the post of Assistant Bartender

Unit 9

UNIT SUMMARY

This unit has explored the cruise sector of the travel and tourism industry, from the early beginnings in the mid-19th century to the present day global industry. You have seen that cruising is undergoing a period of rapid growth and change, with new ships and facilities being developed to cater for new markets around the world. The links between cruising and other sectors of the travel and tourism industry have been fully examined. You have investigated the main cruise areas of the world that are most popular with British cruisers, including the Mediterranean, Caribbean and the Baltic. You have also examined different types of cruises and seen how they appeal to different 'target markets'. Internal and external factors that influence cruising have been explored in depth, for example social and geopolitical issues. The unit has also looked at the many employment opportunities on offer with cruise lines and the qualifications, experience and personal qualities needed to succeed in the sector. Throughout the unit you have been shown many industry examples, while the case studies on Carnival Corporation and plc, the PSA and the impact of cruise tourism in Belize, highlight key issues in the operation and development of the cruise industry.

If you have worked methodically, by the end of this unit you should have:

- Examined the development of the cruise sector of the travel and tourism industry;
- Investigated cruise areas of the world;
- Explored the types of cruises and how they appeal to different markets;
- Investigated employment opportunities within the cruise sector.

You are now in a position to complete the assignment for the unit, under the direction of your tutor. Before you tackle the assignment you may like to have a go at the following questions to help build your knowledge of the cruise sector.

Test your knowledge

1. Describe three recent trends in the cruise sector.
2. Which cruise destination is the most popular with British cruisers?
3. In what ways is the customer profile of cruise passengers changing?
4. Name three companies that offer 'informal cruising'.
5. Which three companies have the biggest share of the global cruise market?
6. Name five cruise brands that are owned by Carnival Corporation and plc.
7. Describe the links that cruising has with other sectors of the travel and tourism industry.
8. What role does the PSA play in the cruise sector?
9. Give two examples of vertical and horizontal integration in the cruise industry.
10. Name ten ports of call used in Mediterranean cruise itineraries.
11. What type of cruise passengers are attracted to cruises in Alaska?

12. Describe some of the environmental impacts of cruise tourism.
13. Describe the features and benefits of five different types of cruises.
14. Describe a variety of external factors that affect the global cruise industry.
15. What personal qualities do the cruise lines look for in new recruits?

UNIT 9 ASSIGNMENT: The cruise sector

Introduction

This assignment is made up of a number of tasks which, when successfully completed, are designed to give you sufficient evidence to meet the Pass (P), Merit (M) and Distinction (D) grading criteria for the unit. If you have carried out the activities and read the case studies throughout this unit, you will already have done a lot of work towards completing the tasks for this assignment.

Scenario

As part of a forthcoming open day for prospective students at your college/school, your group has been asked to prepare some presentations, displays and booklets on different sectors of the travel and tourism industry, to give the students and their parents an idea of the type of work you do on your course. You have been chosen to work on the cruise sector and must complete the following tasks.

Task 1

Prepare and deliver a presentation in which you should:

(a) Describe the development of the cruise sector of the travel and tourism industry;

(b) Analyse the development of the cruise sector;

(c) Critically analyse the current cruise market, making justified predictions for the future of the sector.

These tasks are designed to produce evidence for P1, M1 and D1.

Unit 9

TASK 2

In a separate part of your presentation you should:

(a) Describe the impacts of the cruise sector on ports of call and gateway ports;

(b) Evaluate the impact of cruising on a specific cruise area or port.

These tasks are designed to produce evidence for P2 and D2.

TASK 3

In the final part of your presentation you should:

(a) Describe the appeal of three cruise areas to different types of passengers;

(b) Compare and contrast the appeal of two cruise areas to different markets.

These tasks are designed to produce evidence for P3 and M2.

Task 4

For this task you must produce a display that:

(a) Describes the types of cruises available and explains how they appeal to different markets;

(b) Explains the factors that affect the appeal of different types of cruises to customers, e.g. cost, facilities on board, destinations visited, quality of cabins, etc.

These tasks are designed to produce evidence for P4 and M3.

Task 5

For this task you must produce a booklet that:

Describes employment opportunities available on a cruise ship, expanding on two jobs in detail.

This task is designed to produce evidence for P5.

Unit 10
Tourism Development

INTRODUCTION TO THE UNIT

Travel and tourism is developing rapidly throughout the world. It is seen as an excellent way of creating jobs, generating revenue and helping economic development in destinations from Bradford to Bali, Cardiff to Cancun and Keswick to Kenya. Tourism development has huge potential to help developed countries and developing nations, but it must be managed in a way that is respectful of local people, their cultures and the environment, if it is to be truly sustainable in the long term.

This unit gives you the opportunity to learn more about why and how tourism development takes place at local, national and international levels. You will examine the many objectives of tourism development and the agents involved in the process, i.e. the individuals and organisations that have an interest in developing tourism. You will investigate the positive and negative impacts of tourism development, learning how the positive aspects can be maximised and the negative impacts minimised. Finally, you will explore how sustainable tourism can benefit destinations and their local communities.

WHAT YOU WILL STUDY

During the course of this unit you will:

1. Examine the **objectives** of tourism development in tourist destinations;
2. Examine the **agents** involved in tourism development;
3. Investigate the **impact** of tourism development on the destination;
4. Explore how the **principles of sustainable tourism** can be used to benefit destinations and their communities.

You will be guided through the main topics in this unit with the help of the latest statistics, examples and industry case studies. You should also check out the weblinks throughout the unit for extra information on particular organisations or topic areas and use the activities to help you learn more.

ASSESSMENT FOR THIS UNIT

This unit is internally assessed, meaning that you will be given an assignment (or series of assignments) to complete by your tutor(s) to show that you have fully understood the content of the unit. A grading scale of pass, merit or distinction is used for all internally assessed units, with higher grades awarded to students who show greater depth in analysis and evaluation in their assignments. An assignment for this unit, which covers all the grading criteria, can be found on page 111. Don't forget to visit www.tandtONLine.co.uk for all the latest industry news, developments, statistics and tips to help you with your assignments.

Unit 10

SECTION 1: OBJECTIVES OF TOURISM DEVELOPMENT

Introduction

'Tourism development' is the process by which a destination provides facilities and services for visitors as a way of securing a range of economic, political, environmental, social and cultural benefits. There are a number of important points concerning tourism development that you need to consider before we look in detail at objectives, such as:

- Variations in scale – tourism development can be as small as a village hall committee organising a craft exhibition for summer visitors or as big as a South American nation deciding to invest in tourism and attract overseas visitors;
- Different types – everything from the building of a new hotel, construction of a tourist attraction such as the Eden Project to the extension of a villa complex are all different types of tourism development;
- Pace of development – advances in technology mean that some tourism development can take place very quickly, e.g. the growth of the low-cost airlines in recent years has led to rapid advances in tourism development in countries such as France, Spain and some of the former Soviet states. Other developments occur at a much slower rate, with more planning and a greater concern for reducing the negative impacts of tourism development, for example the controlled tourism development of certain countries bordering the Himalayas, e.g. Bhutan;
- Location of tourism development – whether a developed or developing country, a city or country area, inland or by the coast, all regions of the world now recognise the importance of tourism development;
- Associated infrastructure – tourism development can only take place where there is existing or planned infrastructure, i.e. roads, railways, airports, telecommunications, power supplies and other utilities. Commercial (private sector) developers often look to the public sector to supply these basic facilities and services;
- Positive and negative impacts – tourism development can add significantly to the economic and social well-being of regions around the world, but can also have negative impacts on the people, culture and environment in destination areas. We will look in more detail at these impacts later in this unit.

Much of the UK coast is developed for tourism

Objectives of tourism development

Objectives are the reasons why individuals and organisations decide to get involved with tourism development in the first place and what they hope to achieve as part of the process. You have learned elsewhere on your course that tourism is one of the fastest-growing industries in the world, creating employment and income for destinations in the developed and developing world. Creating jobs and revenue are important economic objectives of tourism development, but political, environmental and socio-cultural objectives play their part as well, as Figure 10.1 demonstrates.

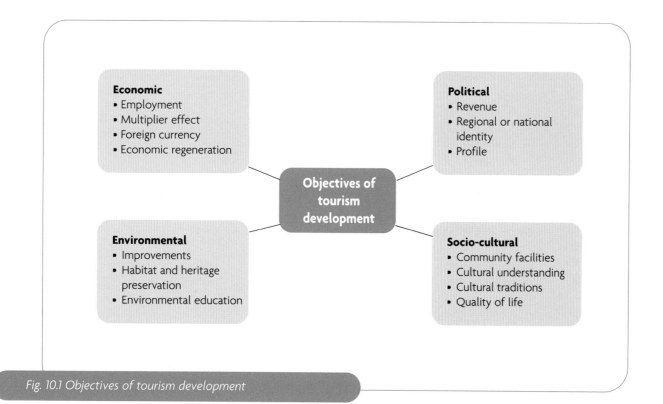

Economic
- Employment
- Multiplier effect
- Foreign currency
- Economic regeneration

Political
- Revenue
- Regional or national identity
- Profile

Objectives of tourism development

Environmental
- Improvements
- Habitat and heritage preservation
- Environmental education

Socio-cultural
- Community facilities
- Cultural understanding
- Cultural traditions
- Quality of life

Fig. 10.1 Objectives of tourism development

It is important to understand that tourism development is not always a smooth and trouble-free process. There are sometimes conflicting objectives amongst the people investing in tourism. Developers, for example, are keen for any tourism developments to take place as quickly as possible in order to get a fast return on their investment. Local people and community groups will want to make sure that any development does not cause environmental, social and cultural problems. Local and national governments will also be concerned about these issues and will impose regulations on the developer to make sure that projects progress in a sustainable manner.

ACTIVITY

Using the information from the following sections of this unit as a guide, carry out some research into the different objectives of tourism development in your own local area (or an area nearby that is developed for tourism). Present your findings as a presentation delivered to the rest of your group, using appropriate visual aids.

This activity is designed to provide evidence for P1.

Economic objectives

It is usually for economic reasons that individuals, organisations and governments first decide to get involved in the tourism development process. Tourism can:

- Create employment;
- Attract revenue to an area and re-circulate it in the local economy via the multiplier effect;
- Increase foreign currency earnings;
- Contribute to economic regeneration.

Employment creation

Creating employment is one of the most important economic objectives of tourism development. The World Travel and Tourism Council (WTTC) estimates that travel and tourism employs over 120 million people worldwide, while employment in UK tourism currently stands at 2.2 million, representing 7 per cent of total employment. Investing in tourism development appeals to many developing nations around the world since jobs in the industry are relatively easy and cheap to establish, particularly when compared to jobs in capital-intensive industries such as engineering, construction and manufacturing. However, jobs in tourism in developing countries are sometimes criticised for being seasonal, poorly-paid and low-skilled – creating a year-round tourism economy should be the goal of all destinations so as to ensure well-paid, full-time jobs in the industry.

Employment in tourism can be direct or indirect. Direct employment includes jobs in hotels and other accommodation, tourist attractions, tour operators, airlines, cruise companies, etc. Indirect jobs are those that are developed in support of the travel and tourism industry, e.g. in construction, food and drink distribution, event management, etc.

Multiplier effect

At local level, revenue generated by tourism development is often vital to the economic well-being of an area and is boosted by an important concept known as the multiplier effect. Research has shown that the amount spent by visitors to an area is re-circulated in the local economy (by, for example, the wages of somebody working in a tourist attraction being spent on goods and services in local shops) and is actually worth more to the area than its face value. For example, £200 spent by a couple on a short break in a hotel, could be worth as much as £200 x 1.4 (the hotel multiplier effect for that area), i.e. a total of £280.

The actual value of the multiplier (1.4 in the above example is merely an illustration), varies between regions and different sectors of the travel and tourism industry. The multiplier for, say, a farm guesthouse is likely to be greater than for a city centre hotel which is part of a large multinational chain. This is because the owners of the farm guesthouse are likely to spend their money locally, buying food and other services for their business, while the goods and services for the large hotel may well be brought in from outside the area as part of a national distribution contract, i.e. income is lost to the area. In economic terms this loss in income is known as a 'leakage' from the local economy.

Foreign currency

If planned and managed effectively, tourism has the ability to generate significant amounts of foreign currency earnings for countries, in the form of direct payments to tourist businesses and taxes collected by local and national governments. Figure 10.2 lists the top 10 countries that earned the most from tourism in 2003 and 2004.

Revenue from tourism contributes to a country's balance

	2003	2004
1. USA	64.3	74.5
2. Spain	39.6	45.2
3. France	36.6	40.8
4. Italy	31.2	35.7
5. Germany	23.1	27.7
6. United Kingdom	22.7	27.3
7. China	17.4	25.7
8. Turkey	13.2	15.9
9. Austria	14.0	15.4
10. Australia	10.3	13.0

Fig. 10.2 Receipts from international tourism (US$ billions)

Source: WTO

of payments, i.e. the flows of money into and out of a country. Tourism is known as an 'invisible' item on a country's balance of payments, along with other services such as banking and insurance ('visible' items include manufactured goods, raw materials, foodstuffs, etc.). Countries that depend heavily on tourism for their foreign currency earnings, such as many of the islands in the Caribbean, usually have a surplus on their balance of payments, i.e. more money is

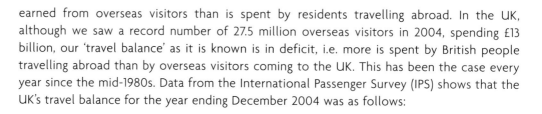

earned from overseas visitors than is spent by residents travelling abroad. In the UK, although we saw a record number of 27.5 million overseas visitors in 2004, spending £13 billion, our 'travel balance' as it is known is in deficit, i.e. more is spent by British people travelling abroad than by overseas visitors coming to the UK. This has been the case every year since the mid-1980s. Data from the International Passenger Survey (IPS) shows that the UK's travel balance for the year ending December 2004 was as follows:

Earnings from overseas visitors	£12.8 billion
Expenditure by British people on visits abroad	£30.0 billion
Travel balance	-£17.2 billion

FOCUS ON INDUSTRY – Chinese tourists to the UK

The first Chinese tourists to travel to Britain on tourist visas arrived in London in July 2005. A group of 80 tourists flew into Heathrow Airport on the first-ever package tour from China – only students and business travellers had hitherto been allowed to travel to the UK, but Beijing granted Britain 'approved destination' status in January 2005, meaning that tourists as well can now visit. British tourism officials are hoping that the new status could generate an extra £500 million for the UK economy by 2020 and increase the current 0.6 per cent share of China's outbound tourism market. The new relaxed rules allow any Chinese citizen to travel to Britain with an approved tour operator.

Overseas visitors are very important to the UK economy

Economic regeneration

Tourism development is often included in multi-purpose regeneration projects, mainly in urban areas where traditional industries have declined. Examples in Britain include the Salford Quays area of Manchester, Albert Dock in Liverpool, developments in Cardiff Bay and the Docklands area of London. The Eden Project in Cornwall, one of the UK's most successful tourist attractions of recent years, is built on former china clay works near St Austell.

Political objectives

Tourism and politics often go hand-in-hand. National and local governments make decisions about whether or not tourism should be encouraged and what tourism facilities should be provided for visitors. They

WEBLINK

www.propoortourism.org.uk

Check out this website for more information on pro-poor tourism.

can control the numbers of visitors to a country or region and use money earned from tourism to invest in other sectors of the economy, for example education, health and welfare services. Many of the former Soviet states that have joined the European Union (EU) see tourism as a way of revitalising their economies and projecting a positive image of their countries, e.g. the Baltic states of Latvia, Lithuania and Estonia. Tourism is used to help alleviate poverty in developing nations, a concept known as 'pro-poor tourism'.

Revenue generation

Politicians see tourism as an excellent way of generating extra wealth for their economies. It is common throughout the world to have to pay hotel, airport and border taxes when travelling. In the UK, the government gains tax revenues from a number of sources related to tourism, including airline passenger duty and VAT on tourist services. Tourism can be used as a springboard for further economic and social developments in urban and rural regions; the regional development and promotion of tourism in France is a good example of this.

Creating an identity

The promotion of tourism in overseas markets and with domestic tourists can help to create or maintain a national or regional identity. Many of the popular Mediterranean tourist destinations used images of their way-of-life and landscapes to encourage tourism from the 1970s onwards. Bilbao in northern Spain has very successfully used tourism to change its identity from an industrialised city to one of the world's foremost tourist destinations, built around the popularity of the Guggenheim Museum.

Raising an area's profile

The global nature of the travel and tourism industry means that it can be used to raise the profile of a country or area on a world scale. Sport and tourism often combine to project positive images of destinations to a global audience and stimulate further tourism development, e.g. the Olympic Games in Atlanta, Sydney and Barcelona were all very successful in increasing tourist numbers and raising tourism expenditure. London is hoping that its success in winning the bid for the Games in 2012 will have a similar effect.

Unit 10

FOCUS ON INDUSTRY – The London Olympic Games in 2012

The staging of the Olympic and Paralympic Games in London in 2012 has been described by Britain's tourism industry as the biggest ever opportunity for the sector. Industry leaders believe that between 50-75 per cent of Britain's net benefit from staging the Games, measured over a 7-10 year period, will be through tourism. Based on Sydney's example, the Games could be worth well over £2 billion to the UK's tourist economy. The Games provide a platform for the international marketing of both London and Britain as leisure, business and sporting destinations, particularly in new and emerging markets such as China, Greece, Korea, Poland and Thailand.

Environmental objectives

Although much tourism development is focused on economic objectives, there are many tourism projects in developed and developing nations that have environmental benefits at their heart, for example:

- Environmental improvements – tourists visiting an area can result in improvements to the natural and built environment, e.g. beach cleaning, new walking and cycling routes, restoration of derelict sites and buildings, more floral displays, etc;
- Habitat and heritage preservation – in many parts of the world, particularly where fragile habitats exist, tourism has highlighted environmental concerns and has led to the preservation of natural habitats, e.g. coral reefs, sand dunes and mountain areas. In many developing countries, especially on the African continent, certain wildlife species are no longer hunted, but conserved as valuable tourism assets – there is a realisation that without the wildlife there would be no tourists;
- Environmental education – tourism can be a powerful force for good in terms of educating people about the environment. Various 'interpretation' methods can be used to get messages across, e.g. guided walks, visitor centres, self-guided trails and explanatory leaflets.

Socio-cultural objectives

To be truly sustainable, tourism development must work in harmony with local people and their traditional ways of life. This holds true for both developed and developing nations. Promoting cultural understanding and maintaining cultural traditions must be a prime objective of all tourism development projects. Communities can benefit from well-planned tourism through the development of new community facilities that may be financed from tourism revenues. These may be tourism-related and non-tourism-related facilities, e.g. a new museum and a new village hall. By making use of such facilities, local communities' quality of life can be significantly improved.

WEBLINK

www.thetravel
foundation.org.uk

*Check out this website
for more information on
this project in Tobago
and the work of the
Travel Foundation in
general.*

FOCUS ON INDUSTRY – The Travel Foundation in Tobago

The Travel Foundation (see case study on page 109) is working with local people in Tobago to develop a number of projects relating to tourism development. Three projects are already underway:

1. A video which explains sustainability issues to visitors arriving at the airport;
2. Reef demarcation buoys that are used to prevent damage caused by boats anchoring on the coral reefs;
3. Turtle awareness – hotel guests and staff are being educated about turtle nesting on hotel beaches.

A medium-term plan is being developed to look at further projects on the island based on research into the economic impact of all-inclusive hotels on Tobago commissioned by the Travel Foundation.

Unit 10

SECTION 2: AGENTS OF TOURISM DEVELOPMENT

Agents of tourism development are the various individuals and organisations that carry out or facilitate tourism developments at international, national, regional and local levels. They may operate in the private, public or voluntary sector a shown in Figure 10.3.

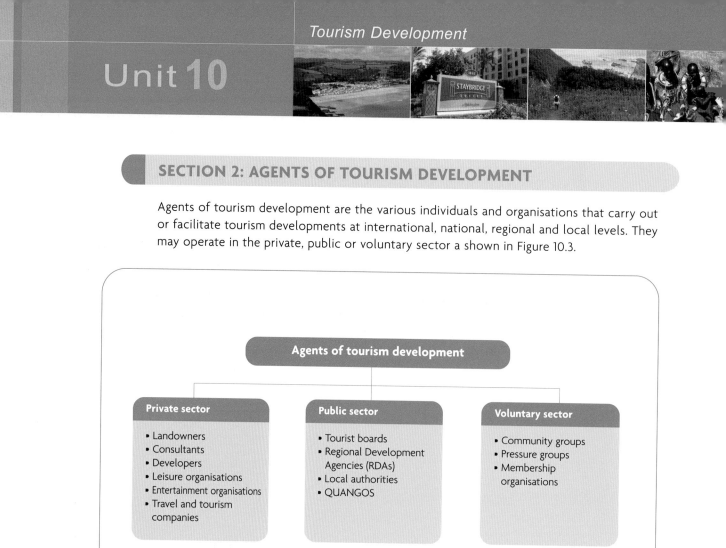

Agents of tourism development

Private sector	**Public sector**	**Voluntary sector**
• Landowners • Consultants • Developers • Leisure organisations • Entertainment organisations • Travel and tourism companies	• Tourist boards • Regional Development Agencies (RDAs) • Local authorities • QUANGOS	• Community groups • Pressure groups • Membership organisations

Fig. 10.3 Agents of tourism development

Although Figure 10.3 separates agents into different groups, it is important to remember that tourism development works best when individuals and organisations work in partnership with each other to achieve common aims and objectives.

Private sector agents

You have learned in other units on your course that the travel and tourism industry is dominated by private sector businesses, whose primary aim is to make a profit. Private sector agents are no different – they invest their money in providing facilities for tourists in the expectation of a good return on their investment. Private sector agents can be single-person operations or large, global companies and include:

- Landowners – individuals and companies can make substantial financial gains when land is needed for tourism development, e.g. new villa and sports complexes;

- Consultants – are specialists who advise governments and private companies on the feasibility of tourism developments. This includes advising on a wide range of issues, such as planning regulations, infrastructure projects, marketing plans, training, financial projections, design solutions, etc. The UK has many tourism consultants, including L & R Consulting, the Tourism Company and Deloitte & Touche, all of which are members of the Tourism Society Consultants' Group;
- Developers – take on the risk of overseeing tourism development projects, e.g. the construction of a new hotel, development of a tourist attraction, etc.
- Leisure and entertainment organisations – provide facilities for tourists when in their destination, e.g. clubs, bars, restaurants, casinos, fitness suites, etc;
- Travel and tourism companies – play an important part in tourism development, often in conjunction with local and national governments, e.g. airlines work with the public sector tourism managers to develop new routes to destinations, while tour operators can significantly increase the numbers of tourists to an area by including it in their programmes.

Public sector agents

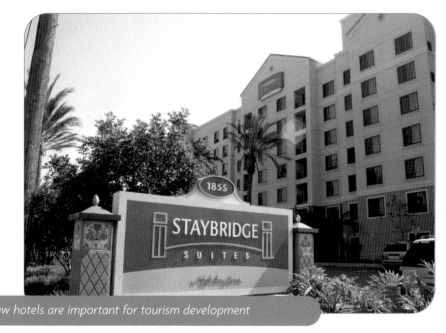

New hotels are important for tourism development

Unlike private sector agents of tourism development, the public sector is not driven by profit maximisation, but has wider social, community and economic objectives. Public sector agents set the policy for tourism and aim to create a favourable business climate within which private sector tourism businesses can operate successfully and grow. They operate at international, national, regional and local levels, for example:

- International – World Tourism Organisation (WTO);
- National – VisitBritain (funded by DCMS – the Department for Culture, Media and Sport);
- Regional – Heart of England Tourist Board;
- Local – Worcester City Council.

The functions carried out by public sector tourism development agents are many and varied, including:

1. Establishment of tourism policy – this is usually the starting point for public sector involvement in tourism development, when policies and priorities for tourism are set, e.g. what type of tourism to encourage, how impacts will be controlled, who will be responsible for tourism development, etc;
2. Marketing and promotion – this is often the most important function of public sector agents, with responsibilities for marketing planning, market research, travel trade promotion and producing promotional materials such as brochures and websites;
3. Infrastructure provision – either independently or in partnership with the private sector, public bodies provide funding for many infrastructure projects that are directly or indirectly associated with tourism, for example road schemes, airports and rail systems;
4. Tourism facilities – some national and local government departments run their own tourist attractions and facilities, such as museums, parks, historic houses, ancient monuments and galleries;
5. Tourist information services – National Tourist Boards usually co-ordinate tourist information centres (TICs) and other services for visitors;
6. Legislation and regulation – public agencies implement a wide variety of laws and regulations relating to tourism, e.g. passport and visa requirements, planning regulations, health and safety, licensing, etc;
7. Finance for development – public agencies can offer grants, loans, tax concessions and tariff reductions as incentives for tourism development;
8. Business advisory services and training – many public bodies at national, regional and local levels provide advice, support and training as a way of raising standards in the tourism industry.

Tourist boards

Tourist boards play a vital role in tourism development in both developed and developing countries. The UK has four National Tourist Boards:

- VisitBritain – responsible for promoting the whole of Britain abroad and England to the British;
- Wales Tourist Board – concerned with improving the economic and social prosperity of Wales through effective marketing and development of tourism;
- VisitScotland – exists to support the development of the tourism industry in Scotland and to market Scotland as a quality destination;
- Northern Ireland Tourist Board – responsible for the development, promotion and marketing of Northern Ireland as a tourist destination.

The national boards are funded mainly from central government sources, channelled through the DCMS, Welsh Assembly Government, Scottish Executive and Northern Ireland Office/Assembly. In developing countries, tourist boards encourage new tourism developments and promote their destinations abroad.

Regional Development Agencies (RDAs)

The launch of Regional Development Agencies (RDAs) in England in 1999 marked a change in government support for regional tourism. Up to that time, Regional Tourist Boards (RTBs) took the lead in all tourism-related matters. Now, the RDAs are funded from central government to promote economic development, including tourism, in their areas. In most regions, the RDAs work with the RTBs to develop future plans for tourism development and marketing. There are currently 9 Regional Tourist Boards in England, 4 Regional Tourism Partnerships (RTPs) in Wales, 14 RTBs in Scotland and 5 Regional Tourism Organisations in Northern Ireland (under review).

Local authorities

Local authorities use their resources to provide as wide a range of tourism facilities and services that finances will allow. In a typical area in the UK, this might include:

- Promotional leaflets, brochures and websites;
- Parks and gardens;
- Theatres;
- Museums;
- Tourist information centres (TICs);
- Accommodation booking services;
- Sports and leisure centres;
- Outdoor activity centres;
- Art and craft galleries.

In developing countries, local agencies work with national governments and the private sector to support the development of tourism.

QUANGOS

QUANGOS (quasi-autonomous, non-governmental organisations) are organisations that are funded from public money, but work separately from government departments. In tourism development, VisitBritain, the South West of England Regional Development Agency and the Wales Tourist Board (WTB) are all examples of QUANGOS, although the WTB is due to be amalgamated into the Welsh Assembly Government in 2006.

ACTIVITY

Gather some information on the public sector agents of tourism development in your own local area, or a nearby tourist area.

This activity is designed to provide evidence for P2 or P3.

Voluntary sector agents

Not all travel and tourism facilities and services are provided solely by private and public sector organisations. A third important source of provision, the voluntary sector, also plays an important part in tourism development. The voluntary sector (sometimes referred to as the not-for-profit sector) includes community groups, charities, trusts and non-governmental organisations (NGOs) involved in:

- Conservation/environmental protection;
- Community activities;
- Sustainable tourism;
- Heritage management;
- Minority groups;
- Youth organisations;
- Cultural organisations.

Voluntary organisations vary enormously in their size and aims. At one end of the scale, a small group of like-minded people may decide to form a community tourism association to develop and promote an area. At the other end we have large organisations such as the National Trust and the Youth Hostels Association (YHA). Pressure groups play an important part in highlighting issues and campaigning for change (see the case study on Tourism Concern on page 87). Voluntary organisations at local, national and international level often receive advice and financial help from both the public and private sector, sometimes in the form of grants or sponsorship.

WEBLINK

www.yha.org.uk

Check out this website for more information on the YHA.

FOCUS ON INDUSTRY – Youth Hostels Association (YHA)

The YHA is one of the UK's leading voluntary organisations serving the needs of young people and a major contributor to Britain's tourism earnings (current annual turnover is in excess of £35 million). The YHA has approximately 300,000 members across all age groups and works hard to maintain its original aim to *'promote love, care and understanding of the countryside in principle and in practice'*. The charity operates 226 Youth Hostels spanning major cities and rural locations, recording over 2 million overnight stays each year.

The following case study highlights the work of Tourism Concern, one of the UK's leading campaigning organisations in the field of tourism development.

Unit 10

CASE STUDY – Tourism Concern

Introduction

Tourism Concern is a membership organisation established in 1989 to bring together people with an active concern for tourism's impact on community and environment, both in the UK and worldwide. The organisation is working for change in tourism and insists that tourism takes account of the rights and interests of those living in the world's tourist areas. It seeks to raise awareness of tourism's impacts, informs and influences decision-makers at all levels, and provides a comprehensive information base. Through its membership network, global contacts and resource collection, Tourism Concern is a respected centre for advice and information on tourism's impacts on environment and culture.

What does Tourism Concern do?

Tourism Concern works with communities in destination countries to reduce social and environmental problems connected to tourism, and with the outbound tourism industry in the UK to find ways of improving tourism so that local benefits are increased. Its mission statement is *'to effect change in the tourism industry by campaigning for fair and ethically-traded tourism'*. Advocacy is a major part of its work and, time and again, the message from its Southern (Third World) partners is that they want tourists, but at present they don't benefit from them.

Tourism for communities

Agencies working overseas are increasingly finding that tourism development impacts on the lives of communities they work with in just the same way as other multinational industries might, such as oil and mining companies. Communities often find that:

- They have tourism imposed on them by governments, foreign developers and tourism businesses;
- There is little linkage between tourism (especially mass tourism) and local industry, such as agriculture;
- Land and other natural resources are frequently co-opted, often illegally;
- Cultural traditions are appropriated and commercialised.

Tourism Concern's links with communities and agencies working in developing countries show that that there is great concern that the trend in tourism development is for greater control by multinational companies, more all-inclusive tourism that excludes local people and businesses, and greater numbers of tourists.

Campaigning

Tourism Concern has been campaigning on human rights and ethical tourism since it was established in 1989. It sees its work in public campaigning as essential to achieving its objectives, not least because public opinion matters increasingly to the well-being of private companies. One of its main campaigns has been to highlight how people lose their homes and livelihoods through the development of tourism, e.g. the displacement of the Maasai people in East Africa, and the poor working conditions of many tourism staff, e.g. the porters who accompany trekkers in many of the world's popular mountain tourist destinations.

Fair trade in tourism

Tourism Concern works with the travel industry to make things fairer for people living in destinations, but is also keen to show that every holidaymaker can play their part in helping achieve fair trade in tourism. It believes that fair trade in tourism could be the way forward and that fair trade will help define a new way of managing tourism which shares its benefits more equitably between tourists, the tourism industry, the governments of the countries visited and, above all, the people who live in the tourist destinations. Tourism Concern has created a Fair Trade in Tourism Network to explore solutions and communicate them worldwide so that communities involved in tourism development can learn from each other.

WEBLINK

www.tourismconcern.org.uk

Check out this website to help answer the questions in this case study and for more information on the work of Tourism Concern.

CASE STUDY QUESTIONS

1. What campaigns is Tourism Concern currently championing?
2. What factors will affect Tourism Concern's success in achieving its aims and objectives?
3. What can Tourism Concern do to persuade governments of the need for well-planned and ethical tourism development?
4. Give some examples of where Tourism Concern's aims are in conflict with tourism developers in developing nations.

Unit 10

SECTION 3: IMPACTS OF TOURISM DEVELOPMENT

An industry the size of travel and tourism cannot fail to have impacts on the people, culture, environment and the economies of destination areas and countries. Often these impacts are positive, for example providing jobs, incomes and environmental improvements, but sometimes tourism has negative impacts, such as congestion, pollution, increased crime and higher prices in tourist areas. The following sections of this unit look in detail at the positive and negative effects of tourism development under the following headings:

- Economic impacts;
- Environmental impacts;
- Social impacts;
- Cultural impacts.

The section concludes by investigating some of the techniques that can be used to maximise tourism's positive impacts and minimise its negative aspects.

Economic impacts

Positive economic impacts

It is often the positive economic impacts that persuade governments, companies and individuals to get involved with tourism development in the first place. Tourism has the potential to generate revenue and provide much-needed jobs. Thinking of your own local area, there may well be hotels, caravan parks, guesthouses or tourist attractions that provide an income for the people who own them and create jobs for local people. Nationally, tourism was worth £74 billion to the British economy in 2003 and provided jobs for 2.2 million people.

At global level, international tourism has been one of the

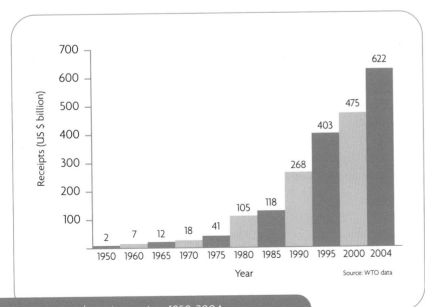

Fig. 10.4 International tourist receipts 1950-2004

world's fastest-growing industries since the end of the Second World War, with the revenue earned from international tourism rising from just US$2 billion in 1950 to a record US$622 billion in 2004 (see Figure 10.4).

The travel and tourism industry has the ability to provide a variety of positive economic impacts, the most important of which are:

- Improved infrastructure;
- Increased income;
- Increased employment.

Improved infrastructure

As well as generating revenue and creating jobs, tourism development also contributes to infrastructure improvements in destination areas, e.g. road and rail improvements, airport developments, improvements in telecommunications and utilities such as water and power supply. In this way, local people can benefit from improved facilities that are provided for tourists. Member states of the European Union can apply for financial help with infrastructure projects from the European Regional Development Fund (ERDF) and other sources, while developing countries are often supported with funding from the World Bank, United Nations and multinational corporations to build new roads, improve water supply and create new tourist facilities.

WEBLINK

www.dft.gov.uk

Check out the Department for Transport website for more information on the Channel Tunnel Rail Link.

FOCUS ON INDUSTRY – Channel Tunnel Rail Link (CTRL)

The CTRL is the first major new railway to be built in the UK for over a century and the first high-speed railway. When fully completed, the 109km of track will stretch from St. Pancras in central London to the Channel Tunnel complex at Cheriton in Kent, connecting Britain with Europe's expanding high-speed rail network. The CTRL is being built in two separate sections. Section 1, which runs for 74km from the Channel Tunnel through Kent to join the existing railway network on the outskirts of London, was opened to train services in September 2003. Section 2 links to section 1 and continues for a further 39km as far as St. Pancras station. It is due for completion in early 2007 and will see the development of new international stations at Stratford in east London and Ebbsfleet in north Kent.

Increased income

The travel and tourism industry generates income and wealth for private individuals, local authorities, companies, voluntary bodies and national governments – from the modest income earned by a couple running a farmhouse bed and breakfast business to the millions of pounds generated by large travel companies and the billions of pounds earned from tourism by many countries around the world. At international level, the money that tourists spend in a country can make a considerable contribution to its balance of payments, i.e. the flows of money into and out of a country. The USA, for example, earned nearly US$75 billion from visiting tourists in 2004. Many developing countries are turning to tourism as a way of increasing their income from foreign visitors and using the money they receive from tourism to improve health, education and social facilities. As well as receiving direct income from visitors, governments also benefit from tax payments made by tourism businesses and tourists themselves, e.g. hotel, aircraft and border taxes.

WEBLINK

www.somerset.gov.uk
/celebratingsomerset
/business/pages/rese
arch.htm

*Check out this website
for more information on
the economic impact of
tourism in Somerset.*

FOCUS ON INDUSTRY – Economic impact of tourism in Somerset

The total number of tourist trips to the county of Somerset in the South West Tourism region totalled 12.1 million in 2003 (9.9 million day trips and 2.2 million staying trips). Total spending by visitors to the county in the same year amounted to £602 million (£262 million from day visitors and £340 million from visitors staying overnight). The number of full-time and part-time jobs in tourism was nearly 23,000.

ACTIVITY

Carry out some research to find out just how much your local area, or a tourist area nearby, benefits from spending by tourists.

This activity is designed to provide evidence for P4.

Increased employment

Tourism's ability to create jobs is one of the main reasons why governments and other public sector bodies encourage the development of tourism. When compared with creating employment in the manufacturing sector, service sector jobs in tourism are seen as a relatively cheap and easy way of making jobs available, since the associated capital start-up costs are usually much lower. Direct employment in tourism occurs in hotels and other types of accommodation, transport operators, travel agencies, tourist attractions, government departments and tour operators, to name but a few. Tourism also creates indirect employment opportunities in sectors not directly associated with the industry, as the following examples from the World Travel and Tourism Council (WTTC) indicate:

- Traditional travel service jobs – includes employment in airlines, hotels, restaurants, attractions, car rental companies, tour operators and travel agents;
- Government travel service jobs – includes employment in tourism promotion and information offices, national park or monument guides, air traffic controllers, road safety and maintenance staff, and lifeguards on tourist destination beaches. They also include customs and immigration officials, plus security staff, at land borders and airports;
- Travel and tourism capital investment jobs – on the public side, these include the design and construction of roads, parks and airports. On the private side, they include employment in the building of aircraft, hotels/resorts, holiday homes, travel company office buildings, cruise ships, and some retail shops and restaurants;
- Travel product jobs – these jobs provide goods and services to travellers and travel companies, ranging from film developers, accountants and dry cleaners to butchers, printers and sign makers.

WEBLINK

www.wttc.org

Check out this website for more details on the global impact of tourism.

At international level, the forecast growth in tourism in the early decades of the 21st century will create additional direct and indirect jobs in the industry. The World Travel and Tourism Council (WTTC) estimates that by the year 2015, international tourism will generate employment for nearly 270 million workers, representing 8.3 per cent of the total global workforce.

ACTIVITY

Make a list of some of the jobs in your local area that are directly associated with travel and tourism. Are there any other businesses that benefit indirectly from tourism?

Negative economic impacts

Although the economic impacts of tourism are generally positive, it can have some negative economic effects, including:

- Increased living costs;
- Decline of traditional employment;
- Economic dependency on tourism.

Increased living costs

An influx of visitors to a holiday area can push up prices of goods and services, particularly when demand is high in peak season. This disadvantages local people who may have to pay higher prices for food, drinks, entertainment, transport, events, etc. Extra charges may be levied on the local community to finance facilities and services for visitors. Through their taxes, local people may have to pay for such facilities as tourist information centres and museums, which are primarily for the benefit of tourists. Local people sometimes resent having to pay for the costs of running travel and tourism facilities that they never use. Areas of the country that become particularly popular with tourists may lose their local shops in favour of retail outlets geared specifically to the needs of the tourists, such as gift shops and cafés. This means that local people have to travel further to buy their staple foods, thus increasing their cost of living. For example, the village of Holmfirth in the West Riding of Yorkshire, which has become famous as the location where the TV programme 'The Last of the Summer Wine' is filmed, has seen many of its village shops being replaced by facilities for visitors.

Some holiday areas have large numbers of second homes that are only used for short periods of the year by their owners. This is particularly the case in National Parks and other countryside and coastal areas of the UK. The demand for second homes often increases the price of all houses in an area, making it difficult for local people, particularly young couples, to buy their first property. Some UK National Park authorities are considering imposing restrictions on who can own homes in their areas as a way of improving the affordability of housing for local people.

Decline of traditional employment

Tourism development can lead to the loss of traditional jobs, when workers move from industries such as farming, forestry, mining and fishing into service jobs in the tourism industry. This was the case in countries such as Spain and Greece in the 1970s and 1980s during the rapid growth in package holidays to the Mediterranean, when people left their work at sea and on the land for jobs with better working conditions in the tourism industry. Developing countries that are working hard to attract tourists experience similar problems in keeping workers in primary industries.

Economic dependency on tourism

In many respects tourism is a very fragile industry, vulnerable to natural disasters, health scares and terrorist activity. Since the horrific attacks on New York's World Trade Centre and the Pentagon in Washington DC in September 2001, the world has experienced an increasing number of natural and man-made incidents, which have had serious implications for international travel and tourism. These include the tsunami on Boxing Day 2004, the

Unit 10

outbreak of SARS in the Far East, terrorist attacks in Bali, Madrid and Kenya, and the bombings in London and the Red Sea resort of Sharm el-Sheikh in July 2005.

For countries that rely heavily on tourism for their income and employment, events such as these can devastate their economies at a stroke. Tourism to the Maldives, for example, dropped by 70 per cent in the period immediately following the tsunami. Also, tourists' needs and tastes change, meaning that a destination or tourism product may not always be in demand, making it doubly important for countries to diversify their economies and not rely too heavily on tourism for their income.

ACTIVITY

Carry out some research into the positive and negative economic impacts of tourism development in your own local area (or a nearby tourist area). Work with a partner to agree some ideas as to how the positive impacts could be maximised and the negative impacts minimised. Present your findings as a presentation to the rest of your group.

This activity is designed to provide evidence for P4.

Environmental impacts

Positive environmental impacts

Although the tourism industry is often criticised for damaging the environment, it can sometimes be a positive force for environmental change – the very fact that tourists come to an area can stimulate activities to conserve the environment for them. Tourism to remote areas of the world, such as the rain forests of South America and Papua New Guinea, plus hitherto undiscovered Pacific islands, can also help expose damaging environmental activities, e.g. destruction of coral reefs, loss of habitats and forest clearance. There is a growing acceptance in many developing countries that it makes good economic sense to conserve the wildlife and natural areas that visitors pay money to see. Pressure groups, such as Tourism Concern (see case study on page 87) and Friends of the Earth, campaign for responsible tourism development that is respectful of local people, their environment and culture. Closer to home, tourism development can lead to the improvement of derelict land and waterways, the restoration of redundant buildings, landscaping and environmental improvements linked to schemes such at the Britain in Bloom campaign, co-ordinated by the Royal Horticultural Society.

WEBLINK

www.rhs.org.uk/
britaininbloom/

Check out this website for more details on the Britain in Bloom campaign.

Unit 10

FOCUS ON INDUSTRY – Kuoni's responsible tourism policy

Kuoni Travel is one of the world's leading long-haul tour operators, employing more than 7,500 staff in 300 offices across the globe. The company is fully-committed to sustainable and environmentally-friendly tourism activities. It regards the environment as an invaluable asset and works with its partners worldwide to help protect it for the future. Kuoni constantly reviews its business in order to apply socially and environmentally-acceptable practices in all areas of its work. As it states on its website, *'As a tour operator, we believe we can contribute to the viability of local economies. However, we are also aware that tourism can have negative impacts on the economy, environment, nature, wildlife, social structures and local cultures. In the long-term interest of host communities and our industry, we will endeavour to prevent or minimise these impacts'.* The company regularly updates its staff and customers on its responsible tourism policy and activities in the UK and overseas.

Negative environmental impacts

We have seen that tourism can have a positive impact on the environment, but it can also impact negatively unless properly managed. On a global scale, tourism can have harmful effects on 'fragile' habitats, such as sand dunes, coral reefs, rain forests and mountain areas. In Britain, the coast, countryside, towns and cities all suffer from the pressures of increasing numbers of visitors and their transportation. Some of the worst environmental problems include:

- Erosion of resources – the wearing away of soil and vegetation by walkers, horse-riders, cyclists, cars, 4 x 4s and motorcycles;
- Litter – both an eyesore and a threat to the safety of people and animals;
- Congestion and overcrowding – in popular holiday areas we all see the effects of too many people and too many cars;
- Pollution – of water and air, not forgetting noise pollution;
- Loss of habitats for flora and fauna;
- Spoiling of the landscape that people have come to see and enjoy.

Better education, improved visitor and traffic management techniques, congestion pricing and better signposting, are some of the possible solutions that are being tried in our towns and countryside to reduce the harmful environmental effects of travel and tourism (see the example of traffic management in York on page 103).

In the UK, the negative environmental impacts of tourism are not confined to countryside areas, but are also to be found in cities and on the coast. Negative impacts in the countryside are most acute in the National Parks, which together accommodate over 100

Path erosion can be a serious problem on coastal paths

million visits per year. Parks close to urban centres come under particular pressure; at summer weekends, some parts of the Peak District and Lake District National Parks reach saturation point, with traffic jams for many miles. The large numbers of people visiting the countryside, most travelling by car, put pressure on the physical environment, resulting in erosion by walkers, cars, cycles, horse-riders and motorcyclists. Litter and the pollution of fields and waterways are also a constant problem, resulting in harm to the natural flora and fauna.

Tourism's harmful effects on the urban environment affect many historic destinations that are popular with tourists, such as York, Bath, Chester, Cambridge, Stratford-upon-Avon and Oxford, as well as our capital cities, Cardiff, London, Belfast and Edinburgh. Congestion, pollution and litter are three of the most common problems concerning tourism in the urban environment. Noise pollution, particularly associated with increased traffic flows, can also affect residents and visitors alike.

On the coast, sensitive areas such as sand dunes and estuaries can be harmed by tourist pressure, while the popular seaside resorts, such as Llandudno, Torquay and Newquay, have to deal with a huge influx of visitors for a relatively short period of time, plus all that they bring with them. In areas of the country that are prone to drought, water supply can be a problem in the peak tourist season, while sewage disposal is a constant challenge to local authorities.

ACTIVITY

Carry out some research into the positive and negative environmental impacts of tourism development in your own local area (or a nearby tourist area). Work with a partner to agree some ideas as to how the positive impacts could be maximised and the negative impacts minimised. Present your findings as a presentation to the rest of your group.

This activity is designed to provide evidence for P4.

Unit 10

Social impacts

Positive social impacts

Given that many of the reasons for visiting tourist destinations are concerned with social experiences, for example meeting new people and learning about different cultures, the travel and tourism industry can be said to have many positive social impacts. Tourism can lead to greater understanding between people of different cultures and help to reduce poverty in developing countries. Although tourism development is often criticised for its negative social impacts on destination areas, other positive social impacts include:

- Improved provision of community facilities and services – local people benefit from new facilities that are provided for tourists, e.g. new attractions and events;
- Education and training – well-managed tourism development gives staff the chance to improve their skills and qualifications, thereby enhancing their career prospects;
- Improved social status for indigenous groups – tourism can help communities improve their livelihoods and gain greater social status, particularly in developing countries that need the income from foreign tourists.

At local level, the provision of tourism facilities for the enjoyment of visitors gives local people the opportunity to improve the quality of their lives and to take part in community activities for the benefit of all. Also, by helping to maintain a clean and attractive environment for visitors, tourism can instil a sense of civic pride in local residents.

Negative social impacts

Some of the most common negative social effects of tourism development include:

- Change in living patterns and displacement – tourism can sometimes distort patterns of living and home ownership in destinations, e.g. in areas that have large numbers of second homes. Also, local people can be forced to move from their homes in order to make way for new tourism developments. This is known as 'displacement' and is an increasingly common feature of tourism development in developing countries;
- Crime – mass tourism often increases the likelihood of criminal activities in destination areas, including prostitution, illegal gambling, robbery and public disturbances. Many of these would occur anyway, but tourism accelerates the problem;
- Conflict with the host community – tourism development that is poorly-planned and managed can give rise to clashes between visitors and the 'host community', i.e. the people who live in the tourist destination. This could occur for a number of reasons, such as excessive noise and congestion in resorts or local people resenting the behaviour of tourists. There can be problems in developing countries when western

tourists come into close contact with people who have totally different cultures and traditions to their own. The indigenous peoples, particularly the young, sometimes try to copy the dress and actions of the visitors, thereby altering their cultural traditions. This is known as the 'demonstration effect';

- Seasonal employment – much employment in tourism is seasonal. This can result in large numbers of unemployed people in tourist resorts for periods of the year, putting extra strain on local government resources. Tourism entrepreneurs work hard to create developments that offer year-round employment, which minimises any problems associated with seasonal work in tourism.

Tourist resorts can become congested in peak season

ACTIVITY

Carry out some research into the positive and negative social impacts of tourism development in your own local area (or a nearby tourist area). Work with a partner to agree some ideas as to how the positive impacts could be maximised and the negative impacts minimised. Present your findings as a presentation to the rest of your group.

This activity is designed to provide evidence for P4.

Cultural impacts

Positive cultural impacts

Tourism development can be a force for good by contributing to cultural activities in destinations. For example, it may help to preserve traditional customs such as dance, music and theatre, and create a demand for locally-produced food and drink. Tourism can also stimulate the production and sale of local arts and crafts to meet the needs of visitors. It has an important role to play in reinforcing an area's cultural identity, particularly amongst the younger generation.

Negative cultural impacts

Many people with an interest in tourism development think that its negative cultural impacts are far more harmful in the long run than the environmental problems associated with the industry. This is because many of tourism's negative environmental impacts can be easily corrected with the correct management and funding. The cultural problems, however, can be far more deep-rooted and may take generations to eradicate, for example:

- An area's cultural identity may be diluted or lost altogether as a result of mass tourism development, e.g. religious codes may be altered to adapt to the needs of visitors or local languages may be lost through under-use;
- In many developing nations, the values of the western visitors may be imposed on the destination area and its people to the detriment of local culture (sometimes known as 'westernisation');
- The staging of events specifically for tourists can sometimes demean cultural traditions that have lasted for centuries, e.g. traditional dance and music.

Tourism can have positive cultural impacts

ACTIVITY

Carry out some research into the positive and negative cultural impacts of tourism development in your own local area (or a nearby tourist area). Work with a partner to agree some ideas as to how the positive impacts could be maximised and the negative impacts minimised. Present your findings as a presentation to the rest of your group.

This activity is designed to provide evidence for P4.

Maximising tourism's positive aspects

It is in the long-term interest of the travel and tourism industry for public, private and voluntary sector organisations to work in partnership to maximise the industry's positive aspects. This can be achieved by giving careful attention to a number of factors, including:

- Avoiding leakages from the local tourism economy;
- Reinvestment of tourism income in public and social projects;
- Education and training.

Tourism can result in a clash of cultures

Leakage avoidance strategies

We saw earlier in this unit that income from tourism is re-circulated in the local economy and is often worth more than its face value; this is known as the multiplier effect (see page 77). Destination managers should aim to keep as much as possible of the money from tourism in the local area by keeping 'leakages' to a minimum, i.e. the money that leaves the local economy to pay for supplies bought outside the area, to pay shareholders or staff who may not live locally, etc. This can be achieved by drawing up tourism development plans that make maximum use of local produce and suppliers, involve local communities in making decisions about tourism and employ local people whenever possible.

WEBLINK

www.atg-oxford.co.uk

Check out this website for more information on ATG and its environmental policies.

FOCUS ON INDUSTRY – ATG and its 'buy local' policy

ATG is an independent tour operator specialising in walking holidays worldwide. Founded in 1979 on principles of environmental conservation and sustainability, its objectives are to ensure environmental best practice throughout its activities, to 'give something back' by undertaking conservation projects in the areas visited, and to involve clients, suppliers, local communities and staff in the process of sustainable tourism. With its 'buy local' policy, 65 per cent of receipts are spent in the locations visited. The company has also invested in local hotels – money that has enabled vital improvements, ensuring their continuation and hence job and wealth creation. Ten per cent of ATG's pre-tax profits are channelled into the ATG Trust, which 'gives something back' by funding conservation projects in the destinations visited. Staff, clients, suppliers and local authorities and communities are all involved in the selection of the projects, which aim to sustain the areas for the benefit of future generations.

Unit 10

Reinvestment of tourism income in public and social projects

As we saw earlier in this unit when examining the objectives of tourism development, most investment in tourism takes place for commercial reasons – an individual or organisation hopes to make a financial return on their investment in the industry. However, some governments undertake investment in tourism for non-commercial reasons, to benefit local communities and improve their quality of life. For example, public investment in leisure centres, parks, tourist information centres, transport infrastructure and visitor attractions, may be justifiable on social if not always commercial grounds. Some developing countries levy tourist taxes on visitors and use the money collected to invest directly in improvements to education, health and housing in the destination area. In some parts of the UK, money from tourists is used to maintain the areas that they visit, e.g. car parking charges are used to maintain footpaths and dry stone walls. The Lake District Tourism and Conservation Partnership is a good example of this, raising more than £230,000 from visitors and tourism businesses for conservation projects in 2004-5.

Tourism education and training

One of the most cost-effective ways of maximising tourism's positive impacts is to invest in education and training of local people for employment in tourism-related activities, e.g. in hotels and other accommodation, tourist attractions, tour guiding, hospitality, etc. Education and training of local people not only helps destinations to retain more tourism revenue in the area, but also provides visitors with higher standards of service, thereby contributing towards more repeat business and a sustainable tourism industry.

ACTIVITY

Working with a partner, carry out some research to find examples of developing countries that are investing in tourism education and training as part of their tourism development process. Present your findings as case study information sheets.

Minimising tourism's negative aspects

The performance of organisations in relation to the impact that they have on the environment and on host communities is becoming a major issue for the 21st century. No travel and tourism organisation can operate without having positive and negative effects on its immediate natural environment and, in many cases, on the environment thousands of miles away. Western societies are becoming increasingly concerned about the threats to the environment posed by many tourism developments. The 1980s saw the growth of the 'green consumer' who not only looks for environmentally friendly products in the supermarkets,

but also for tourism products that are developed in harmony with the environment. Many tourism developments have been criticised for their lack of concern for environmental, social and cultural impacts, while many argue that the whole of the tourism industry is, by its very nature, environmentally and culturally destructive.

Techniques for minimising the negative impacts of tourism development are many and varied, and include:

- Planning controls;
- Implementing the principles of sustainable tourism;
- Visitor and traffic management;
- Environmental auditing;
- Community involvement in the tourism development process.

Planning controls

Planners are responsible for making sure that any tourism development is acceptable to local people and respectful of the local environment. In the UK, local authorities have the power to refuse planning permission for tourism developments if they do not meet certain criteria, for example their impact on the landscape, scale and location. Planners are called upon to make judgements about a wide variety of developments in tourism, for example:

- The building of a hotel or holiday complex;
- Signposting of hotels and tourist facilities;
- Change of use of buildings and land for tourism purposes;
- The development of tourist attractions;
- Car parking associated with tourism projects.

In all cases, planning authorities have to balance the economic benefits of tourism projects with the possible damage to the local environment and communities.

Implementing the principles of sustainable tourism

The World Tourism Organisation (WTO) defines sustainable tourism as 'tourism that meets the needs of present tourists and host regions while protecting and enhancing opportunity for the future'. Section 4 of this unit investigates the concept and principles of sustainable tourism in greater detail (see page 105).

Visitor and traffic management

The pressures on many of our most beautiful landscapes and historic cities from the growth in visitor numbers, has led to a range of measures to control the impact of people and their cars on the environment. Initiatives in rural areas try to encourage visitors to leave their cars at home and use public transport instead, for example in the Peak District National Park. Some of the busiest roads in the National Parks are closed to traffic altogether at peak times, encouraging walkers and cyclists to explore areas free from noise and pollution. Historic cities such as Canterbury, Cambridge and York have developed integrated transport policies aimed at reducing cars in the city centres and encouraging cycling and the use of public transport, including park-and-ride schemes.

WEBLINK

www.york.gov.uk

Check out this website for more information on traffic and visitor management in York.

FOCUS ON INDUSTRY – Traffic management in the city of York

In its Local Transport Plan 2001-2006, York City Council announced a series of measures to manage traffic flows and encourage sustainable transport in this popular tourist city, including:

- The introduction of high frequency bus services on 10 radial routes through the city centre designed specifically to promote a shift away from car use;
- A supporting network of conventional, local bus services;
- Bus priority measures to guarantee bus journey times to the heart of the city;
- The development of park-and-ride sites as transport interchanges for all forms of travel to and from the city centre;
- Acceleration of the existing cycling and pedestrian safety schemes.

Environmental auditing

An environmental audit is an investigation of an organisation's policies and practices from the point of view of their impact on the local and global environment. Following on from some pioneering work carried out by the Inter-Continental Hotels Group, which produced a manual of procedures on the environmental consequences of all its business activities, many large hotel companies, airlines and tour operators are now investigating their activities and processes from an environmental standpoint. They examine everything from the fuel used in their cars to the type of detergents used for cleaning. Some organisations have used their concern for the environment as a marketing tool, hoping to capitalise on the growing market for tourism products and services that are truly respectful of the world in which we live.

Many major travel and tourism companies, including TUI Thomson, British Airways and easyJet, have developed environmental policies and train staff in their implementation. The 'Tourism for Tomorrow Awards', launched in 1991 by British Airways and administered since 2004 by the World Travel and Tourism Council (WTTC), recognise environmentally responsible tourism developments on a worldwide basis. Recent global winners have

Unit 10

WEBLINK

www.tourismfortomorrow.com

Check out this website for more information on the 'Tourism for Tomorrow Awards'.

included Damaraland Camp in Namibia, Casuarina Beach Club Barbados and the UK's Jurassic Coast.

Community involvement in the tourism development process

Local people should be involved from the outset in any new tourism developments, whether in a developed or developing country. Failure to consult local communities can result in conflict between host communities and visitors. Community involvement in tourism development is one of the key principles of sustainable tourism development, which is examined in the next section of this unit.

SECTION 4: PRINCIPLES OF SUSTAINABLE TOURISM

Sustainable tourism is an emerging concept that has grown out of increased concern about the negative environmental and socio-cultural impacts of unplanned tourism development. An extension of 'green tourism', which developed out of concern for the environment, sustainable tourism is part of a much wider global debate on sustainable development, highlighted by the Brundtland Report in 1987 and the first Earth Summit in Rio in 1992.

The World Tourism Organisation (WTO) offers the following definition:

'Sustainable tourism development meets the needs of the present tourists and host regions while protecting and enhancing the opportunity for the future. It is envisaged as leading to management of all resources in such a way that economic, social and aesthetic needs can be fulfilled, while maintaining cultural integrity, essential ecological processes, biological diversity and life support systems'.

It goes on to state that sustainable tourism should:

1. Make optimal use of environmental resources that constitute a key element in tourism development, maintaining essential ecological processes and helping to conserve natural heritage and biodiversity;
2. Respect the socio-cultural authenticity of host communities, conserve their built and living cultural heritage and traditional values, and contribute to inter-cultural understanding and tolerance;
3. Ensure viable, long-term economic operations, providing socio-economic benefits to all stakeholders that are fairly distributed, including stable employment and income-earning opportunities and social services to host communities, and contributing to poverty alleviation.

Principles of sustainable tourism

Various bodies concerned with travel and tourism have developed policies on sustainable development, including the former English Tourist Board 'Tourism and the Environment Task Force', whose principles for sustainable tourism developed in 1991, and quoted extensively today, state that:

1. The environment has an intrinsic value which outweighs its value as a tourism asset. Its enjoyment by future generations and its long-term survival must not be prejudiced by short-term considerations;
2. Tourism should be recognised as a positive activity with the potential to benefit the community and the place as well as the visitor;
3. The relationship between tourism and the environment must be managed so that the environment is sustainable in the long term. Tourism must not be allowed to damage the resource, prejudice its future enjoyment or bring unacceptable impacts;

4. Tourism activities and developments should respect the scale, nature and character of the place in which they are sited;
5. In any location, harmony must be sought between the needs of the visitor, the place and the host community;
6. In a dynamic world some change is inevitable and change can often be beneficial. Adaptation to change, however, should not be at the expense of any of these principles;
7. The tourism industry, local authorities and environmental agencies all have a duty to respect the above principles and to work together to achieve their practical realisation.

The challenge facing the travel and tourism industry, especially the mass market tour operators, is to implement the principles of sustainable tourism for the benefit of present and future destinations and their host communities. Many communities in the UK and elsewhere have developed action plans, known as Local Agenda 21, to promote the idea of sustainable development locally.

ACTIVITY

Carry out some research to learn more about Agenda 21 and Local Agenda 21. In relation to your own area, find out if the local authority has a policy on sustainable tourism development or a Local Agenda 21 group.

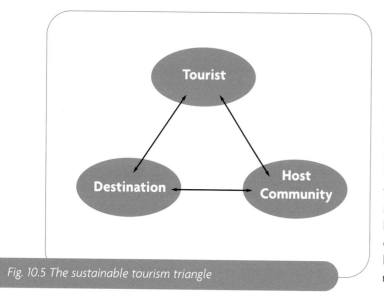

Fig. 10.5 The sustainable tourism triangle

The mainstream travel and tourism industry is slowing waking up to the fact that it needs to give consideration to the potentially damaging effect that its operations can have on the environment and host communities. Pressure from a travelling public that is more environmentally and culturally aware is forcing airlines, tour operators, destination planners and accommodation providers to implement the principles of sustainable tourism. It is no longer uncommon to find statements of environmental policy in the holiday brochures of the mass-market tour operators, giving advice to holidaymakers on how to protect local environments and respect local cultures and traditions.

Unit 10

Benefits of sustainable tourism

Figure 10.5 demonstrates the three core aspects – the tourist, the host community and the destination – that must operate in harmony for tourism development to be truly sustainable. All three interact with one another and create the positive and negative tourism impacts that were discussed earlier in this unit.

Adopting a sustainable approach to tourism development brings benefits to each of the three parties shown in Figure 10.5, as explained in the following sections of this unit.

Benefits to the destination

Sustainable tourism can offer a number of benefits to destinations, such as:

- A protected natural environment;
- Greater appeal to visitors generally, particularly those who are looking for a more authentic experience while on holiday;
- Sustainable use of resources, e.g. water, land and energy.

Benefits to the host community

Host communities can benefit in a number of ways from a sustainable approach to tourism development, for example there is likely to be:

- More opportunities for community involvement in tourism development;
- Greater support for local goods and services;
- New business opportunities;
- More local pride.

Benefits to the tourist

Sustainable tourism offers a number of benefits to tourists, including:

- A high quality experience;
- Better relationships with the local people in destinations;
- The opportunity to learn about local cultures and traditions;
- Closer understanding of the host community.

The travel and tourism industry also benefits from sustainable tourism in a number of ways, including:

- Reduced operating costs by recycling and adopting energy- efficient practices;
- Better working relationships with the local community;
- Greater understanding of visitor needs;
- More business from tourists who are looking for a more authentic holiday experience;
- Opportunities to develop new business ventures linked to environmentally-friendly activities, e.g. cycling, wildlife watching, walking and conservation holidays.

Incorporating sustainable tourism into tourism planning

Sustainable tourism helps to promote local customs and traditions

There are few people who would disagree that sustainable tourism is 'a good thing'. The difficulties arise when the principles of sustainable tourism have to be put into practice by incorporating them into plans and strategies – this is when some people begin to question whether sustainable tourism is actually achievable.

Many public and voluntary sector tourism organisations incorporate sustainability principles into their long-term planning as a matter of course. This occurs at international level, e.g. the World Tourism Organisation (WTO) and the World Travel and Tourism Council (WTTC), at national level with the National Tourist Boards and locally, where local authorities promote sustainable tourism principles and practices.

The majority of private sector tourism operators are supportive of sustainable tourism principles, but often find it hard to incorporate them into their commercial activities. The following case study highlights the work of the Travel Foundation, which works with the travel and tourism industry to find ways of implementing sustainable tourism principles into business practices.

CASE STUDY – The Travel Foundation

Introduction

The Travel Foundation is an independent UK charity that aims to help the outbound travel and tourism industry manage its activities in a more sustainable manner. The Foundation's focus is on protecting and enhancing the environment and improving the well-being of destination communities, enriching the tourism experience now and into the future.

Who benefits from the Foundation's work?

On its website, the Travel Foundation lists the following as beneficiaries of its work:

- Consumers – get higher quality and an enriched holiday experience, as well as the reassurance that their favourite destinations will be protected for generations to come;
- Businesses – are better able to meet the needs of their customers, at the same time as protecting the resources on which their future depends;
- Destination communities – receive greater benefit from tourism, with a boost to their local economy and conservation of the natural environment, local traditions and culture;
- Local and national governments have evidence to develop effective tourism policies and support destination communities and environments.

Projects sponsored by the Foundation

The Foundation provides funding for research work and practical projects to encourage sustainable tourism principles. Current projects include work in Tobago and Mexico, plus the development of practical tools to guide best practice in the industry. Previous projects have focused on developments in the Gambia and Cyprus. The Foundation also works in partnership with the industry to develop programmes to train staff about sustainable tourism.

WEBLINK

www.thetravel
foundation.org.uk

Check out this website to help answer these questions and for more information on the work of the Travel Foundation.

CASE STUDY QUESTIONS

1. How does the work carried out by the Travel Foundation differ from that undertaken by Tourism Concern?
2. Who are the main beneficiaries of the Foundation's work?
3. What tools does the Foundation use to encourage the travel and tourism industry to sign up to the principles of sustainable tourism?
4. Which other organisations work with the Foundation to help achieve its objectives?

Unit 10

UNIT SUMMARY

This unit has introduced you to the concept of tourism development in developed and developing countries of the world. You have explored the different objectives of tourism development and found that it is often the economic benefits of tourism that encourage individuals, organisations and governments to become involved in tourism. You have learned about the various 'agents' of tourism, which operate at international, national, regional and local levels. The unit has looked in detail at the positive and negative impacts of tourism development – economic, environmental, social and cultural – and examined how tourism's positive aspects can be maximised and its negative effects minimised through careful planning and management. You have also explored the concept of sustainable tourism and found that implementing its principles is a major challenge for the global travel and tourism industry. Throughout the unit you have been shown many industry examples, while the case studies on Tourism Concern and the Travel Foundation highlight key issues in tourism development worldwide.

If you have worked methodically, by the end of this unit you should have:

- Examined the objectives of tourism development in tourist destinations;
- Examined the agents involved in tourism development;
- Investigated the impact of tourism development on the destination;
- Explored how the principles of sustainable tourism can be used to benefit destinations and their communities.

You are now in a position to complete the assignment for the unit, under the direction of your tutor. Before you tackle the assignment you may like to have a go at the following questions to help build your knowledge on tourism development.

Test your knowledge

1. What is 'tourism development'?
2. What are the four key objectives of tourism development?
3. What is the 'multiplier effect' and why is it important in tourism development?
4. Giving examples, explain how tourism development can help economic regeneration.
5. How and to what extent will staging the Olympic and Paralympic Games in London in 2012 help the tourism industry in the UK?
6. What is an 'agent' of tourism development?
7. List four key private sector agents of tourism development and explain their roles.
8. What are the main functions carried out by public sector agents of tourism development?
9. How does Tourism Concern help communities in tourist destinations achieve 'fair trade tourism'?
10. What are the four main categories of tourism development impacts?
11. Name three negative economic impacts of tourism development.

12. Name three positive social impacts of tourism development.
13. What are 'leakages' from the tourism economy and how can they be avoided?
14. Why is it important to involve local communities in the tourism development process?
15. What is 'sustainable tourism' and how can mainstream travel and tourism companies be persuaded to operate in a sustainable manner?

UNIT 10 ASSIGNMENT: Tourism development

Introduction

This assignment is made up of a number of tasks which, when successfully completed, are designed to give you sufficient evidence to meet the Pass (P), Merit (M) and Distinction (D) grading criteria for the unit. If you have carried out the activities and read the case studies throughout this unit, you will already have done a lot of work towards completing the tasks for this assignment.

Scenario

In your gap year before going to university to study Tourism Management you are working for a UK-based tourism development consultancy that specialises in carrying out feasibility studies for new tourism projects all over the world. You have been asked to work with Jed Sanders, one of the junior consultants, on an EU-funded project concerning tourism development in the developing countries of the world. Jed wants you to carry out some research into the subject.

The project focuses on three main areas:

1. The objectives and agents of tourism development;
2. The positive and negative impacts of tourism development;
3. The principles of sustainable tourism.

He wants you to complete the following three tasks that consider both developed and developing tourist destinations. In order to complete the tasks you must research a range of aspects of tourism development in one specified developed destination and one specified developing destination. You have a free choice of countries, but for your developed destination you may like to consider researching one of the top ten earners of tourism revenue shown in Figure 10.2 on page 77. Your developing destination needs to be one that is not yet fully geared up for tourism. This could be one of the former Communist states that joined the European Union in 2004, e.g. Czech Republic, Latvia, Lithuania, Estonia or Slovakia, or perhaps a country in Africa whose government is keen to develop tourism, for example Botswana, Libya or Ethiopia.

Task 1

Jed wants you to prepare a booklet on the objectives and agents of tourism development that could be used by local and national government officials in developing countries that are keen to develop tourism. Your booklet will compare tourism development in developed and developing countries so that the officials can learn from good practice. The booklet must:

(a) Describe the objectives of tourism development for one specified developed tourist destination and one specified developing tourist destination;

(b) Describe the agents of tourism development in your chosen developed destination and explain their role;

(c) Explain the agents of tourism development that could be involved in your selected developing tourist destination and their role.

These tasks are designed to provide evidence for P1, P2 and P3.

The booklet should also:

(d) Discuss the conflicting objectives and positions of agents of tourism and the impact of these upon tourism development in your selected developed and developing destination;

(e) Use examples of good practice drawn from other destinations to suggest and justify possible improvements within your selected developing tourist destination.

These tasks are designed to provide evidence for M1 and D1.

Task 2

Jed wants you to prepare a presentation on the positive and negative impacts of tourism development. Your presentation must:

(a) Describe the positive and negative impacts of tourism development in your specified developed destination;

(b) Explain how your chosen developed tourist destination can minimise the negative impacts and maximise the positive impacts of tourism;

(c) Evaluate the effectiveness of measures undertaken in your selected developed tourist destination to minimise the negative impacts and maximise the positive impacts of tourism.

These tasks are designed to provide evidence for P4, M2 and D2.

Task 3

Jed has asked you to prepare a short written report on sustainable tourism. Your report must:

(a) Describe the principles of sustainable tourism and show how they can be used to benefit destinations and their host communities;

(b) Explain how the principles of sustainable tourism can be used to benefit your selected developing tourist destination and its communities.

These tasks are designed to provide evidence for P5 and M3.

Unit 10

Unit 12
Special Interest Tourism

INTRODUCTION TO THE UNIT

Special interest tourism is growing rapidly throughout the world, giving people the chance to enjoy their hobby or take part in an activity in a holiday setting. Special interest tourism is very wide-ranging and can include a number of different activities – everything from wine tours in Australia and trekking holidays in the Himalayas to cookery courses in Tuscany and art appreciation holidays to Italy. Changes in society, such as the ageing of the population, greater use of technology, increased concern for the environment and a desire to learn more about different cultures, are fuelling an increased demand for special interest tourism.

In this unit you will learn about the relationship between special interests and tourism, focusing on key events in the historical development of tourism and the changes in consumer interests and demands. You will also explore the factors that affect participation in special interest tourism. You will investigate the location of special interest tourism and the nature of the activities that it includes. The unit gives you the opportunity of examining one specific area of special interest tourism in detail, investigating both the providers and the range of services offered.

WHAT YOU WILL STUDY

During the course of this unit you will:

1. Examine the **relationship between special interests and tourism;**
2. Explore the **factors that affect participation** in special interest tourism;
3. Investigate the **location** of special interest tourism and the **nature of activities** included;
4. Examine the tourism **provision** for a specific special interest.

You will be guided through the main topics in this unit with the help of the latest statistics, examples and industry case studies. You should also check out the weblinks throughout the unit for extra information on particular organisations or topic areas and use the activities to help you learn more.

ASSESSMENT FOR THIS UNIT

This unit is internally assessed, meaning that you will be given an assignment (or series of assignments) to complete by your tutor(s) to show that you have fully understood the content of the unit. A grading scale of pass, merit or distinction is used for all internally assessed units, with higher grades awarded to students who show greater depth in analysis and evaluation in their assignments. An assignment for this unit, which covers all the grading criteria, can be found on page 147. Don't forget to visit www.tandtONLine.co.uk for all the latest industry news, developments, statistics and tips to help you with your assignments.

Unit 12

SECTION 1: RELATIONSHIP BETWEEN SPECIAL INTERESTS AND TOURISM

Special interest tourism is one of the fastest-growing sectors of the travel and tourism industry. People are becoming better educated, have more spending power and are seeking out new experiences to take part in during their leisure time. At the same time, the travel and tourism industry is responding by offering an ever-wider choice of holidays and activities to meeting this growing demand. In the opening sections of this unit we look at the relationship between special interests and tourism, beginning with an overview of key milestones in the development of tourism.

Development of tourism

The 'mass tourism' that exists in many parts of the world today has its origins in the years immediately following the end of the 1939-1945 Second World War, but throughout history, people have travelled the world for purposes of trade, education, religion and to fight in battles. The early origins of tourism can be traced back to pre-Egyptian times, when there was a limited amount of travel associated with festivals and celebrations of a religious or spiritual nature. The early Egyptian civilisation displayed a primitive social structure and rewarded the privileged classes with leisure time to enjoy activities such as dance, music, drama and archery. So, even in Egyptian times, taking part in special interests and activities was an important part of life for some.

The Greeks and Romans

The Greek civilisation was the first to promote the benefits of a healthy balance between work and leisure. There is evidence of travel for purely recreational purposes, with the Greeks hosting international visitors during the first Olympic Games help in 776 BC.

The Romans were keen to promote 'leisure with a purpose' to their citizens. Roman engineers built public leisure facilities for the masses living in urban areas, who practised recreation for physical fitness and in preparation for war. The extensive road network developed by the Romans allowed faster and more convenient travel for business and leisure purposes. There was growth in international travel within the Roman Empire for trade, while the wealthier Romans made visits to friends and relations, and began to appreciate the healing powers of near and distant spa waters for the first time.

The 'Grand Tour'

From 1670 onwards, young gentlemen of the aristocracy were sent on the 'Grand Tour' of the great cultural cities of Europe to widen their education and experiences of life, prior to

Unit 12

seeking positions at court on their return home. Cities such as Paris, Venice, Rome and Florence gave these young tourists the opportunity of sampling different cultures and societies. The popularity of the 'Grand Tour' reached its peak in the mid-18th century, but was halted abruptly by the onset of the French Revolution and the Napoleonic Wars.

The rise of spa resorts

Although the medicinal benefits of spa waters had been recognised in Roman times, it was not until the 16th century that their full tourist potential began to be exploited and spa resorts grew in popularity. The healing potential of spa waters became widely accepted amongst the aristocracy, leading to the development of spa resorts in Britain and on the Continent. Towns such as Buxton, Cheltenham, Leamington Spa, Llandrindod Wells and Bath prospered until well into the 18th century. Baden-Baden in Germany was one of the most popular spa destinations in Europe.

Early transport developments

The introduction of steam power was to have a very important effect of the development of tourism from the middle of the 19th century onwards. The first steam-powered passenger train service linking Liverpool and Manchester was introduced in 1830, and the network expanded rapidly to service the growing number of manufacturing heartlands in Britain. The growth of the rail network also brought many seaside resorts within easy travelling distance of the main centres of population. Resorts such as Brighton, Margate and Blackpool grew in popularity; Brighton was a notable success with some 132,000 visitors recorded on Easter Monday in 1862.

In 1841, Thomas Cook organised his first excursion by train from Leicester to Loughborough for his local Temperance Association. Within 15 years, spurred on by the success of his first trip, Cook was running a fully-commercial travel company arranging tours and excursions both at home and overseas, including visits to the Great Exhibition in London in 1851 and inclusive tours to the Paris Exhibition in 1855. The completion of the Suez Canal in 1869 provided Cook with the opportunity of organising his first tours to Egypt.

In the early 19th century, just as steam power on land was radically changing the patterns of tourism and travel, the same was true at sea, with the introduction of a new generation of steam-powered ships serving North America, the Continent and the Far East. The Peninsular and Oriental Steam Navigation Company (P & O) introduced the first, regular, long-distance services to India and the Far East in 1838. The Cunard Steamship Company started services to North America in 1840. Following his successes in Britain and on the Continent, Thomas Cook organised the first steamship excursion to America in 1866.

Unit 12

The Industrial Revolution

The Industrial Revolution, which had been the catalyst for the development of the railways, also led to improvements in the road and canal networks in the UK. What the Industrial Revolution also began was the desire for workers to escape from their normal harsh routines and often dirty environments, in favour of relaxation and entertainment in the relative purity of the countryside and coast.

The 1938 Holidays with Pay Act gave a stimulus to mass tourism in the UK, with 80 per cent of workers being entitled to paid holidays by 1945. Holiday camps flourished immediately before the outbreak of the Second World War, the first having been opened by Billy Butlin in 1936 at Skegness. Two years later, there were around 200 camps offering self-contained 'package' holidays to 30,000 people per week. In the early 1950s, two-thirds of all domestic holidays were taken at the seaside and the majority of holidaymakers travelled to their destinations by coach or train.

Tourism developments post-World War Two

The type of 'mass tourism' that is such a prominent feature of life in the 21st century began to develop after the end of the Second World War. Three important elements of post-World War Two society in the UK – the development of jet aircraft, the growth of the overseas package tour and increasing car ownership – were to have far-reaching implications on the UK domestic tourism scene.

The late 1950s saw the establishment of the British Travel Association, forerunner to the British Tourist Authority (now VisitBritain), which was given the role of encouraging the development of hotels and resorts. The 1960s can be chronicled as the time when UK tourism came of age. The government passed the Development of Tourism Act in 1969, establishing the English, Wales and Scottish Tourist Boards, plus the British Tourist Authority, which was charged with promoting the whole of Britain to overseas visitors.

ACTIVITY

Read through the first sections of this unit up to this point and make a list of the points that you think have had an impact on the development of special interest tourism. One example could be the rise in car ownership in the 20th century.

This activity is designed to provide evidence for P1.

Unit 12

Current developments in travel and tourism

The travel and tourism industry of the 21st century is experiencing a period of rapid change, driven by a number of factors, including:

1. Developments in technology – the Internet is having a dramatic effect on the way people gather information on holidays and buy travel and tourism products. Technology is also influencing developments in different types of transport;
2. Demographic changes – e.g. the ageing of the population, more lone-parent households, marriage later in life, etc;
3. Lifestyle changes – e.g. more part-time working, search for enlightenment, desire to learn about different cultures and take part in new experiences;
4. Globalisation – the move towards ever-larger corporations with influence that stretches across continents;
5. Consumer behaviour – people are demanding higher standards of service and higher quality products;
6. Economic changes – e.g. lower inflation rates, higher levels of disposable income, lower unemployment levels, free movement of people across borders;
7. Environmental issues – e.g. greater concern for the environment, management of the earth's resources and sustainability.

The effects of these factors on the industry itself include:

The Eden Project reflects a greater concern for the environment amongst tourists

- Growth in online sales of travel and tourism products – and the impact this is having on traditional sales outlets, including travel agencies;
- New developments in transportation, e.g. high-speed rail networks, growth of low-cost airlines, bigger cruise ships, etc;
- Increase in popularity of long-haul destinations;
- Development of 'niche' products to meet the needs of particular types of holidaymakers, including those with special interests;
- Restructuring of the travel and tourism industry into smaller numbers of large companies, offering a range of 'brands';

- Higher quality products and better service standards for customers;
- Greater demand generally for travel and tourism products, especially short breaks and additional holidays;
- Development of 'responsible' holidays and travel products that are respectful of the environment and local communities in destination areas.

Special interests

As people become better educated, have more disposable income and make more use of new technology, the range of special interests that many want to experience grows all the time. Taking part in special activities in their leisure time gives people a sense of achievement, may help to keep them fit and can forge new friendships. Special interests can be categorised into three different types, as shown in Figure 12.1.

Dog sledding is a 'niche' product *(courtesy Exodus Travel)*

Passive activities are those that require very little physical effort from those who take part and include:

- Painting;
- Cooking;
- Reading;
- Arts and crafts;
- Taking part in drama;
- Spiritual experiences;
- Sports spectating;
- Watching television and listening to the radio.

Active pursuits, where physical effort is required from the participants, include:

- Team events such as playing football and cricket;
- Walking;

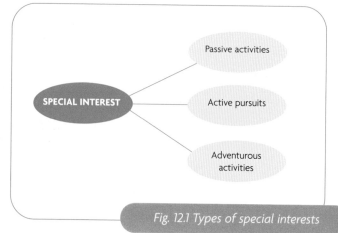

Fig. 12.1 Types of special interests

Unit 12

- Cycling;
- Camping and caravanning;
- Youth camps;
- Orienteering;
- Sailing;
- Horse riding.

Adventurous activities take active pursuits one stage further, by adding a degree of danger when taking part. These 'extreme sports' as they are sometimes known include:

- Climbing and abseiling;
- Airsports, e.g. paragliding, parascending, flying, sky diving;
- Canoeing;
- White water rafting;
- Canyoning;
- Surfing and kite surfing;
- Bungee jumping;
- Mountain biking;
- 4 X 4 motorised activities.

Trekking in the Everest region (courtesy of Himalayan Kingdoms)

Popularity of special interests

It is difficult to estimate the total numbers of people taking part in special interests and activities in the UK, given that there are so many different types. The Office for National Statistics collects data on participation in leisure and sports activities as part of the General Household Survey (GHS) and, in 2002, the survey found that 75 per cent of all adults had taken part in some type of sport, game or physical activity during the 12 months prior to interview. Another measure of the popularity of special interests is the growth in membership of organisations such as the National Trust, Royal Society for the Protection of Birds (RSPB), English Heritage, Ramblers' Association, Cyclists' Touring Club and the many wildlife trusts and local conservation groups across the country.

Unit 12

Passive activities

Figures from the General Household Survey show that participation in passive activities in 2002 by those interviewed was as follows:

- 99 per cent watched television;
- 88 per cent listened to the radio;
- 83 per cent listened to records/tapes;
- 65 per cent read books;
- 11 per cent sang or played a musical instrument;
- 11 per cent danced;
- 9 per cent painted or did drawing, printmaking or sculpture;
- 4 per cent wrote stories, plays or poetry;
- 3 per cent helped with the running of an arts/cultural event or organisation on a voluntary basis;
- 2 per cent performed in a play, drama or rehearsed for a performance.

The trend over a 30-year period shows that participation in most passive activities has increased, but dressmaking, needlework and knitting have decreased in popularity.

Active pursuits

Statistics from the same GHS survey indicate that the five most popular activities undertaken in 2002 (with participation rates in brackets) were:

1. Walking   (43 per cent)
2. Swimming   (35 per cent)
3. Keep fit/yoga   (22 per cent)
4. Cycling   (19 per cent)
5. Billiards/snooker/pool   (17 per cent)

Compared with the other activities, keep fit/yoga was the most likely activity to be done regularly. Eight per cent of adults said that they had taken part in keep fit/yoga four or more times over a four-week period, while three per cent said that they participated in it twelve or more times over the same period. Swimming was the next most frequent activity. For the first time in 2002, interviewees in the General Household Survey were asked which activity that they currently do not take part in would they like to try. The most popular activities mentioned were:

1. Swimming   (13 per cent)
2. Keep fit/yoga   (12 per cent)
3. Golf   (5 per cent)
4. Skiing/snowboarding   (5 per cent)
5. Horse riding   (5 per cent)

Adventurous activities

Adventurous activities combine active pursuits with an element of danger. We saw earlier that these include airsports, land and water-based activities. There are no comprehensive figures on participation in adventurous activities in the UK. The United Kingdom Tourism Survey (UKTS) includes data on participation in some types of adventurous activities, including watersports and climbing. Figures for hill walking and mountain biking are, however, included in more general walking and cycling categories, and UKTS includes no data on motorised adventure sports. An article in the March 2003 edition of *Insights* (VisitBritain) points out that the UKTS data that is available indicates that:

- Over 10 per cent of UK holiday trips involve participation in adventurous activities (15 per cent in Scotland and 17 per cent in Wales);
- At least 11 million UK holidays each year include taking part in some type of adventurous activity;
- Annual spending by UK holiday visitors who take part in adventurous activities during their stay is at least as much as £2 million;
- Adventure holidays currently account for approximately 4 per cent of all UK holidays.

Research quoted in the same article suggests that hill walking, non-motorised watersports (in particular canoeing, surfing, windsurfing and dinghy sailing), climbing and mountain biking are currently the most popular adventurous activities in the UK. Other types of adventurous activities (caving, motorised watersports, motorised land sports, diving, airsports and

Adventure tourism in action (courtesy Outward Bound Trust)

other land-based activities) appear to be much more 'niche' products, appealing to very specific sectors of the market. Some adventurous activities, such as rope courses and quad biking, often have more appeal as part of a multi-activity holiday or as incidental holiday activities.

Relationship between special interests and tourism

Having considered key aspects of the development of tourism and identified a range of special interests, we are now in a position to bring these together by examining the relationship between special interests and tourism. It is perhaps not surprising that people want to carry on their special interest or activity while on holiday, particularly if it is in a warmer climate! People who participate in specialist interests and activities can be very inquisitive by nature, wanting to learn about different areas, meet new people and take part in new experiences. All the available evidence on special interest tourism is that it is a major growth area of the travel and tourism industry – meeting the specialist needs of increasing numbers of travellers.

ACTIVITY

Choose one of the five active pursuits listed on page 122 and examine the provision for the activity in holidays and short breaks, e.g. which companies offer walking tours, to which destinations, prices charged, types of products, etc.

This activity is designed to provide evidence for P1.

What is special interest tourism?

Given that there are so many different interests and activities that people can take part in while on holiday or a day visit, finding a suitable definition of 'special interest tourism' is not an easy task! A simple definition is that special interest tourism is 'tourism with a purpose'. Taking this a little further, we can say that it is a type of tourism that appeals to people who have a particular interest that they with to pursue in a holiday setting – it is often the hub around which their total holiday experience is built. Some people think of 'activity tourism' and 'special interest tourism' as one and the same, but as we saw earlier in this unit, the term 'special interest' can cover a variety of pastimes which are very far from active, for example painting, reading books and playing a musical instrument. Activity tourism is just one of the many different types of special interest tourism, alongside wildlife tourism, cultural tourism and health tourism, to name but a few.

Unit 12

Motivation	Special interest tourism products
Learning a new skill or activity	• Watercolour painting holidays • Spinning and weaving tours • Wine tasting tours • Cookery holidays • Pottery holidays
Attending sports events	• Motor racing Grands Prix trips • Tours to football matches in Europe • Wimbledon Lawn Tennis Championships • Corporate hospitality at the FA Cup Final • Holiday packages to the Ryder Cup
Taking part in adventures	• Mountain trekking holidays • Quad biking events • Canyoning • Bungee jumping • Kite surfing
Self-improvement and relaxation	• Spa tourism • Pilgrimages • Yoga holidays • Health breaks • Retreats
Learning about wildlife, nature and the environment	• Wildlife safaris • Conservation holidays • Whale watching tours • Walking holidays • Bird watching tours
Investigating heritage and culture	• Cultural holidays • Industrial heritage tours • Art appreciation holidays • Garden tours • Farm holidays

Fig. 12.2 Motivations and products in special interest tourism

Unit 12

The wide variety of special interest tourism products on offer is the result of the industry responding to the very different motivations of individuals. For example, special interest tourism can be associated with somebody wanting to:

- Learn a new skill or activity;
- Attend a sports event;
- Take part in adventures;
- Relax and investigate self-improvement;
- Learn about nature, wildlife and the environment;
- Investigate different cultures.

These motivations, with examples of associated special interest tourism products, are shown in Figure 12.2. The examples of special interest tourism products given in the table are by no means exhaustive, but give a flavour of how different motivations are satisfied by particular products and services.

Learning about different cultures in Bhutan (courtesy Himalayan Kingdoms)

Unit 12

SECTION 2: FACTORS AFFECTING PARTICIPATION

Special interest tourism is a very dynamic sector of the travel and tourism industry. New products are being developed all the time and people are keen to try out new experiences as soon as they are developed. In this section we look at the factors that influence whether or not people take part in special interest tourism and, if they do, what affects their choice of special interest or activity. Some of these factors are specific to the industry (industry factors), while others are concerned with the characteristics of the tourists themselves (participant factors).

Industry factors

Factors that organisations working in the special interest tourism sector need to take into account include:

1. Demographics and social changes;
2. Market segmentation;
3. Product appeal and development;
4. Consumer behaviour.

Demographics and social changes

'Demographics' is the term used to describe the characteristics and trends of the population, for example age, family composition, gender and ethnicity. It is important for special interest tourism companies to monitor changes in demographics and changes in society so that they can either adapt their products to changing circumstances or even introduce new products in a growth area. Some of the most important demographic and social changes that are occurring in the UK include:

- The ageing of the population;
- More lone-parent households — the proportion of children living in lone-parent families more than trebled between 1972 and 2004;
- Marriage later in life — the average age for first marriages in 2003 was 31 for men and 29 for women, compared with 26 and 23 respectively 40 years ago;
- More part-time and flexible working;
- Increased working from home.

The ageing of the population is perhaps the most significant of all the demographic changes taking place in the UK today. Figures from the Office for National Statistics (ONS) show that the proportion of the population aged 65 and over has increased over the last 30 years, while the proportion below 16 years of age has fallen. The percentage of people under 16

Unit 12

fell from 25 per cent in mid-1971 to 19 per cent in mid-2004, whereas the proportion of people aged 65 and over rose from 13 per cent to 16 per cent over the same time period. Also, older people are living longer – the proportion of people aged 85 and over increased from 7 per cent in mid-1971 to 12 per cent in mid-2004. These figures are important for the special interest tourism sector, which can look to the future in the knowledge that there will be more older people with the time to take part in all types of special interests and activities while on holiday. It is not such good news for companies that offer special interest products aimed at children and young people, since the proportion of the population in younger age categories is falling.

ACTIVITY

Carry out some research into three companies that offer holidays for older people. Make notes on the types of products they offer, destinations used and activities/special interests catered for. Explain how the companies meet the needs of this particular group of tourists in their products and services.

This activity is designed to provide evidence for P2.

Market segmentation

Market segmentation is the process of dividing the total market for a product or service, i.e. all the people who could buy it, into different 'segments', each with broadly similar characteristics. Holiday companies carry out segmentation because it allows them to focus more clearly on the needs and wants of particular groups, for example older people, young people wanting an activity holiday of high spenders looking for the ultimate in luxury while on holiday. Special interest tourism lends itself particularly well to market segmentation, since it is made up of very many specialised interests and activities. Figure 12.3 shows how market segmentation can be applied to the special interest tourism sector – six popular areas have been selected, each made up of providers that try to match the segments' needs to the products they offer. The 'wildlife tourism' segment, for example, offers products such as whale watching tours, wildlife safaris and jungle expeditions to a variety of clients. Segmenting the market for special interest tourism is not always straightforward and there is often overlap between sectors. For example, taking part in a tour of spa towns in Europe could be both health tourism and cultural tourism. The important point is that companies are clear about the products they offer and the needs of their particular customers.

Unit 12

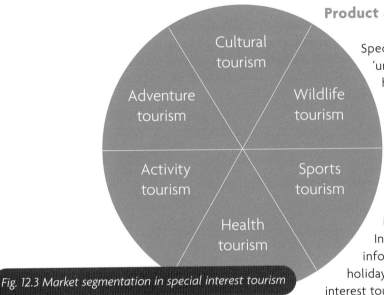

Fig. 12.3 Market segmentation in special interest tourism

Cultural tourism

Adventure tourism

Wildlife tourism

Activity tourism

Sports tourism

Health tourism

Product appeal and development

Special interest tourism is in many respects an 'unpackaged holiday' – companies often tailor holidays to customers' particular requirements rather than selling something 'off the shelf'. The specialist nature of some activities often makes it impossible to offer a standardised holiday product. Companies work hard to make their products as appealing as possible to their target audience, using a variety of promotional techniques, including brochures with high quality images of activities and special interests. The Internet is a particularly useful tool for providing information and selling special interest tourism holidays and breaks, given that the customers for special interest tourism tend to be very computer-literate.

The media plays an important part in stimulating demand for special interest tourism. The growing numbers of terrestrial and digital TV channels showing programmes covering a variety of special interests, from gardening and watercolour painting to custom cars and cookery, are partly responsible for the increasing popularity and appeal of special interest tourism. Specialist magazines and newspaper articles also play an important role in stimulating demand.

Consumer behaviour

We have seen that society is changing rapidly in the UK, with greater use of new technology, increased disposable incomes, changes in population characteristics and different work patterns. These changes are altering the purchasing behaviour of consumers in many ways. People expect to be able to buy products easily and quickly, whether in a

Exploring in the Himalayas (courtesy Himalayan Kingdoms)

Unit 12

shop or online, they are looking for high quality products and services, good value for money and 24/7 access to facilities whenever possible. These same requirements apply equally well to all types of tourist products, including special interest tourism. Companies must strive to meet customer needs at all stages of the holiday experience, from initial enquiry through to the departure for home.

Participant factors

Factors that influence special interest tourism customers include:

1. Socio-economic factors;
2. Status, image and fashion;
3. Political stability and security;
4. Motivation.

Socio-economic factors

A person's disposable income, i.e. what is left over after all necessary expenses have been met, influences their choice of holiday, short break or day trip. Clearly, the more disposable income a person has, the more they have available to spend on their holiday. We saw earlier in this unit that special interest tourism is a 'niche' product, i.e. it appeals to small, specialist groups of people with particular interests. Research shows that people who take part in specialist interest tourism have higher levels of disposable income than the population as a whole, tend to be younger and are in professional occupations. Some people say they are 'money rich, but time poor' because although they earn good salaries, they have little leisure time in which to spend their money. They tend to take part in challenging, active pursuits for short periods of time. Retired professional people are also attracted to special interest tourism and, as well as having the time, also have reasonable levels of disposable income.

Status, image and fashion

Some types of special interest tourism activities are considered to be very fashionable and appeal to people who relish a challenge, value status symbols and like to impress their friends! Activities like sky diving, bungee jumping, kite surfing and microlighting fall into this category. The introduction of outdoor clothing into high street fashion, the growing numbers of adventure sports magazines and increasing coverage of special interests and activities on TV, all illustrate the fashionable image associated with some types of special interest tourism.

Unit 12

Political stability and security

As with all kinds of tourist activity, special interest tourism needs a secure and stable political situation in a country of destination in order to prosper. Areas that have been the scene of terrorist attacks of civil wars cannot hope to attract and retain special interest tourists. Some types of special interest tourism, particularly adventure and exploration activities, take place in remote parts of the world that are prone to political unrest. Companies that operate in these areas need to be kept fully aware of the situation at all times and follow the advice from the Foreign and Commonwealth Office (FCO) on whether or not it is safe to travel.

Motivation

Figure 12.2 on page 125 gave some examples of what motivates people to take part in special interest tourism, but motivation is a complex subject. There are complex psychological influences at work within individuals that affect their choice of holidays. Probably the most widely quoted work on motivation theory is that of Maslow, who developed the 'hierarchy of needs' (see Figure 12.4).

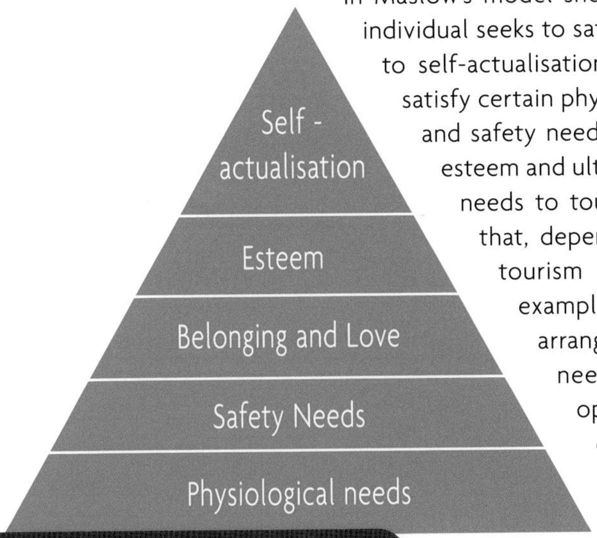

In Maslow's model shown in Figure 12.4 there are five levels of needs that an individual seeks to satisfy, from physiological needs at the base of the pyramid to self-actualisation at the pinnacle. Maslow argues that individuals must satisfy certain physiological needs, such as shelter, warmth, water and food, and safety needs before moving on to the need for belonging and love, esteem and ultimately self-actualisation. Applying Maslow's hierarchy of needs to tourists' motivation for special interest tourism, it is clear that, depending on the particular circumstances of the individual, tourism can satisfy all levels of needs. A holidaymaker, for example, will choose accommodation, hospitality and travel arrangements that meet his or her physiological and safety needs. Special interest holidays can certainly provide opportunities for developing social relationships, thereby contributing towards the need for belonging and love. Tourists sometimes use their travel experiences as a way of boosting their esteem among peers and the fashionable nature of some special interest tourism activities can contribute to this. Particular types of special interest tourism experiences may also contribute to a person's achievement of self-actualisation or self-fulfilment, perhaps becoming spiritually enlightened or learning a new language while on holiday, or taking part in health and spa tourism.

Self - actualisation

Esteem

Belonging and Love

Safety Needs

Physiological needs

Fig. 12.4 Maslow's hierarchy of needs

Unit 12

ACTIVITY

Choose one type of special interest tourism and make notes on the factors (industry and participant) that influence participation in the activity.

This activity is designed to provide evidence for P2.

SECTION 3: LOCATION AND NATURE OF ACTIVITIES

This section investigates the nature of special interest tourism activities and where they take place. It includes case studies on two specific types of special interest tourism – cycling tourism, and health and spa tourism, which you will find useful when completing your assignment for this unit. You can also find a case study on adventure tourism on page 143. As well as considering the nature and location of these activities, each case study includes information on companies and organisations that operate in each of these specialist markets.

Nature of activities

We saw earlier in this unit that people take part in many different activities during their leisure time – some passive, some active and some involving a degree of risk or danger (see page 120). The types of activities included in special interest tourism can be divided into three categories – those that take place on water, land-based activities and airsports, as shown in Figure 12.5.

People can take part in these activities in many different circumstances, for example on an individual basis, as part of a group or as a member of a team or club.

Land-based	Water-based	Airsports
• Visiting historic sites	• Canoeing	• Hang gliding
• Quad biking	• Kayaking	• Paragliding
• Mountain trekking	• Sailing	• Sky diving
• Art appreciation	• Surfing	• Gliding
• Pottery	• Windsurfing	• Flying
• Cycling	• Kite surfing	• Parachuting
• Walking	• Canyoning	• Bungee jumping
• Bird watching	• Scuba diving	
• Visiting spas	• Jet skiing	
• Visiting gardens		

Fig. 12.5 Types of activities in special interest tourism

ACTIVITY

Choose three different types of special interest tourism and describe the occasions when a person may take part in each activity (1) on an individual basis; (2) as part of a group; (3) as a member of a team or club. Name companies or organisations that provide products and services for each of the activities and circumstances that you have described. Present your findings as a chart.

This activity is designed to provide evidence for P4.

Unit 12

We saw earlier in this unit that there are many different reasons why people want to take part in special interest tourism (see Figure 12.2). These motivations include:

- For educational reasons – e.g. a group of garden enthusiasts visiting the Royal Horticultural Society's gardens at Wisley in Surrey to learn about varieties of fruit;
- To explore different cultures – e.g. a backpacker spending a gap year in Thailand to work and learn about Thai culture;
- For reasons of discovery – e.g. a couple going on a cruise in the Norwegian fjords;
- To pursue a hobby – e.g. a person attending a watercolour painting course in Provence;
- To face a challenge and danger – e.g. abseiling in the Swiss Alps or sky diving in the USA;
- For excitement – e.g. a family holiday to the theme parks in Florida;
- For relaxation – e.g. a family enjoying a short break at a health spa.

Location of activities

Special interest tourism takes place in many different indoor and outdoor settings, in the UK and abroad. Adventure and activity tourism makes use of natural resources, so is usually

located in countryside and coastal areas. Access to locations is important, both from the point of view of guest convenience in reaching the facility and the need for swift access by the emergency services in the event of an accident or incident. Distance from major centres of population is a consideration for special interest tourism providers, with those located close to cities benefiting from increased trade. Some adventure tourism activities take place under cover, for example in centres with indoor climbing walls.

Special interest tourism concerned with hobbies or learning a new skill, for example cooking, painting, pottery, stained-glass making, spinning and weaving, may need purpose-built facilities.

The High Pyrenees is a spectacular location for special interest tourism (courtesy Exodus Travel)

Unit 12

CASE STUDY – Cycling tourism

Introduction

Cycling tourism can be defined as a holiday or day visit that involves participation in cycling, either as a primary or secondary purpose of the visit. It is an environmentally sustainable type of tourist activity, which has minimal negative impact on the environment and local communities. It can also make a positive contribution towards encouraging visitors to use their cars less and can makes good use of under-utilised and redundant resources, such as by-roads and disused railway lines. It also generates income for a variety of tourism businesses and destination areas, helping to create jobs and contribute to economic development. A recent study in Scotland has shown that cycling is worth £39 million to the economy of the Highlands and Islands region, while in Wales, cycling currently contributes £18 million to the economy and could be worth as much as £34 by 2007.

Cycling on the NCN route 64 near Lincoln (courtesy Sustrans/Paul Rea)

Nature of the activities

There are a number of different types of cycling tourism 'products', for example:

1. Family cycling – all members of a family can enjoy the benefits of cycling while on holiday or day trip;
2. Off-road cycling – tends to appeal to younger people looking for a challenge on mountain biking routes;
3. Cycle touring – holidays covering long distances in the UK and overseas, with overnight stays en route, perhaps using the National Cycle Network (NCN);
4. Cycle racing – combining racing with a holiday, for example a group of UK enthusiasts following the route of the Tour de France.

Cycling tourism products take different forms, for example:

- A cycling holiday or short break – where cycling is the main purpose of the trip;
- Cycling for a short period while on holiday – perhaps hiring a bike;
- A day visit that involves cycling – for example, visiting a forest area with mountain biking trails.

Unit 12

Location and destinations

The great appeal of cycling is that it can take place virtually anywhere. In the UK, cycling tourism takes place along country lanes, disused railway lines and canal towpaths, as well as in forests and moorland areas. It is particularly popular in National Parks, where many authorities promote cycling as way of reducing the number of cars in the parks. The National Cycle Network is a countrywide series of signed cycling routes linking communities to schools, stations and city centres, as well as to countryside areas. Co-ordinated by the charity Sustrans, the network currently extends to 10,000 miles of routes throughout the UK, with further expansion planned.

There are increasing numbers of companies that offer cycling holidays in European countries, especially France and Spain. Regions such as the Loire, Dordogne, Brittany and northern Spain are popular with cycle tourists from the UK. Mountain bikers travel to areas such as the French Alps in the summer, riding on the runs that are used for skiing in the winter. Outside of Europe, cycling tourism is more of a specialist activity, but it is possible to book a cycling holiday to South America, Africa, Thailand, India and even cycle across Russia! Many charities organise long-distance bike rides to attract sponsorship.

Cycling tourism providers

The increasing popularity of cycling in recent years has led to an increase in the numbers of providers. Most are private companies offering a specialist service on a relatively small scale, but many of the large, well-known tour operators now offer activities, including cycling, as part of their holiday packages. Examples of specialist cycling tourism providers offering holidays in the UK and overseas include:

Cycling in Vietnam (courtesy Exodus Travel)

- Bicycle Beano Cycling Holidays;
- Cycleactive;
- Susi Madron's Cycling for Softies;
- Headwater Holidays;
- Breton Bikes Cycling Holidays;
- CTC Cycling Holidays (part of the Cyclists' Touring Club);

- Nielson;
- Sherpa Expeditions;
- Exodus Travel;
- Explore Worldwide;
- Bents Bicycle Tours.

Cycling often forms part of multi-activity holidays for children at holiday activity centres and outdoor pursuits' centres operated by local authority education departments.

WEBLINK

www.ctc.org.uk;
www.sustrans.org.uk;
www.aito.co.uk

Check out these websites to help answer the questions in this case study and for more information on cycling tourism.

CASE STUDY QUESTIONS

1. What is the National Cycle Network and what is it trying to achieve?
2. Choose one of the cycling tourism providers listed above and carry out some further research into the products and services it offers, including destinations visited, types of holidays, costs, travel details, etc.
3. Research the provision for cycling tourism in one of the UK's National Parks.
4. Provide details of three companies that offer cycling tours in France, including the areas visited, types of holidays on offer, costs and travel arrangements.

CASE STUDY – Health and spa tourism

Introduction

The healing power of spa waters was recognised as long ago as Roman times and in the 18th century, spa towns such as Bath, Buxton and Tunbridge Wells were welcoming visitors to sample the waters. Today, spas across Europe offer a range of facilities from casinos and leisure pools to luxury hotels and beauty salons. Over the last 10 years, the word 'spa' has broadened out in new directions to encompass virtually any place, facility, treatment or product that is connected with physical, mental or spiritual health. Over the same time period there has been a rapid growth in spa facilities of all types, to meet the growing demand from customers who need guidance on wellness and well-being, as well as somewhere to escape from the pressures of modern life and re-energise their physical and mental processes. This demand has resulted in health and spa tourism becoming one of the fastest-growing sectors of the UK travel and tourism industry.

Unit **12**

Nature of the activities

Health and spa tourism can be divided into five distinct categories:

1. Destination spas;
2. Day spas;
3. Hotel spas;
4. Spa towns;
5. Spa travel.

Destination spas

Sometimes known as 'health farms' or hydros, these are popular with clients who need a relaxing break to take time out from the world, to be pampered, to experience new therapies and activities, to eat healthily and possibly to lose weight or 'detox'. Destination spas provide comfortable accommodation and a wide range of spa facilities, e.g. steam rooms, bubble-jet pools, sauna and relaxation areas. They are often located in a countryside setting and offer clients tailor-made packages to suit their needs. Companies in this sector of the health and spa market include Ragdale Hall Health Hydro in Leicestershire and the Celtic Manor Resort near Newport in south Wales.

Day spas

These cater for people who want to take a few hours out of their busy schedule or demanding home life to 'recharge their batteries'. Day spas can be located in a historic building, a new purpose-built facility or within an existing health club. They offer steam rooms and sauna, relaxation areas, some gym facilities and classes such as yoga or pilates with qualified instructors. Companies offering day spa facilities include Aqua Sana at Center Parc's Oasis Whinfell Forest centre in the Lake District and the Academy Spa in Harrogate, North Yorkshire.

Hotel spas

More and more hotels are adding spas and spa treatments to their leisure facilities and some of the best are of a very high quality. Clients can expect steam rooms, bubble-jet pools, sauna and relaxation areas, a range of therapeutic treatments and some gym or fitness equipment. Weekday business guests in the hotel can make use of the spa facilities, while spa breaks help to fill rooms at weekends with leisure tourists. Companies offering hotel spa facilities include Chewton Glen Hotel, Spa and Country Club in Hampshire and Calcot Manor Spa in the Cotswolds.

Unit 12

Spa towns

Britain's spa towns are undergoing something of a revival in popularity. Places as far apart as Llandrindod Wells in Wales, Leamington Spa in Warwickshire, Moffatt in Scotland and Harrogate in North Yorkshire are using their long association with spa waters to encourage tourism. All have a water source, often rich in minerals and legend, and sometimes credited with specific healing properties. Many spa towns are rejuvenating their spa architecture, renovating historic facilities and staging cultural activities and festivals to attract visitors.

Hotel spas are growing in popularity (courtesy St Davids Hotel and Spa, Cardiff)

Spa travel

Holidays are for leisure, pleasure and relaxation – three ideals that are in keeping with the philosophy of spas and spa treatments. Increasing numbers of people are using their holidays and short breaks to concentrate on improving their well-being using health and spa tourism facilities. Companies that specialise in spa travel include Erna Low and Thermalia Travel, both operating tours in a wide variety of destinations across the world.

WEBLINK

www.britishspas.co.uk

Check out this website to help answer the questions in this case study and for more information on health and spa tourism.

CASE STUDY QUESTIONS

1. What factors are likely to influence the future development of the health and spa tourism sector?
2. Choose one of the spa travel companies listed above (Erna Low or Thermalia) and carry out some further research into the products and services it offers, including destinations visited, types of holidays, costs, travel details, etc.
3. What changes in society have led to increased demand for health and spa tourism products and services?
4. What are the objectives of the Spa Business Association?

Unit 12

SECTION 4: PROVISION OF SPECIAL INTEREST TOURISM

Special interest tourism providers

The growing popularity of special interest tourism has resulted in a growing number of UK-based providers of products and services. Special interest tourism providers are found in the private sector, public sector and voluntary sector. There is sometimes overlap between these sectors – the Ramblers' Association, for example, is a voluntary sector organisation, but it operates a commercial (private sector) division known as Ramblers' Holidays.

Private sector providers

Private sector special interest tourism providers are either companies running facilities such as outdoor activity centres and walking tours, or tour operators selling special interest holiday packages in the UK and overseas. Many of the tour operators are small, specialist companies offering a limited number of tours to small groups of travellers. However, the rising popularity of special interest tourism has led the major, vertically-integrated holiday companies to enter the market. Thomas Cook, for example, has a number of special interest products including Neilson (skiing, sailing and mountain biking), Thomas Cook Signature and Thomas Cook Sport. Thomson/TUI owns Headwater Holidays and Crystal Holidays, both operating in the special interest tourism sector. Even mid-size tour operators have a variety of special interest tourism products, as the following example from Kuoni demonstrates.

WEBLINK

www.kuoni.co.uk

Check out this website for more information on Kuoni and its special interest tourism products and services.

FOCUS ON INDUSTRY – Special interest tourism at Kuoni

Kuoni is one of the world's leading tour operators, specialising in long-haul travel. In addition to its mainstream travel and tourism products, the company operates a number of divisions that feature special interest tourism of all kinds, for example:

- Kuoni Sport Abroad – a specialist sports division offering tours to major sports events throughout the world, e.g. cricket, motor sports, rugby and golf;
- Far East Travel Centre – specialising in tailor-made holidays to the Far East, Australia and the Pacific islands;
- The Travel Collection – offering bespoke travel experiences for the more discerning clients;
- Voyages Jules Verne – a comprehensive range of journeys incorporating various themes throughout the world, travelling by air, rail and sea;
- Kuoni Leisure Groups – specialist division handling charity challenge groups, bird watching tours, ad hoc group travel and celebratory travel for special events;
- Kuoni Events – conference and incentive travel division offering a personalised and tailor-made service for corporate clients;

- Perform Europe – professional organisers of incoming performance group itineraries to major UK international festivals and outbound workshop programmes for music, dance and drama groups;
- UK Connection – specialising in fully-inclusive group tours for schools and colleges to destinations in the UK, continental Europe and further afield;
- Kuoni Schools – specialists in budget tailor-made tours, student conferences and technical visits for collegiate groups travelling within the UK, continental Europe and around the world.

ACTIVITY

Carry out some research into the holidays offered by the 'big four' UK tour operators – Thomas Cook, First Choice, TUI/Thomson and MyTravel – and find out what products and services they offer for customers wanting a special interest holiday. Present your findings as a chart comparing what the four companies offer.

This activity is designed to provide evidence for P5.

WEBLINK

www.aito.co.uk

Check out this website for more information on AITO and its member companies offering specialist interest tourism products and services.

Many of the holiday companies offering special interest and activity products are members of AITO, the Association of Independent Tour Operators. They offer packages based on a variety of themes and interests, and most can produce tailor-made itineraries based on customers' individual requirements.

Public sector providers

WEBLINK

www.aala.org.uk

Check out this website for more information on the Adventure Activities Licensing Authority and the activities that it licenses.

The public sector's role in special interest tourism is mainly concerned with local education authorities (LEAs) providing outdoor activity centres for use by schools under their control. Many inner city councils run centres in National Parks and other countryside areas in England, Wales, Scotland and Northern Ireland. Safety is a key concern at these centres and, at present, all LEA centres, as well as those in the private sector, that cater for people under the age of 18 are required by law to be licensed by the Adventure Activities Licensing Authority (AALA).

Unit 12

WEBLINK

www.thurrock.gov.uk/
grangewaters

*Check out this website
for more information on
Grangewaters Outdoor
Education Centre in
Essex.*

FOCUS ON INDUSTRY – Grangewaters Outdoor Education Centre

Grangewaters is a typical outdoor education centre run by a local authority, in this case managed on behalf of Thurrock Council in Essex. It is licensed by the AALA and offers a wide range of activities, including dingy sailing, canoeing, high ropes, camp craft, orienteering and climbing. The centre caters for school and college groups, youth groups and visitors with special needs.

Voluntary sector providers

The voluntary sector plays an important role in special interest tourism provision, through organisations such as:

- The National Trust – offers working holidays in the UK, covering anything from dry stone walling to planting trees;
- Youth Hostels Association – with more than 220 hostels in England and Wales;
- British Trust for Conservation Volunteers (BTCV) – organises around 250 conservation holidays each year in the UK and in 25 countries worldwide. Tasks include pond clearing, beach cleaning and hedge laying;
- Outward Bound Trust – has centres in more than 30 countries offering special interest and activity holidays;
- Royal Society for the Protection of Birds (RSPB) – offers a range of leisure breaks in association with tour operators.

Local communities also contribute to special interest tourism provision by organising events and courses that attract visitors as well as local people.

Services

By their very nature, special interests often need specialist equipment. This includes safety equipment for many of the adventure activities we have mentioned elsewhere in this unit. Some people who take part in activities prefer to use their own equipment, while others are happy to use what is supplied by the company or hire equipment from specialist suppliers.

Many specialist interest tourism holidays involve companies providing tuition and instruction to guests. Depending on the type of special interest or activity concerned, staff need to be to be fully trained to deliver the activities in a safe and efficient manner. Many staff at activity and adventure centres have to be trained to National Governing Body standards in their respective sports and activities.

CASE STUDY – Adventure tourism

Introduction

Adventure tourism is a growing 'niche' sector of the UK travel and tourism industry that is capitalising on people's increased interest in fitness and desire to accept a challenge. It consists of holidays, short breaks and day visits that involve taking part in active or adventurous outdoor activities, either as a primary or secondary purpose of the visit. Adventure tourism is particularly popular in Scotland and Wales, but also in many English destinations such as the Lake District, Peak District, Yorkshire and the south west, especially Cornwall. Adventure tourism activities involve a degree of risk and danger and appeal particularly to young, professional people, who have sufficient disposable income to buy the (often expensive) equipment needed to take part in the activity.

Nature of the activities

Adventure tourism includes a wide range of outdoor activities, such as:

- Mountain biking;
- Canoeing and kayaking;
- Caving and pot-holing;
- Rock climbing of all types;
- Surfing, windsurfing and kite surfing;
- Hang-gliding, paragliding, parascending, sky diving and microlighting;
- Mountain trekking, gorge walking and canyoning;
- Motorised land sports, e.g. 4 x 4 driving, rally driving and quad biking;
- Scuba diving;
- Orienteering, snowboarding, land yachting, bungee jumping and other land-based activities.

Adventure tourism products can take different forms, for example:

- Adventure holidays or short breaks – where taking part in adventure activities is the main purpose of the trip, e.g. a trekking holiday in the Himalayas;
- Taking part in adventure activities as part of a holiday, e.g. having a half-day kite surfing lesson while on a family holiday in mid Wales;
- Adventure day visits – where taking part in adventure activities is the main purpose of the visit, e.g. a group from Exeter taking part in multi-activity adventure day course on the south Devon coast.

Unit 12

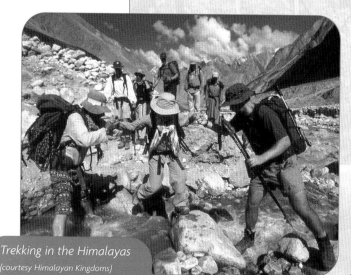

Trekking in the Himalayas
(courtesy Himalayan Kingdoms)

Location and destinations

Adventure tourism takes place in the UK and overseas. In the UK, many adventure holidays take place in National Parks and other areas of outstanding natural beauty. Part of the experience of an adventure tourism holiday is being in close contact with nature and the environment, so these areas are well-suited to adventure tourism activities. The precise location will depend on the requirements of the activity, e.g. access to water for canoeing and kayaking, access to crags for climbing, access to beaches for surfing, kite surfing and windsurfing, etc. As for adventure tourism destinations abroad, the sky is literally the limit! Every world continent has destinations that are popular with adventure tourists, for example:

- Europe – e.g. the Alps, Scandinavia and the Mediterranean islands;
- Asia – e.g. the Himalayas, Cambodia, Thailand and Vietnam;
- South America – e.g. the Amazon rainforest, the Andes and coastal regions;
- North America – e.g. the Rocky Mountains, National Parks and British Columbia;
- Africa – e.g. game reserves, Sahara Desert and the Victoria Falls;
- Australia/New Zealand – e.g. the Great Barrier Reef, Tasmania and South Island New Zealand;
- Antarctica and the South Pole.

Adventure tourism providers

The UK adventure tourism industry is made up of mainly small activity businesses catering for a specialist adventure activity or offering a multi-activity experience for customers. Some have their own self-catering or serviced accommodation, while others use nearby hotels, guesthouses, campsites, bunkhouse barns and hostels. There are increasing numbers of tour operators offering adventure holidays in the UK and to all parts of the world, usually taking small numbers of travellers in groups under the direction of an experienced tour leader. Examples of larger adventure tourism providers offering holidays in the UK and overseas include:

- PGL;
- Acorn Adventures;
- Dragoman Overland;

- Exodus Travel;
- Explore Worldwide;
- Guerba Worldwide;
- Himalayan Kingdoms;
- Adrift;
- Discover the World;
- Audley Travel;
- Naturetrek.

Adventure activities sometimes form part of multi-activity holidays for children at holiday activity centres and outdoor pursuits' centres operated by local authority education departments.

WEBLINK

www.aito.co.uk

Check out this website to help answer the questions in this case study and for more information on adventure tour operators.

CASE STUDY QUESTIONS

1. Choose one of the adventure tourism providers listed above and carry out some further research into the products and services it offers, including destinations visited, types of holidays, costs, travel details, etc.
2. Provide details of three companies that offer trekking holidays in the Himalayas, including the areas visited, types of holidays on offer, costs and travel arrangements?
3. Compare and contrast the provision for mountain biking holidays in the UK and the French Alps, covering providers, product details, costs, travel and accommodation options, etc;
4. Research the provision for adventure tourism in one of the UK's National Parks.

UNIT SUMMARY

This unit has investigated the growth area of special interest tourism. You have seen that the term 'special interest tourism' covers a variety of activities and special interests that people carry out while on holiday or on a day visit, either in the UK or overseas. You have investigated the relationship between special interests and tourism, delving back in history to illustrate key points. The many factors that affect participation in special interest tourism – both industry factors and participant factors – have been explored in detail. Factors such as the ageing of the population, changing social structures and increasing disposable incomes were seen to be important in affecting the development of special interest tourism. You have considered the location of special interest tourism activities and the nature of the activities themselves. Finally, the unit has examined the provision of special interest tourism products and services, from private, public and voluntary sector organisations.

Throughout the unit you have been shown many industry examples, while the case studies on cycling tourism, health and spa tourism, and adventure tourism provide three in-depth examples of the nature of different aspects of special interest tourism.

If you have worked methodically, by the end of this unit you should have:

- Examined the relationship between special interests and tourism;
- Explored the factors that affect participation in special interest tourism;
- Investigated the location of special interest tourism and the nature of the activities included;
- Examined the tourism provision for a specific special interest.

You are now in a position to complete the assignment for the unit, under the direction of your tutor. Before you tackle the assignment you may like to have a go at the following questions to help build your knowledge of special interest tourism.

Test your knowledge

1. What is 'special interest tourism'?
2. Which points about the historical development of tourism have had an impact on the development of special interest tourism?
3. What are 'niche' tourism products and why is special interest tourism considered to be one?
4. List five passive and five adventurous activities that can form part of a special interest tourism product.
5. Which is the most popular active pursuit in the UK?
6. How do adventurous activities contribute to economic development in the destinations where they take place?
7. List three motivations of people who take part in special interest tourism.
8. What are 'demographics' and how do they affect special interest tourism?
9. Name six different segments found in special interest tourism.
10. Which socio-economic factors affect participation in special interest tourism?
11. Explain how Maslow's hierarchy of needs relates to special interest tourism.
12. Describe the locations of three different types of special interest tourism.
13. Name six companies that offer cycling tourism holidays and breaks.
14. Describe private sector provision for special interest tourism in the UK.
15. Name six UK-based adventure tourism companies that offer holidays within the UK and overseas.

UNIT 12 ASSIGNMENT: Special interest tourism

Introduction

This assignment is made up of a number of tasks which, when successfully completed, are designed to give you sufficient evidence to meet the Pass (P), Merit (M) and Distinction (D) grading criteria for the unit. If you have carried out the activities and read the case studies throughout this unit, you will already have done a lot of work towards completing the tasks for this assignment.

Scenario

In your first job since leaving college you are working in the Marketing Department of a mid-size tour operator that has been selling villa holidays to Spain, Greece and Turkey for the last six years. The Head of Marketing, Jenni Frost, has been asked by senior management to investigate the possibility of introducing special interest tourism holidays into the company's programme to capitalise on the growth in popularity of activities and special interests amongst clients. Jenni has asked you to help out on the project, which focuses on four main areas:

1.   The relationship between special interests and tourism;
2.   The factors which affect participation in special interest tourism;
3.   The location of destinations and nature of the activities of different types of special interest tourism;
4.   The tourism provision for a specific special interest that the company may wish to introduce.

She wants you to complete the following four tasks.

Task 1

Jenni needs some background evidence on special interest tourism and would like you to produce a written report in which you should:

(a) Describe the relationship between special interests and tourism;

(b) Explain how the relationship between special interests and tourism developed;

(c) Analyse the relationship between special interests and tourism, the participants and providers, and the locations and activities.

These tasks are designed to produce evidence for P1, M1 and D1.

Task 2

Jenni would like you to prepare and deliver an illustrated presentation in which you should describe the factors which affect participation in special interest tourism.

This task is designed to produce evidence for P2.

Task 3

For this task, Jenni would like you to produce three special interest tourism case studies in which you should:

(a) Describe the location of destinations for three different types of special interest tourism;

(b) Describe the nature of the activities included in the three different types of special interest tourism you selected in task 3 (a);

(c) Explain how the factors which affect participation in special interest tourism that you covered in your presentation for task 2, plus the location and nature of the activities in tasks 3 (a) and 3 (b), affect participation in the three different types of special interest tourism you have selected.

These tasks are designed to produce evidence for P3, P4 and M2.

Task 4

Finally, Jenni would like you to carry out a thorough investigation into one area of special interest tourism. She would like you to compile a portfolio in which you should:

(a) Describe the tourism provision for a specific special interest;

(b) Analyse the provision for the special interest that you chose in task 4 (a), explaining any gaps in provision;

(c) Evaluate the provision for the special interest that you chose in task 4 (a), suggesting strategies to eliminate any gaps, and explaining and justifying your suggestions.

These tasks are designed to produce evidence for P5, M3 and D2.

Unit 13
Holiday Representatives

INTRODUCTION TO THE UNIT

Holiday representatives play a vital role in the successful operation of a tour operator's programme of holidays. A holiday representative ('rep') is the holidaymakers' first, and probably only, direct point of contact with the tour company. Working as a holiday rep is a very appealing job to many people thinking of a career in travel and tourism. It offers the chance to work in all parts of the UK or abroad and help all types of customers enjoy their holidays to the full, but it is a very demanding and responsible job. Reps have to work very long hours, deal with a host of enquiries from customers and sort out problems in a professional and efficient manner. Time off in the resort is very limited during the season and the job entails a certain amount of administration and basic accounting.

In this unit you will learn about the roles and responsibilities of different types of holiday representatives. The unit also gives you the opportunity to examine the legal responsibilities of reps and the part they play in relation to health and safety in the holiday environment. You will also have the chance to practise your communication techniques and customer service skills in different situations commonly found by people working as holiday representatives.

WHAT YOU WILL STUDY

During the course of this unit you will:

1. Investigate the roles and responsibilities of **different categories of holiday representatives;**
2. Examine the **legal responsibilities** of the holiday representative and the role they play in relation to **health and safety** in the holiday environment;
3. Use a range of **communication techniques** to meet customer needs;
4. Apply **social and customer service skills** in different situations.

You will be guided through the main topics in this unit with the help of the latest statistics, examples and industry case studies. You should also check out the weblinks throughout the unit for extra information on particular organisations or topic areas and use the activities to help you learn more.

ASSESSMENT FOR THIS UNIT

This unit is internally assessed, meaning that you will be given an assignment (or series of assignments) to complete by your tutor(s) to show that you have fully understood the content of the unit. A grading scale of pass, merit or distinction is used for all internally assessed units, with higher grades awarded to students who show greater depth in analysis and evaluation in their assignments. An assignment for this unit, which covers all the grading criteria, can be found on page 183. Don't forget to visit www.tandtONLine.co.uk for all the latest industry news, developments, statistics and tips to help you with your assignments.

Unit 13

SECTION 1: CATEGORIES OF HOLIDAY REPRESENTATIVES

Working as a holiday representative is many people's idea of the perfect job – the chance to work abroad in the sun, socialise while you work and visit exciting places all sound very appealing, particularly to many young people. However, working as a rep is very hard work and may not suit everybody, as the advice from Thomson shown in Figure 13.1 explains.

LIVING AND WORKING OVERSEAS

Working and living in a different country is a completely different experience to being at home. The food, the language, the culture and the working hours, to name but a few, will all be new to you. Taking a big step and leaving all your friends and family behind is therefore not for the faint-hearted!

The nature of the holiday business also requires a large degree of flexibility. You will work six out of seven days. However, you may be contacted at any time if there is an emergency, so you will need to be willing and available to help if the need arises. We do our best to place you in the country of your choice, especially if you speak the language; however, this is not always possible, so you will need to be prepared to work anywhere in our programme.

Although leaving your home to work in a different country is a big step, it is also a completely different life experience and on offer is great job satisfaction and excellent career opportunities. So if you want adventure in your life, take a small step towards making a big leap!

Fig. 13.1 Advice from Thomson Holidays

Tour operators look for people who have a responsible and sensible outlook when recruiting holiday reps. Applicants need to be tactful, flexible and patient, with a lot of drive, enthusiasm and stamina, plus excellent organisational skills.

Although the image of a person working in a sunny Mediterranean resort is the one that comes most readily to mind when you think about the work of a holiday representative, there are actually many different types of reps working in the UK and abroad, serving all types of customers in many different kinds of accommodation and various resort areas. Reps can be classified into:

1. Property representatives;
2. Transfer representatives;
3. Children's representatives;
4. Tourist guides.

In the following sections of this unit we will investigate these categories in turn, examining the key roles and responsibilities of each.

Property representatives

These are the types of reps that are familiar to most of us who have been on a holiday abroad or seen TV programmes about working in travel and tourism. Property representatives look after customers staying in a range of different types of accommodation – hotels, villas, apartments, forest lodges, campsites, timeshare accommodation, caravan parks, holiday centres, etc. A property representative has three key roles:

1. To represent the company – holiday reps are the public face of the holiday company. Customers on a Thomas Cook holiday, for example, will not meet the senior managers or directors based in the UK, but they will have regular contact with their rep, expecting him or her to provide information and be able to handle any problems or enquiries speedily and efficiently. How good reps are at their jobs can have a significant impact on a holidaymaker's enjoyment of their holiday and the overall image of the company;

2. To provide excellent customer service – it goes without saying that holiday reps must deliver very high standards of customer service if they are going to satisfy their customers' needs. They must be available at all reasonable times to inform and entertain their customers, deal with complaints and handle sometimes difficult situations with tact and diplomacy;

3. To generate revenue – travel and tourism is a commercial operation, so reps are expected to sell extras to holidaymakers while in the resort, for example day and evening excursions, accommodation and travel upgrades, car hire and activities, for which they normally earn a commission.

The responsibilities of property reps are very varied and include:

- Conducting welcome meetings;
- Visiting properties to meet customers;
- Accompanying holidaymakers on transfers between airport and accommodation;
- Providing and maintaining local information boards for holidaymakers;
- Ensuring health and safety requirements;
- Running entertainments and events for customers
- Selling and organising excursions;
- Calculating payments, currency conversions and commissions;
- Carrying out routine administration;
- Liaising with hotel owners and managers;
- Solving problems for guests;
- Handling complaints;
- Dealing with non-routine incidents, illness and emergencies.

These three key roles and responsibilities are summed up well in the following case study on the roles and responsibilities of Thomas Cook Overseas Representatives, taken from the Thomas Cook website.

Unit 13

CASE STUDY – Thomas Cook Overseas Representatives

Overview

As an Overseas Representative you will be the public face of the company, always on hand to help. One minute you might be recommending a nice quiet spot to sunbathe, the next you could be dealing with a guest to solve their issue or complaint. The sheer variety and unpredictability of the job will call for some very special qualities. So whilst you won't require specific qualifications or experience, you do need bags of personality, a knack for dealing with people and the ability to stay calm under pressure and still keep smiling.

Key responsibilities and outputs

- To professionally and efficiently accompany customers to and from the airport;
- To deliver 'introductions' to customers after their arrival, with the objective of providing customers with practical and interesting information in accordance with the company's guidelines;
- To deliver exceptional customer service in order to achieve the customer service targets given by the destination management;
- To actively sell Thomas Cook events, car hire and ad hoc events in order to achieve the income targets given by the destination management;
- To actively monitor health, safety and quality standards;
- To accurately complete weekly/fortnightly paperwork in accordance with the company guidelines and the resort deadlines;
- To establish a friendly, respectful relationship with all hotel staff, suppliers and airport officials;
- To guide both day and night events as required;
- To take an active role in any in-house entertainment/activity where possible;
- To conduct police and clinic visits as required.

People skills

- Good communication skills and the ability to hold conversations with customers;
- The ability to work either as part of a team or independently;
- The ability to listen and respond sympathetically to customers' requests/needs;
- An enthusiastic, positive personality – must like working with people.

Decision-making skills

- The initiative to escalate problems and incidents to the destination management;
- The ability to resolve problems.

Development skills

- A willingness to learn and participate in any given training.

CASE STUDY QUESTIONS

1. What specific qualities do Thomas Cook staff look for when recruiting holiday representatives?
2. What different types of rep jobs does Thomas Cook offer?
3. Find a vacancy for a holiday representative's job with Thomas Cook and write a short report on how you feel you meet the key requirements of the post and in which areas you would need further development and training before taking the job;
4. Which aspects of being a Thomas Cook overseas representative appeal most to you and what responsibilities would you be least comfortable with?

WEBLINK

www.thomascookjobs.co.uk

Check out this website to help answer these questions and for more information on holiday representative job opportunities with Thomas Cook.

Property representatives work in a variety of different locations and meet the needs of many different types of customers, as the following sections of this unit explain.

Hotel representatives

The work of most overseas holiday reps working for the big, mass-market tour operators is hotel or apartment-based. The large numbers of holidaymakers in a hotel or apartment complex means that it makes sense for a rep to spend most of his or her time in a single location or a group of properties that are close together, thereby keeping in regular contact with holidaymakers. This also cuts down travelling time between properties, which may be by public transport, moped, car, bicycle or walking, depending on the circumstances. Applicants for these jobs usually need to be over 20 or 21 years of age, are provided with accommodation and a company uniform, and receive training before starting the job and while working in-resort.

Unit **13**

A Thomas Cook Overseas Representative

Villa representatives

Villas tend to be more spread out than hotels or apartments, so reps have to spend more time travelling between properties and may not see villa-based customers quite as often during their holiday. They are likely to be given some form of transport for their work, either a car or moped. Roles and responsibilities are very similar to those of hotel/apartment reps, although information about what to do in the resort is likely to be given on a one-to-one or small group basis rather than by using the type of information board used in a hotel or apartment complex. Villa reps working for the big holiday companies are employed full-time for the season, but smaller tour operators offering villa holidays sometimes use the services of a freelance rep based in the resort, i.e. somebody who is self-employed and looks after the customers of a number of different companies.

Campsite couriers

Campsite couriers work overseas or in the UK and are responsible for looking after customers during their holiday in a tent or mobile home. Major companies that recruit couriers for overseas work include Keycamp and Eurocamp (both part of Holidaybreak plc) and Canvas Holidays. Most jobs are from May to September, so they appeal

CAMPSITE COURIERS AT HOLIDAYBREAK PLC

The role of a courier is a varied one, however your main responsibility is to ensure that our customers have a great holiday! You will welcome newly-arrived customers after preparing and cleaning their accommodation to the correct standard. You are the customers' main point of contact, so helping with local area information, acting as interpreter and generally helping customers is very important. Other areas of responsibility are: making minor repairs to accommodation and equipment, completing reports and basic accounts, montage and demontage work at the beginning and end of the season.

A friendly and helpful approach with the maturity and initiative to deal with any situation is essential. You will be providing high a high level of service handled with professionalism, all with a willing attitude and of course a smile!

Fig. 13.2 Working as a Campsite Courier for Holidaybreak plc

particularly to students; the normal minimum age for recruitment is 18 years of age. Couriers spend a lot of time cleaning and preparing tents and mobile homes for new guests, plus making their stay as enjoyable as possible when they arrive, as the example from Holidaybreak plc in Figure 13.2 explains.

There are a number of different jobs available as campsite couriers, for example:

- Courier – the most common position, ensuring customers enjoy their holiday to the full (as described in Figure 13.2);
- Senior courier – required to organise the daily workload of a small team of couriers and children's couriers, as well as being able to carry out full courier duties as required. Positions tend to be for the full season only;
- Mature courier – some companies welcome mature couple and single applicants as couriers. Mature couriers provide invaluable benefits to customers, since many of them have considerable experience of camping and travelling in Europe. Mature couriers can choose to live in company tents or their own caravan or motorhome;
- Site manager – people with proven supervisory experience are recruited to lead the largest teams for the major camping tour operators. They are expected to set and maintain excellent standards of service and behaviour amongst staff;
- Team leader – responsible for managing the work of a team of couriers, with responsibility for customer service and accommodation standards;
- Children's courier – responsible for organising and delivering a regular programme of events for children on site, as well as being available for general courier duties as required.

WEBLINK

www.keycamp.co.uk;
www.eurocamp.co.uk;
www.canvasholidays.co.uk

Check out these websites for more information on campsite courier job opportunities.

A Keycamp courier greets new arrivals

In addition to these posts, the larger companies offer jobs at the beginning and end of each season in montage (erecting tents) and demontage (dismantling tents), including team leaders, assistants and drivers.

Ski reps

Ski tour operators offer a range of overseas appointments throughout the season, most of which involve close contact with customers. Positions include chalet hosts, bar managers, chefs, receptionists, chalet managers and resort

Unit 13

managers. Working as a chalet host is a common first appointment in a ski resort, giving a good grounding for career progression within the company or industry. Chalet hosts employed by Inghams, a specialist ski tour operator, have the following responsibilities:

1. Running a catered chalet;
2. Catering and cleaning to a very high standard;
3. Looking after guests;
4. Menu planning;
5. Budgeting and basic administration.

The company's chalets vary in size from those accommodating up to 8 people, which may be managed by a single chalet host, to larger chalets suitable for friends and couples to run together. Inghams look for individuals who are outgoing and cheerful, with a sense of humour and a basic love of cooking. The specific requirements for the post of chalet host are:

- A cooking diploma or proven experience of catering;
- Basic hygiene knowledge;
- Minimum age of 19 years;
- Previous experience within the hospitality industry;
- Excellent customer service skills.

> ## WEBLINK
>
> www.inghams.co.uk
>
> *Check out this website for more information on job opportunities at Inghams.*

Ski reps in the French Alps

Ski reps who do well in their winter season jobs may be offered summer season positions in different resorts or a job in the UK company headquarters.

Different types of holidaymakers

You've learned in other units on your course that tour operators provide holidays and travel products for a wide variety of customers. This is known as 'market segmentation', i.e. dividing the market for holidays into different segments, each of which has similar characteristics. For example, there are holidays geared specifically to the needs of young people, families, senior citizens, people who like activities and so on. This means that there are jobs for representatives looking after all types of holidaymakers, as the following sections of this unit demonstrate.

Families on holiday

Holidays for families are the backbone of the package holiday market; they offer good value for money at an all-inclusive price in a safe and secure environment. Reps help families to settle in to what are likely to be unfamiliar surroundings in the resort accommodation and point out activities and attractions that are geared particularly to families. They may be asked to help families who have special dietary or other requirements, by liaising with hotel management. Families with young children tend not to go on late night excursions, so reps should point out the day trips that are likely to appeal most to this segment of the market. Many tour operators offer clubs and activities for children, to keep them entertained and give their parents a rest. These are usually divided by age groups and full details are normally given out at the welcome meeting at the start of the holiday. Reps play an important part in making the sometimes stressful activity of taking children on holiday as carefree and enjoyable as possible.

Holidays for young people

Holidays for young people are an altogether different affair! These involve partying until the small hours, meeting lots of new people and having a good time in the resort. Reps working for holiday companies that offer young people's holidays, for example Club 18-30 (part of the Thomas Cook Group) and 2wentys (owned by First Choice Holidays), look for very outgoing personalities in the people they employ. Reps are expected to take part in all the activities on offer to the young holidaymakers, so need boundless energy, enthusiasm and stamina. These include trips to clubs, pubs and bars, plus beach and pool games and activities. Such a volatile mix of alcohol, activities and hot sun can sometimes lead to problems, so reps often have to 'think on their feet' and handle awkward situations in a professional manner. Although sometimes difficult, reps working on young people's holidays must remain professional at all times and not be tempted to get too involved with their clients. For people with the right attitude and skills, these jobs give young reps the chance to visit the 'hot spots' of Europe, such as Ayia Napa, Faliraki and Kavos.

ACTIVITY

Carry out some research into holiday reps' jobs with companies that offer holidays for young people and make a list of the key roles and responsibilities of the jobs, plus the skills, qualities and experience needed to do the job well.

This activity is designed to provide evidence for P1.

Unit 13

Holidays for seniors

Holidays for the over 50s and 'seniors' in general tend to be much more sedate, although there is a growing trend for older people to be far more active in later life. Recent research commissioned by Saga, Britain's leading travel company for the over 50s, indicated that the top ten most popular activities that over 50s would like to try include learning to fly, rally car driving, white water rafting, surfing and even sky diving! Holiday reps working with senior holidaymakers need to understand the particular needs of older people on holiday, which may include more time needed when travelling on excursions, help with access to facilities and empathy with their particular circumstances. For this reason, many tour operators recruit older and more mature people to fill these posts, making it easier for the holidaymakers to relate to their reps.

Travelsphere clients enjoying their holiday

Transfer representatives

If a tour operator has a very large number of passengers regularly arriving at a particular airport or airports, they may employ a transfer rep specifically to organise client transfers between the airport and their accommodation, thereby releasing the resort reps to carry out their normal duties. In most cases, however, resort reps carry out airport transfers on a rota basis. The role of the transfer rep is to meet and greet customers as they arrive at the airport and transfer them safely and speedily to their holiday accommodation. This is normally by coach, but could be by taxi or even a hired car. At the end of their holiday, the process is reversed and the transfer rep supervises the collection of passengers from their accommodation and transfers them to the airport to catch their flight home. Specific responsibilities of the transfer rep include:

- Meeting and greeting customers at the airport;
- Checking the passengers against a manifest (a list of passengers' names);
- Escorting the customers to the coach;
- Giving a welcoming speech on the coach;
- Checking the holidaymakers into to their accommodation;
- At the end of their holiday, collecting guests from their accommodation;
- Transferring the customers to the airport;
- Directing guests to the check-in desks;
- Waiting at check-in until all guests have departed safely.

Unit 13

Transfer reps are the very first representative of the holiday company that the customer meets, so they play a very important part in ensuring that customers get their holidays off to a good start. Sometimes, however, transfer reps have to deal with problems, such as lost luggage, delayed flights, long queues at check-in and passengers arriving late for their return flight. These situations can be very stressful and call for a great deal of patience, tact and diplomacy on the part of the transfer rep.

Children's representatives

Becoming a children's rep is a good way to start a career as a representative since the starting age is often lower (over 18 years) than for a property or resort rep. If you enjoy the life as a children's rep and do well in your job, you may decide to stay on in the travel and tourism industry by applying for a resort rep's position when you are older. Jobs as a children's rep are offered by the major holiday companies and campsite operators, some of which ask for an NNEB, BTEC or NVQ level 3 in Childcare, a Diploma in Nursery Nursing or an equivalent UK qualification from applicants.

The main role of a children's rep is to carry out a varied programme of activities for children, which provides them with a valuable social experience while on holiday. Children's reps need to create a child-friendly environment that is safe, clean and effectively managed so as to ensure maximum enjoyment for all children. Specific responsibilities include:

- Providing a variety of stimulating activities for children in different age ranges;
- Maintaining and promoting an informative and attractive notice board of events;
- Attending welcome meetings to explain the services available for children;
- Managing groups of children during activities and events;
- Maintaining appropriate health, safety and security measures;
- Completing report forms and carrying out basic accounting in line with company procedures;
- Control and manage stock effectively;
- Liaising with and helping other reps as and when required;
- Offering a baby-sitting service.

Children enjoying themselves at a Keycamp Fun Station

Successful candidates for children's courier jobs are screened via an enhanced disclosure check from the Criminal Records' Bureau to satisfy all concerned that there are no good reasons why they should not carry out the role.

Tourist guides

Tourist guides accompany visitors on tours, explaining points of interest, answering questions and generally 'adding value' to the customers' holiday experience. Tourist guides work in the UK and overseas in many different situations, for example:

- A guide providing a service for tour operators in overseas resorts by accompanying guests on excursions;
- A tour guide leading a party of overseas visitors on a walking tour of Cambridge;
- A guide working for a UK coach company leading a week-long tour of the Scottish Highlands;
- A tour guide leading tourists in the foothills of the Himalayas;
- A guide working independently and offering guided tours of the Egyptian pyramids;
- A tour guide leading a party of school children on a minibus tour of Liverpool.

Their main role is to make sure that clients have an enjoyable, safe and informative tour, as described in the following case study on the work of a tourist guide.

CASE STUDY – The work of a tourist guide

Introduction

Jenny Sanderson is a Blue Badge registered guide working in London. As well as English, she speaks French and German fluently, and is learning Japanese in order be able to work with tourists and tour companies from that country. Here she explains her role and responsibilities.

What does a tourist guide do?

My main role is to ensure that my clients have an enjoyable, safe and informative tour. This involves meeting and greeting the group, leading them safely during their tour, explaining points of interest on the tour, answering questions and finishing the tour at the agreed time and location.

Unit 13

Who are your clients?

I work with groups of all sizes and from all parts of the world, including the UK. Most are on holiday, but some are educational groups and people visiting London on business. Tours take place on coaches, in taxis, hire cars or on foot. I've even given a tour of London in a chauffer-driven car for a wealthy prince from Saudi Arabia!

What happens in a typical day?

The first thing to say is that no two days are the same! You never quite know how a tour will turn out; so much depends on the type of people and how they react. Some groups are very quiet, while others love to talk and it's very difficult to keep to time! I normally meet a group at their hotel at about 9 am. The first thing I check is that everybody has had breakfast and that all the people who should be on the tour have turned up! I always check the itinerary carefully with the party's tour manager or leader, making sure we cover everything in the group's programme. A typical panoramic coach tour of London would cover all the famous sights, including Buckingham Palace, the Houses of Parliament, the Changing of the Guard, Big Ben, the Tower of London. St Paul's Cathedral and Tower Bridge. It might also include a visit to the London Eye, the British Museum or a shopping trip, according to what has been agreed in advance.

What happens on the tour?

If it's a coach tour, I give a running commentary as we progress along the tour. At the same time, I interact with the clients to see what they are interested in and ask them questions. I think audience participation is very important! I try to maintain people's interest by finding things that they can relate to. For example, if I'm with a German group and we are passing Downing Street, I point out the last time that the German Chancellor visited the Prime Minister. Usually, the tour is made up of a number of planned stops to see points of interest. Sometimes our stops are very brief – just long enough to take photographs and for me to give a quick round up of the main facts. On a one-day trip to London, everybody wants to take pictures of Buckingham Palace and Big Ben!

What skills and qualities do you need to be a good tourist guide?

First and foremost you must like working with people – if you're not a 'people person', then don't get a job as a guide. Also, you need very good communications skills, both verbally and in writing. Knowledge of at least one foreign language as well as your mother tongue is pretty much a necessity. You also need to be quite persuasive to make sure that people stick to time and don't wander off by themselves. Having the Blue Badge qualification is a definite bonus – it sets you apart as being professional in what you do. Finally, a good sense of humour, an outgoing personality and good organisational skills come in very handy.

CASE STUDY QUESTIONS

1. What qualities are needed to be a successful tourist guide?
2. What techniques can tourist guides use to establish rapport with their customers?
3. What measures should tourist guides employ to make sure that customers are safe and secure when taking part in walking tours and coach tours of historic cities?
4. Which aspects of being a tourist guide appeal most to you and what responsibilities would you be least comfortable with?

Tourist guides working in the UK can take an industry qualification and become Blue Badge registered guides after completing the course successfully.

WEBLINK

www.blue-badge-guides.com

Check out this website for more information on Blue Badge Guides.

FOCUS ON INDUSTRY – Blue Badge Guides

The Guild of Registered Tourist Guides is the national, professional association for registered Blue Badge Guides within the British Isles. It represents around 2,100 guides in England, Wales, Scotland, Northern Ireland, Jersey and the Isle of Man. Since its foundation in 1950, the Guild has been dedicated to raising and maintaining the highest professional standards of its members. It provides professional support to its members, including day-to-day issues involving users of guide services, sites, coach operators and health and safety. All Guild members hold the coveted Blue Badge, the British national standard guiding qualification and internationally-recognised benchmark of excellence. Blue Badge Guides are selected, trained and examined by the official British tourist boards. The training is detailed and comprehensive, lasting for 18 months.

Tourist guides perform a valuable service for visitors

Unit 13

SECTION 2: LEGAL RESPONSIBILITIES

You are probably aware that society is becoming ever more conscious of the law and what happens if legal responsibilities are not carried out. Customers are much more willing to complain about products and services, including holidays and other travel products, and are prepared to fight for their rights, going as far as court action if necessary. Travel and tourism companies have to follow their legal responsibilities to the letter, whether this is to do with the quality of products and services they sell, issues to do with employing staff, health and safety matters, and consumer rights when things go wrong.

Legal responsibilities

Tour operators, and the staff they employ, must work within the legal framework when supplying holidays and other travel products to customers. All staff, including holiday reps working in the UK and overseas, have a general 'duty of care' to everybody they come into contact with as part of their work, such as customers, colleagues, contractors and suppliers. Over and above this duty of care, the work of holiday reps is governed by a number of important pieces of legislation, including:

- The Package Travel Regulations 1992;
- Trade Descriptions Act 1968 and 1972;
- Supply of Goods and Services Act 1982.

Package Travel Regulations

The Package Travel Regulations came into operation on 1st January 1993 in the then 12 Member States of the European Union. The main aim of the Regulations is to give people buying package holidays more protection and access to compensation when things go wrong, while at the same time harmonising the rules covering packages operated throughout European Union countries. Up to the introduction of the Regulations, tour operators had been able to disclaim responsibility when holiday arrangements went wrong, for example overbooking at a hotel or the failure of a coach transfer to arrive, on the grounds that they had no control over these unfortunate events. Under the terms of the Package Travel Regulations, tour organisers must accept legal responsibility for all the services they offer to travellers. Exceptions would be made in circumstances which could neither have been foreseen nor overcome, although in such circumstances, organisers must give all necessary assistance to consumers.

The Package Travel Regulations place a number of duties and responsibilities on tour operators, for example:

- Providing information to customers on who is responsible for the package they have booked. That person or organisation is then liable in the event of failure to deliver any elements of the package;
- Providing clear contract terms;
- Giving emergency telephone numbers;
- Providing proof of the organiser's security against insolvency and information on any available insurance policies;
- Giving immediate notification with explanation of any increase in prices permitted within the terms of the contract;
- Providing a variety of compensation options if agreed services are not supplied;
- Producing accurate promotional material including brochures.

Holiday representatives are not expected to know every detail of the Package Travel Regulations, but must be aware of their existence and why they have been put in place. The sorts of circumstances when the Regulations could come into force include overbooking of accommodation, leading to some customers' rooms being unavailable, and serious flight delays.

Trade Descriptions Act 1968 and 1972

This Act protects consumers against false descriptions made knowingly or recklessly by anybody selling products and services, including holidays and other travel products. Any description of, for example, a hotel or resort must be truthful at the time it was written (if circumstances change, then the company must inform the customer of the nature of the changes). The Act places a duty on owners and operators of travel and tourism facilities to produce brochures, websites and other promotional materials that are not intended to deceive customers.

Supply of Goods and Services Act 1982 (as amended by the Sale and Supply of Goods Act 1994)

This legislation states that any contract for a holiday should be carried out using 'reasonable care and skill'. The tour operator and travel agent should ensure that the booking is carried out correctly and that the holiday itself should be of a generally satisfactory standard, complying with any descriptions made. Tour operators must take great care when selecting accommodation, transport and any services they provide as part of their package holidays.

Unit 13

Booking conditions and contracts

Tour operators' booking terms and conditions are explained in their brochures and customers are deemed to have accepted these, and enter into a contract with the tour operator, when they sign their holiday booking form. The circumstances when customers can claim refunds and compensation are included in the booking conditions and reflect the need to comply with the Package Travel Regulations described earlier in this unit. Payments can be made when, for example, holidaymakers are forced to take a lower standard of accommodation than they had booked as a result of overbooking by the hotel.

Drivers' hours

There are separate regulations governing how long drivers of passenger vehicles can drive on UK and European trips, so as to ensure safety for all concerned. The UK domestic rules state that drivers are allowed to drive for a maximum of 10 hours in any working day, and must drive for no longer than 5.5 hours continuously before having a break of at least 30 minutes for rest and refreshment. The regulations are very complicated and there are exemptions for certain circumstances.

WEBLINK

www.dft.gov.uk

Check out this Department for Transport website for the full drivers' hours' rules and regulations.

The European rules are extremely complex, but a simple starting point is that drivers of passenger vehicles are allowed to drive for a maximum of 9 hours in any working day, which can be increased to 10 hours per day twice a week. After 4.5 hours of continuous driving, the driver must take a break of at least 45 minutes before continuing the journey. A tachograph, which records the driver's hours, must be used by drivers of vehicles with 18 or more seats on domestic journeys and 10 or more seat on international journeys.

Holiday reps need to be aware of these regulations when planning coach and minibus excursions.

Health and safety

Under the terms of the Package Travel Regulations, and other legislation, tour operators have a legal duty to ensure that the holidays and other services they offer to customers meet all current health and safety regulations. It is no longer acceptable for a tour operator to say that it is not responsible for parts of its programmes that are delivered by other companies.

Health and safety inspections

Before signing contracts with any of its suppliers before the start of a holiday season, for example hoteliers and coach operators, tour companies inspect premises and vehicles to

Unit 13

make sure they comply with health and safety guidelines. Once the contracts have been signed and the season is underway, it is the responsibility of reps to carry out regular checks to make sure that health and safety standards are being maintained. This involves systematic inspections of a number of items, including:

- Fire alarms and evacuation signs and procedures;
- Swimming pool safety equipment and notices;
- Electrical, gas and water systems;
- The safety of balconies in rooms;
- Warning flags on beaches;
- Hygiene standards in accommodation, eating areas, public areas and toilets;
- Safety equipment used for activities, including children's clubs.

HEALTH AND SAFETY REPORT

Form completed by _____

Property _____

Date form completed _____

Date faxed to Area Office _____

Description of defect	Reported to	Action to be taken	Target date for completion

Signed _____ (Representative)

Signed _____ (Hotel Management)

An example of a health and safety report that reps have to complete is shown in Figure 13.3.

The Federation of Tour Operators (FTO) provides its members, which include all the leading UK holiday companies, with practical help and information on managing health and safety in resort areas. To ensure consistency in regulations and standards of health, hygiene and safety between destinations, the FTO has appointed a health and safety co-ordinator and developed a code of practice. This publication contains advice on a range of issues, including:

- Fire safety;
- Food safety;
- Pool safety;
- General safety;
- Beach safety;

Fig. 13.3 A health and safety report

WEBLINK

www.fto.co.uk

Check out this website for more information on the FTO health and safety guidelines.

- Legionella (legionnaire's disease) management;
- Children's clubs;
- Incident management.

The Federation has also developed a health and safety training video to complement the code of practice.

ACTIVITY

Under the direction of your tutor, carry out a health and safety inspection, and complete a health and safety report form. This could take place in your college/school, a nearby tourist facility or while investigating accommodation as part of a study tour in the UK or overseas.

This activity is designed to provide evidence for P3.

WATER PARK RISK ASSESSMENT

Location _____ Carried out by _____

Date _____ Checked by _____

Location	Hazard	Risk	Control measures
Travel to park	Safety of coach/minibus	Low	• Visual inspection • Check seatbelts • Check emergency doors
Swimming pool	Injury caused by trips and slips Possibility of drowning	Medium	• Verbal warning to customers • Inspection of safety aids • Monitoring behaviour
Flumes and slides	Injury caused by falls and slips Possibility of drowning	Medium	• Verbal warning to customers • Inspection of safety aids • Monitoring behaviour
Across the park	Injury from traffic	Low	• Verbal warning to customers • Inspection of speed restriction measures • Supervision of customers
Across the park	Possibility of loss, abduction or assault of children	Low	• Verbal warning to customers • Supervision of children • Checks on procedures

Fig. 13.4 A risk assessment form

Risk assessments

A risk assessment is a systematic investigation of the potential hazards in a given situation. Holiday reps may be required to carry out risk assessments when planning an excursion, for example a trip to a water park as part of an activity for children's club members. Reps complete a form that lists potential hazards and the action that needs to be taken to minimise risks. An example of a risk assessment form is given in Figure 13.4.

Reporting accidents

Reps are trained to report all serious accidents and incidents involving holidaymakers in the resort, by completing an accident report form (see Figure 13.5) or logging the details in an accident book. The reports must be as detailed as possible, since they may be needed for future claims against the tour operator by customers.

ACCIDENT REPORT FORM

Form completed by _____

Property/location _____

Date form completed _____

The accident	Date and time Location Was a photograph taken? Yes/No
Full description of the incident and any injuries	 Was medical treatment needed? Yes/No
The injured party	Name Holiday ref: Home address Tel. No:
Witnesses	Name Address Name Address

Fig. 13.5 An accident report form

SECTION 3: COMMUNICATION TECHNIQUES

Communication is an essential part of a holiday representative's job, whether dealing with customers, hoteliers, work colleagues, contractors or suppliers. For most of the time, communicating with these people is a straightforward and pleasant affair, but there are occasions when reps have to use their communication skills to deal with difficult and awkward situations. There are many techniques that can be used in these situations, as we shall see in the following sections of this unit.

Communication techniques

The two most important techniques used by reps in the work situation are verbal communication and written/visual communication.

Verbal communication

It's fair to say that reps have to talk a lot while doing their jobs, so good verbal communication skills are essential. Verbal communication can be formal or informal. Examples of formal communication involving reps include:

- Conducting a welcome meeting for new arrivals in a resort;
- Telling customers about health and safety procedures in a hotel;
- Making a speech to thank your work colleagues at the end of the season;
- Complaining to a supplier that some equipment is faulty;
- Providing a commentary on a coach excursion.

Reps communicate informally when they are talking to customers and colleagues in a more relaxed manner, perhaps while on an excursion or in a hotel lobby.

ACTIVITY

Working with a partner, make a list of other situations when a rep would communicate formally and informally with a range of people while at work.

This activity is designed to provide evidence for P3.

Unit 13

Verbal communication is an important aspect of a rep's job

Using a microphone

Although daunting at first, most holiday reps need to be able to use a microphone, usually on a tour bus or at a welcome meeting, to communicate with large groups of clients. Many tour operators include developing this skill in their reps' pre-resort training, where staff role play the sort of situations they are likely to find themselves in when abroad. The same general rules that are followed when communicating using your natural voice also hold good when using a microphone, for example making sure that you can be heard by everybody, speaking slowly in a clear tone and giving people time to ask questions or clarify points.

Communicating with different types of customers

Reps come into contact with all sorts of customers while at work, e.g. groups, individuals, adults, children, youths, people whose first language isn't English, mixed age groups, people with special needs, etc. Reps must be able to assess customers' needs quickly and provide appropriate help, advice and guidance.

Dealing with groups can be an altogether more challenging task than communicating with an individual customer. Handling group situations calls for good organisational and

Dealing with children can be challenging and fun!

communication skills, so that every member of the group turns up in the right place at the right time! Although the group you are dealing with may be very large, it is important to make every effort to treat the members of the group as individuals by, for example, addressing people by name and taking time to talk to them on a one-to-one basis, particularly those that you feel may need a little more attention or support.

There are certain ground rules that you need to adopt when communicating information to a group of customers, including:

- Making sure that members of the group can see, hear and understand you;
- Communicating effectively using simple language in a clear, confident tone of voice;
- Making sure that everybody has understood what you have said by allowing time for questions;
- Making yourself available afterwards if people want further clarification on a one-to-one basis.

Dealing with groups of clients is an important part of the work of a holiday representative, for example when organising transfers, conducting excursions or on guiding duties. Developing group handling skills will ensure that you can:

- Ensure the safety and welfare of groups of clients;
- Handle mixed groups, e.g. by age, gender, language;
- Handle difficult groups, e.g. rowdy, under the influence of alcohol or complaining;
- Deal with medical and emergency situations.

ACTIVITY

Take turns at playing the role of a tour guide by taking the rest of your group on a tour of your college/school or the local area. When the tour has finished, the 'customers' should discuss the strengths and weaknesses of each guide, concentrating on communication with the group as a whole as well as with individual group members. You may also like to role play the situation of a group of rowdy holidaymakers to practise some different group handling skills!

This activity is designed to provide evidence for P3.

Unit 13

Communicating with suppliers and colleagues

For most of their time at work reps are dealing with customers. However, working as a rep is very much a team job, so there is plenty of contact with work colleagues, either in the resort or with people in head office back in the UK. There are also occasions when reps need to contact suppliers. Much of this contact is by telephone, often using a mobile 'phone. Clients are given contact numbers of the resort office and/or UK head office in case of difficulty or emergency. Some smaller, specialist operators, who may not have a fully-staffed overseas office, may also give their reps' mobile numbers to clients. Whatever the circumstances, there are a number of important points to bear in mind when dealing with incoming telephone calls from other members of staff or clients, for example:

- Answer all calls quickly – leaving a call for more than 5 rings is considered inefficient;
- Greet the caller with your name and/or your organisation and ask how you can help;
- Smile while you are talking! This may sound crazy, but it really does help you to project a welcoming tone to the person on the other end of the 'phone;
- Listen carefully to what the caller is saying;
- Always speak clearly and use language appropriate to the caller;
- Take notes if there is a message for another member of staff;
- Transfer calls to another appropriate member of staff if you cannot deal with the customer yourself;
- If you promise to call a customer later, make sure you do it!

Similar rules apply if you are making an outgoing telephone call to a supplier or work colleague.

Non-verbal communication and body language

Non-verbal communication is the process by which we send and receive signals and messages without the use of the spoken word. When at work, reps are always in the public eye, not just in formal situations such as while hosting a welcome meeting, but every minute while on duty. This means that they have to conduct themselves appropriately and professionally at all times, by projecting a positive and welcoming image, making eye contact while talking, maintaining a good posture and keeping any irritating habits or mannerisms to a minimum!

Written and visual communication

Many of the responsibilities of holiday reps are concerned with gathering local information and communicating this information in written and visual form to customers, for example:

- Giving holidaymakers leaflets about local facilities and attractions at the welcome meeting;
- Passing on information during transfers to and from the airport;
- Compiling information books and folders for guests to use while in-resort;
- Maintaining informative and attractive notice boards with information on resort attractions and activities;
- Making posters to advertise events.

Sources of local information include tourist offices, guidebooks, the Internet, local hoteliers, attractions and restaurateurs, as well as other overseas staff. As well as investigating what local attractions, facilities and events a resort has to offer holidaymakers, reps also need to know about local laws and customs, such as religious codes and festivals.

Notice boards are an excellent way for customers to keep up to date with what's happening in their resort and for reps to provide important information, as well as promoting and selling excursions and other travel services. The board needs to be located in a central position where holidaymakers regularly congregate, for example in a hotel foyer or by the welcome tent or mobile home on a campsite. Notice boards differ from one company to another, but minimum requirements are:

- Photographs, regular visiting times and details of how to contact the reps;
- Emergency contact details;
- Details of excursions and events;
- Details of return flights and any changes to travel arrangements;
- Facilities available in any children's clubs.

At the beginning of the season, reps usually prepare an information book or file for use by guests. This includes a great deal of useful local information such as an overview of the resort, public transport information, details of attractions, where to eat, doctor and dentist contact information, details of excursions, car and moped hire, foreign exchange, etc.

Notice boards and information books must look professional and business-like. When designing them, reps must make sure that:

- There are no spelling or grammar mistakes;
- All the information is current and not out of date;
- Where possible, information is typed or word processed;
- There is good use of colour to attract attention;
- There is not too much information on the notice board.

Unit 13

ACTIVITY

Working as part of a team, choose a popular overseas holiday destination and gather together information on its attractions, facilities and events. Use the information you collect to make a notice board that could be used by British people on holiday in the resort. Use a range of information sources, such as brochures, guidebooks, tourist offices and the Internet, to gather your information. Many of the major tour operators' websites have destination guides.

This activity is designed to provide evidence for P4.

You saw earlier in this unit that reps have to complete quite a lot of paperwork as part of their job, e.g. health and safety reports, customer complaint forms, risk assessments, etc. Tour operators provide guidance on how these should be completed during rep training and while in-resort. Reps must ensure that all written documents are completed accurately and written in a clearly understood manner.

Communication situations

Having examined the various communication techniques available to reps, we must now see how these can be put into action in the following situations:

1. During transfers;
2. At welcome meetings;
3. Guiding groups.

Transfers

We saw at the beginning of this unit that transfers between airport and accommodation are an important part of a rep's job, carried out on a rota basis amongst staff in the resort. After welcoming the holidaymakers, the rep on duty escorts the customers to their waiting coach and makes sure that they are all safely on board before setting off for the accommodation. On the journey to the accommodation the rep will use the microphone on the coach to talk to the passengers. On a typical transfer trip the rep will:

- Welcome the customers on behalf of the tour company;
- Introduce himself/herself and the coach driver;
- Give the local time and indicate how long the transfer should take;
- Point out the emergency exits and other safety features on the coach;
- Explain that a number of different stops will be made to various accommodation bases;

- Give an overview of the local area and resort facilities;
- Give the time and location of the welcome meeting;
- Distribute welcome packs;
- Provide information about the weather, safety of drinking water, banking facilities, etc;
- Give details of check-in procedures at the accommodation.

Reps should give customers the opportunity to ask any questions they may have or to clarify any points they are not sure about.

ACTIVITY

Assume that you are a rep working for First Choice Holidays. Role play a coach transfer between Palma Airport and the Hotel Don Paco in Magaluf. The rest of your group should critically evaluate your performance based on the information on communication techniques already covered in this unit.

This activity is designed to provide evidence for P3.

Welcome meetings

Welcome meetings are normally held the morning after the holidaymakers arrive in the resort, to allow them time to get over the journey and settle into their accommodation. Refreshments are normally served at the meeting, which should be conducted in a friendly and welcoming manner by the rep.

At the welcome meeting, the rep will cover a number of items, including:

- An introduction to the rep, the resort and accommodation on behalf of the tour company and the hotel management;
- Rep's availability and the location of the notice board;
- Details of local attractions in the resort;
- 'Housekeeping' items such as the times of meals and pool opening in the accommodation, use and cost of telephones, baby changing facilities, availability and cost of safes, etc;
- Information on facilities in the resort, including the location of banks, shops, medical facilities, car hire, beaches, public transport, etc;
- Details of the type and cost of excursions offered by the tour company, and how they can be booked;
- Any questions or concerns from the holidaymakers.

Unit 13

ACTIVITY

Still assuming that you are working as a resort rep for First Choice Holidays, plan and deliver a welcome meeting for the Magaluf holidaymakers who were on the coach transfer in the previous activity in this unit. The rest of your group should critically evaluate your performance based on the information on communication techniques already covered in this unit.

This activity is designed to provide evidence for P3.

Guiding groups

You've already learned that reps are called upon to look after groups on certain occasions, for example when carrying out airport transfers or leading an excursion by coach. The skills needed to deal effectively with groups was covered earlier in this unit (see page 171). The secrets to guiding groups effectively are thorough preparation and attention to detail. When leading an excursion, for example, time spent in researching the area you are exploring with your passengers will pay dividends when you deliver a polished, professional and knowledgeable commentary. As well as being informative, it's a good idea to inject a little humour into the tour in order to 'break the ice' and get some responses from the holidaymakers. You need to pay attention to health and safety issues during your guided tour, by pointing out safety features on the coach and continually being aware of potential hazards when leading the group on walks away from the coach and visiting attractions. People with special needs, including the elderly and those with children, may need particular attention and it is a good idea to have a word with them before the start of the excursion to find out what's needed.

SECTION 4: SOCIAL AND CUSTOMER SERVICE SKILLS

Social skills in the workplace

So far in this unit we've seen that the role of representatives revolves around dealing with people in a pleasant and professional manner. Social skills play a big part in a rep's role and are extremely important in:

- Creating rapport – with customers, work colleagues, suppliers, contractors, etc. in a variety of different situations;
- Providing a welcome – to customers, from the time they arrive in the resort to their departure flight home;
- Empathising – reps need to be able to understand issues from the customers' point of view;
- Providing a friendly and helpful service – should be the prime motivation for taking a job as a rep;
- Using appropriate language – social and communication skills will vary depending on the type of customer, e.g. language used when talking with young people on holiday is likely to be different from that used to deal with senior customers.

Some people naturally have a more sociable nature, but it's important to remember that social skills can be learned and improved through training and practice.

Customer service skills

Elsewhere on your course you have learned about the importance of developing and delivering excellent customer service skills in the workplace – meeting the needs of customers is the number one goal for travel and tourism companies that want to succeed in business. The effects of NOT providing acceptable levels of customer service can be very damaging to the company concerned, resulting in fewer sales, lost revenue and a poor image. Reps who are found to have poorly-developed customer service skills can be helped with extra training, but if this fails to improve matters they may well be advised to consider a career outside of travel and tourism.

There are a number of occasions when reps need to use customer service skills, for example:

- Providing information;
- Dealing with queries;
- Handling complaints;
- Dealing with customers with special needs;
- Dealing with non-routine incidents such as accidents or illness.

Unit 13

Providing information and dealing with queries

Reps will tell you that the range of queries they have to deal with is immense – everything from where to find a good seafood restaurant to where can I get my dentures repaired! Dealing with customers' queries and providing them with information is a key role for reps, who must always respond in a positive, polite and helpful way.

Handling complaints

Although the great majority of holidaymakers have a trouble-free holiday, there are occasions when reps have to deal with complaints from clients. This may result from a number of causes, including overbooking, flight delays, accommodation of a poor standard, noise or poor quality food.

The key actions to take when handling complaints are:

- Listen attentively so that you get the whole story first time;
- Thank the customer for bringing the problem to your attention;
- Apologise in general terms for the inconvenience but do not grovel;
- Provide support for the customer by saying that the complaint will be fully investigated and matters put right as soon as possible;
- Sympathise with the customer and try to see the situation from their point of view;
- Don't justify the circumstances that led up to the complaint and go on the defensive;
- Ask questions if you are not clear on any points of the customer's complaint;
- Find a solution to the problem;
- Agree the solution with the customer;
- Follow through to make sure that what you promised has been done;
- In future, try and anticipate complaints before they happen!

One step on from somebody who has a justifiable complaint is the customer who is intent on 'causing a scene'. Just like handling complaints, there are tried and tested ways of dealing with these individuals:

1. Try not to let them get you down or get under your skin. The fact that they wish to cause a fuss may be a sign of their own insecurity;
2. Never argue with them – it can often get the member of staff into deeper trouble;
3. Never be rude to the customer, however rude they are being to you!
4. Try not to take any remarks personally – you may have had nothing to do with the alleged incident but are simply the nearest member of staff;
5. Let the customer do the talking and listen to what they have to say.

If a situation appears to be getting out of hand, it is wise to seek help from another rep or senior member of the overseas team.

ACTIVITY

Working with other members of your group, role play the following situations that reps sometimes encounter:

1. A customer complaining about the poor quality food in her hotel;
2. The leader of a school group complaining about the time his pupils have to queue to use the hotel's games room;
3. A couple complaining to the transfer rep when they arrive in their resort about the long delay in their outward flight from Manchester.

You should take it in turns to play the person complaining and the rep dealing with the complaint. Members of the group should make notes on how well the 'rep' handles the complaint, in line with the key points discussed above.

This activity is designed to provide evidence for P3 and P5.

Customers with special needs

Travel and tourism organisations must strive to provide excellent standards of service to ALL their customers, regardless of their circumstances, age, abilities or disabilities. Some customers have specific needs which may need a particular type of customer service. This may be because of:

- The need for wheelchair access;
- Sensory disabilities;
- Mobility problems;
- People with young children.

Research has shown that around 14 per cent of all people living in Europe have some form of disability. Added to this are the many millions who, through age or circumstances, have a particular special need. The ageing population means that there are increasing numbers of people with deteriorating eyesight and hearing, and an inability to move around with ease.

The important point for reps to remember is that visitors with specific needs don't want to be made to feel a nuisance or different from other customers, but do welcome a little extra appreciation of, and respect for, their particular circumstances. Remember too that disabled people's ability to carry out their normal day-to-day activities is very often constrained by the environment in which they find themselves, rather than the disability they live with, for example, problems with getting on and off buses, coaches, trains and aircraft, and narrow doorways that do not allow wheelchair access.

Dealing with non-routine incidents

When incidents such as accidents, illness, crimes or serious disturbances occur involving customers in-resort, reps have to be able to handle these situations in a clam and professional manner, seeking assistance from colleagues or the emergency services as required. Dealing with non-routine incidents is one of the areas covered in reps' training before they start work in the resort.

Personal presentation

First impressions count in any business and even more so in the travel and tourism industry where dealing with people is such an important part of the work. It is vital for holiday reps to understand that the way they present themselves to customers has a direct influence on the clients' enjoyment, as well as the rep's job satisfaction and the future success of the tour company. In particular, reps need to appreciate the importance of the following:

- Company image;
- Codes of dress and behaviour;
- Personal appearance.

Company image

Tour operators spend a great deal of money developing their image or 'brand', which is used on all advertising, promotional work, aircraft, stationery, etc. Reps play an important part in reinforcing the company's image, not just with the uniform that they wear, but in the way they deal with customers. If treated well by reps while on holiday, customers come away with a positive impression of the tour operator and will tell their friends about the good time that they had, leading to extra business for the company.

Codes of dress and behaviour

Nearly all holiday companies provide uniforms for their holiday reps. Uniforms help to create a positive first impression with customers and make staff easily identifiable if customers need help or advice. The wearing of a uniform also presents a consistent image to the public and helps to build customer loyalty. However, it is important to remember that the word 'uniform' does not necessarily mean a very formal dress code. Holiday reps working on campsites or as children's reps, for example, wear a company 'uniform', but it often consists of a polo shirt, shorts and trainers. The important point about a uniform is that it should be appropriate and functional, i.e. suited to the nature and demands of the job. Overseas staff should be informed at interview about the dress code for the job and what type of uniform is supplied.

Training of representatives before they start work in the resort covers a number of sensitive issues concerning behaviour in the workplace. Reps are reminded about using appropriate language at all times with clients and other members of staff, including not swearing or using slang. Tour operators have different policies on staff smoking and drinking while on duty. The overriding concern of all companies is that reps must not be under the influence of alcohol while at work. With many companies, this is an offence for which staff can be instantly dismissed. Holiday reps must also comply with the tour operator's policies on relationships with colleagues and customers. As with drinking while on duty, inappropriate relationships with clients and colleagues are to be avoided.

Uniforms create a good impression with holidaymakers

Personal appearance

All reps must report for work in a presentable fashion, well groomed and with a smart uniform. Personal appearance can be a sensitive area, particularly when supervisors and managers have to remind staff about the importance of arriving at work in a clean, hygienic and presentable fashion. All staff working in travel and tourism, but especially reps whose work brings them into close contact with customers, must:

- Be generally clean;
- Have hair that is clean and tidy;
- Have fresh breath.

Customers will not tolerate staff with poor body odour or bad breath and may well take their custom elsewhere. It is important to remember that the staff are the outward image of an organisation. For example, if you are greeted at an airport by a representative who smells of stale cigarettes or whose hair is unkempt, your first impressions of the company and your holiday are likely to be negative. If, on the other hand, the rep is smartly presented, with a pleasant smile and tidy hair, you are much more likely to be impressed with the tour company from the outset.

Unit 13

UNIT SUMMARY

In this unit you have examined many aspects of the work of holiday representatives, particularly those working overseas. You have found that there are actually many different types of holiday representatives, from campsite couriers to children's reps. All need the same qualities to succeed – a pleasant and welcoming manner, excellent presentation and communication skills, a willingness to help others, bags of initiative and enthusiasm, plus good organisational skills. The unit has examined legal aspects of the rep's role and found that ensuring a safe and secure environment for holidaymakers is a very important part of the job, involving carrying out health and safety inspections and completing the necessary paperwork and reports. You have leaned about, and practised, a range of verbal and written communication techniques to do with working as a holiday rep and explored the importance of social and customer service skills in the workplace. Throughout the unit you have been shown many industry examples, while the case studies on Overseas Representatives at Thomas Cook and the work of a tourist guide, highlight key roles and responsibilities of different types of reps.

If you have worked methodically, by the end of this unit you should have:

- Investigated the roles and responsibilities of different categories of holiday representatives;
- Examined the legal responsibilities of holiday representatives and the role they play in relation to health and safety in the holiday environment;
- Used a range of communication techniques to meet customer needs;
- Applied social and customer service skills in different situations.

You are now in a position to complete the assignment for the unit, under the direction of your tutor. Before you tackle the assignment you may like to have a go at the following questions to help build your knowledge of the work of holiday reps.

Test your knowledge

1. What are the three key roles of a property representative?
2. List five responsibilities of property reps.
3. Describe three of the different courier jobs available on campsites.
4. What are the specific requirements for the post of chalet host in a ski resort?
5. Explain how a rep would go about meeting the needs of young people on holiday and holidaymakers aged over 50.
6. Name three companies that offer jobs as campsite couriers.
7. What qualities does a children's rep need to succeed in his or her job?
8. What is a Blue Badge Guide?
9. Explain how a rep's job is influenced by the requirements of the Package Travel Regulations.

10. List five items that are normally inspected by reps on a health and safety check of a hotel or apartment complex.
11. What is a 'risk assessment' and when might a rep have to carry one out?
12. What are the key points to bear in mind when communicating with a group?
13. What duties does a rep carry out on a typical transfer between airport and accommodation?
14. What aspects of personal presentation are particularly important to reps while on duty?
15. What are the key points to follow when dealing with complaints from customers?

UNIT 13 ASSIGNMENT: Holiday representatives

Introduction

This assignment is made up of a number of tasks which, when successfully completed, are designed to give you sufficient evidence to meet the Pass (P), Merit (M) and Distinction (D) grading criteria for the unit. If you have carried out the activities and read the case studies throughout this unit, you will already have done a lot of work towards completing the tasks for this assignment.

Scenario

Since completing your BTEC course you have worked in a Birmingham hotel for 15 months on reception duties. You feel that the time is right to make a career move and you have applied for a job as an overseas resort representative with one of the major holiday companies. You put in an excellent application and have been invited to an interview and selection day at the company's head office. During the day, you are asked to complete a number of tasks to assess your suitability for the job. The first two tasks involve making a presentation and writing a short report, while tasks 3 and 4 are role plays involving other applicants for representative jobs.

Task 1

For this task you must make a presentation to the selection panel and the rest of the applicants in which you should:

(a) Describe in detail the roles and responsibilities of one type of property representative and one other type of holiday representative;

(b) Compare and contrast the roles and responsibilities of the two different types of representatives that you chose for task 1 (a);

(c) Analyse the contribution that holiday representatives can make to enhance the customer's holiday experience and the potential effects of the representative's failure to provide an appropriate level of service.

These tasks are designed to produce evidence for P1, M1 and D1.

Task 2

This task asks you to write a short report that could be read by your resort manager. In the report you should:

(a) Explain the legal responsibilities of representatives and the role they play in relation to health and safety in the holiday environment;

(b) Explain how the legal and health and safety responsibilities affect the role of the two different representatives that you chose for task 1 (a).

These tasks are designed to produce evidence for P2 and M2.

Task 3

The selection panel would like you to role play this task, in which you should:

(a) Use appropriate communication techniques when carrying out an airport transfer, a welcome meeting and a coach journey to and from an evening barbecue excursion;

(b) Use appropriate communication techniques to produce an information booklet and a notice board to provide information for customers who are staying in a Mediterranean resort of your choice. Design and complete a booking form for the excursion described in task 3 (a).

These tasks are designed to produce evidence for P3 and P4. Task 3(a) can also produce evidence for P5 if social and customer service skills are used to deal effectively with customers while carrying out the airport transfer, welcome meeting and coach journey to and from the evening barbecue excursion.

Task 4

The members of the selection panel have given you a series of different customer service situations to deal with in role plays (your tutor will provide you with these). They are based on the same resort that you chose for task 3 (b). The situations are:

(a) Providing information to a small group of customers about attractions in the resort;

(b) Dealing with a query from a customer about getting an early flight home to visit a sick relative;

(c) Handling a complaint from a customer who is unhappy that she hasn't been given a room with a sea view in her hotel although she paid a supplement for this;

(d) Dealing with a customer who has had her passport and credit cards stolen from her room in the hotel;

(e) Comforting a child who has cut his toe on some glass on the side of the hotel swimming pool.

These tasks are designed to produce evidence for M3 if you consistently deal effectively with the range of customers in the different types of situations, and evidence for D2 if you consistently project a professional company image in all communications with customers, dealing confidently and communicating positively when dealing with the range of customers in the different types of situations.

Unit 14
Passenger Transport Operations

INTRODUCTION TO THE UNIT

The passenger transport industry provides leisure and business travellers with the means of reaching their destinations and is the hub around which the whole of the travel and tourism industry revolves. Passenger transport is a very dynamic sector, making use of new technologies to supply faster, more convenient, better value, more accessible and safer means of travel to and within the UK and overseas. Having good transport networks is essential for the development of a successful travel and tourism industry.

This unit gives you the opportunity to examine the passenger transport environment in detail, looking at the history and development of the sector, as well as issues relating to economic and social dimensions. You will investigate the different types of passenger transport and the features associated with each of them. Current issues to do with passenger transport will also be explored. Finally, the unit will introduce you to the concept of passenger flows, examining the different types and how they are managed.

WHAT YOU WILL STUDY

During the course of this unit you will:

1. Examine the **passenger transport environment;**
2. Investigate the **features** of different modes of passenger transport;
3. Explore current **issues** affecting passenger transport operations;
4. Examine how organisations manage **passenger flows**.

You will be guided through the main topics in this unit with the help of the latest statistics, examples and industry case studies. You should also check out the weblinks throughout the unit for extra information on particular organisations or topic areas and use the activities to help you learn more.

ASSESSMENT FOR THIS UNIT

This unit is internally assessed, meaning that you will be given an assignment (or series of assignments) to complete by your tutor(s) to show that you have fully understood the content of the unit. A grading scale of pass, merit or distinction is used for all internally assessed units, with higher grades awarded to students who show greater depth in analysis and evaluation in their assignments. An assignment for this unit, which covers all the grading criteria, can be found on page 216. Don't forget to visit www.tandtONLine.co.uk for all the latest industry news, developments, statistics and tips to help you with your assignments.

Unit 14

SECTION 1: PASSENGER TRANSPORT ENVIRONMENT

By its very nature, the travel and tourism industry involves travelling to, from and around destinations in the UK and overseas. Transport, therefore, is a vital component of travel and tourism. Transport for tourism covers a variety of water, air and land-based services, including travel by coach, train, private car, taxi, hired car, bicycle, aircraft, cruise ship, ferry and canal craft. It also includes the infrastructure that supports the means of travel, such as roads, motorway service areas, ferry terminals, airports and railway stations. Much of this infrastructure is provided by public agencies, or by public/private sector partnership arrangements. As demand for travel has grown, many transport terminals have developed into large, integrated complexes offering a range of catering, currency exchange, business, retail and entertainment facilities.

Historical development of transport

Using transport to travel for purposes of trade, religion, leisure and to fight in battles goes far back in history, from pre-Egyptian times and the beginning of the Greek civilisation. The Romans were great travellers, building an extensive road network across all parts of the Roman Empire. From the middle of the 17th century, young gentlemen of the aristocracy travelled to the capital cities of Europe as part of the 'Grand Tour', to broaden their education and experiences of life. Travel to spa towns became popular in the 17th and 18th centuries with visitors experiencing the healing power of their spa waters.

The development of rail transport from 1830 onwards was to have a far-reaching effect on travel for business and leisure purposes. Thomas Cook organised his first excursion by train on 5 July 1841, taking a group of 500 Temperance Association members from Leicester to Loughborough for a meeting. During the next three summers he arranged a succession of trips between Leicester, Nottingham, Derby and Birmingham. Rail travel in steam-driven locomotives also played a very significant role in the growth of seaside resorts around the UK coast.

Steam also played an important part in the development of long-distance travel by boat. In the 1880s, the Orient Line and North of Scotland Company, both later to be taken over by P&O, pioneered modern-style cruises and in 1904 P&O offered its first cruise holiday programme, arranged by Thomas Cook. The tour used the liner *Rome*, renaming her *Vectis* in her new role as a 'cruising yacht'.

The development of the car in the 20th century began to give people greater freedom to explore the coast and countryside, while the introduction of passenger services in jet aircraft after World War Two was to stimulate the rapid growth of the 'mass tourism' that exists around the world today. The following sections of this unit investigate how different modes of transport evolved in days gone by.

Unit 14

evolution of modes

Air transport

International air transport grew at double-digit rates from its earliest post-World War Two days until the first oil crisis in 1973. Much of the impetus for this growth came from technical innovation. The introduction of turbo-propeller aircraft in the early 1950s, trans-Atlantic jets in 1958, wide-bodied aircraft and high by-pass engines in 1970, and advanced avionics were the main innovations. They resulted in higher speeds, bigger aircraft, better unit cost control and, as a result, lower fares for passengers. Combined with increased real incomes and more leisure time, the effect was an explosion in demand for air travel.

The rapid growth in international tourism since the end of the Second World War has been closely allied to the expansion of air travel services. Advances in aircraft technology have led to increases in aircraft capacity and the development of aircraft with a far greater flying range. These two factors, coupled with increased demand for air travel generally, have enabled airlines to reduce prices and provide the stimulus for the growth of scheduled services and package holidays to all parts of the world. Allied to the growth in air services has been the rapid expansion of the associated infrastructure needed to cope with business and leisure tourists as well as freight traffic, including airports, terminals and runways. London-Heathrow alone handles more than 65 million passengers per year and is one of the world's busiest airports.

The Boeing 747 'jumbo jet' was introduced in 1970
(courtesy
Boeing Corporation)

Rail transport

From the mid-18th century onwards, railways were the dominant type of mass transportation in the UK and many industrialised nations. However, the rise in car ownership of the early twentieth century and the later introduction of air travel services from the 1950s onwards, reduced the numbers of people travelling by train for leisure and business purposes. It is true that passenger and freight rail transport still has an important role to play in some developed nations and is the principal form of long-distance travel for people living in the developing countries of the world. In western societies, travel by rail still occupies a small

Unit 14

share of most country's domestic tourism transport statistics. From an international tourism viewpoint, rail travel finds itself unable to compete with other travel types for the mass movement of tourists to their holiday destinations.

The general fall in demand for tourist travel by rail is not just a consequence of the rise in popularity of the private car and the introduction of travel by air. It is also a function of government approaches to rail travel, which vary considerably in different regions of the world. If we compare rail travel in the United Kingdom and France, for example, we see a UK rail transport network that has suffered from insufficient investment in rolling stock, signalling and track upgrading for many years. As such, demand for tourist travel by rail has fallen sharply since the 1950s, although there is some evidence of an upward turn in recent years. The French government, on the other hand, has invested considerable public funds in the rail system, with its 'flagship' TGV (train de grande vitesse) network offering a high-speed service across the country. The French rail system is used extensively for tourist travel and the TGV is regarded as a viable alternative to domestic air services for business travel within the country. A similar situation exists in Japan, where the so-called 'bullet' trains link major centres of population. One notable exception to the poorly-developed UK rail network is the Eurostar service linking London with Paris, Lille, Brussels and other major European cities via the Channel Tunnel, offering a high-speed service to business and leisure travellers. When the high-speed rail link from London to the Channel Tunnel is completed in 2007, journey times will be reduced even further. The European Union has recently agreed plans to develop an integrated transport network throughout the continent by the year 2010, including a trans-European rail network. Rail links to airports are also growing in popularity, allowing travellers to leave their cars at home.

WEBLINK

www.eurostar.com

*Check out this website
for more information on
Eurostar services.*

Eurostar at Waterloo

Despite the best efforts of countries such as France, international tourist travel by rail has become a 'niche market' product, serving the needs of two particular categories of travellers, namely young people travelling on cheap discount tickets often over a long period of time and older people who can afford the luxury of nostalgic trips on the great railway journeys of the world, for example the Venice-Simplon Orient Express, the trans-Siberian route and tourist trains operating in the North American Rocky Mountains.

Sea transport

In the same way that rail transport was the dominant mode of surface travel up to the time of the rapid growth in car ownership and the introduction of air travel services, so the ocean-going liners were the most popular form of sea transport for long-distance international travel up to the middle of the 20th century. Passenger shipping services suffered badly when air travel services were introduced from the 1950s onwards. Companies such as P&O, Union-Castle Line and Cunard withdrew their services to the USA, South Africa and the Far East; such routes were to be serviced by the more accessible and affordable scheduled air travel services.

The demise of the ocean-going liners forced the passenger shipping industry to diversify into cruise shipping. Today, cruising is growing in popularity, with the Caribbean, Florida, the Mediterranean, the Baltic, the Far East and Australasia among the principal cruise destinations of the world. Paradoxically, the introduction of the very same air services that signalled the demise of the international passenger shipping industry has boosted cruising, with the development of the fly-cruise holiday, where tourists combine a charter or scheduled flight to and/or from a port with their sea cruise. Whereas in the past cruising tended to be the preserve of rich and famous senior citizens, today's cruising industry has products geared to all ages and budgets. The arrival of mass market tour operators and new generation vessels onto the cruising scene has heralded a new era of packaged cruises at bargain basement prices.

Road transport

The road transport element within the transport sector of tourism includes travel by private car, bus and coach, taxi, hired car and bicycle. The private car has grown into the world's dominant form of travel for tourist purposes, especially for domestic tourism and intra-continental travel. The number of private cars on Britain's roads has increased sharply from just 2 million in 1950 to 25 million in 2003, and continues to grow. The government is keen to reduce the impact of cars on the environment, as discussed in its recent White Paper.

ACTIVITY

In July 2004, the UK government launched the *Future of Transport White Paper*, a long-term strategy for a modern, efficient and sustainable transport system over the next 15 years. The strategy looks at the factors that will shape travel and transport in the near future and sets out how the government will respond to the increasing demand for travel, maximising the benefits of transport while minimising the negative impacts on people and the environment.

Carry out some research and write a short newspaper article on the key points in the White Paper concerning travel by road, rail, sea and air travel, plus the recommendations for encouraging more walking and cycling. You may like to start your research at the Department for Transport website www.dft.gov.uk where there is an executive summary of the White Paper.

This activity is designed to provide evidence for P1.

Unit 14

③ **Relationship between transport and tourism**

From the construction of the first road networks in Roman times, the introduction of the railways in the mid-19th century, the growth of private motoring throughout the 20th century to the development of jet aircraft from the 1950s onwards, the growth of the travel and tourism industry has been closely linked to developments in transport. The provision of safe, reliable, comfortable, fast, convenient and accessible modes of transport, plus an adequate transport infrastructure, is a vital prerequisite for successful tourism development, whether in the UK or any overseas country.

One of the problems concerning the relationship between transport and tourism is that many of the places that tourists want to visit are often the most inaccessible, e.g. picturesque mountain areas, quaint fishing villages and out-of-the-way towns and villages. Places like these are not well-served by public transport, forcing visitors to use their cars if they want to visit. More than seven out of every ten tourist trips taken by British people in the UK are by car. For most destinations, the perfect compromise between transport and tourism is to have a range of good road and rail links to the area, plus alternatives to the car once people have arrived, such as park-and-ride schemes, cycle hire and minibus services.

④ **Social benefits**

The development of the UK transport system over the last 150 years has created a variety of social benefits for people travelling on holidays, short breaks and day visits, including:

- Increased mobility – people now have greater freedom to explore town and country areas on public transport and in their private cars. However, figures from the Department for Transport indicate that nearly 30 per cent of the UK population do not own or have access to a car, relying instead on public transport;
- Equality – falling real prices of travel and cars have opened up transport opportunities to people from all income levels, religious backgrounds and ethnic origins, whether living in urban or rural areas. People with mobility problems have benefited from the greater freedom offered by the private car and improving facilities on public transport services;
- Enhanced holiday/leisure experience – developments in transport have played a crucial role in the development of a travel and tourism industry that is responsive to customer needs, provides a wide range of products and services to destinations throughout the world, and enhances people's quality of life.

⑤ **Geographical dimensions**

Developments in a variety of transport modes have given tourists the opportunity of travelling quickly to faraway places at a relatively low cost in comparative safety. New locations and destinations have been opened up for tourism, particularly since the introduction of jet aircraft and the dramatic growth in the popularity of package holidays since the 1970s onwards. However, the development of transport has contributed to often inappropriate tourism development around the world, lacking respect for the environment, culture and people of overseas destinations. Different types of transport are also criticised for their harmful environmental impacts, for example emissions from aircraft and cars. Just as the travel and tourism industry must work towards greater sustainability, so too must the transport sector on which it relies so heavily.

Transport opens up faraway destinations
(courtesy InterContinental Hotels)

Transport developments have also played an important part in the 'globalisation' of the world, i.e. the move away from local and national trade to an economy that spans the whole of the world. Globalisation is driven by technology and is an important issue in the travel and tourism industry, where companies such as airlines, car hire firms and hotel groups try to gain an advantage over their competitors by operating at a global level. Many of the larger transport companies enter into alliances and partnerships with other companies or governments, e.g. airline alliances such as Star, Oneworld and Skyteam (see page 12 unit 8).

⑥ Economic issues

Economic issues to do with investment and jobs have always been at the forefront of transport developments. Entrepreneurs such as Thomas Cook, Samuel Cunard, Harold Bamberg of Eagle Airways, Freddie Laker of Skytrain (the first trans-Atlantic low-cost airline) and Richard Branson of Virgin, have invested heavily in transport services that have been used by millions of tourists. Transport is the lifeblood of the travel and tourism industry, helping to create thousands of service jobs in the UK and in tourist destinations across the globe. Transport has allowed destinations to develop their travel and tourism potential to the full, stimulating investment in airports, hotels, tourist attractions, travel agencies, tour operators, restaurants, night clubs, etc. In developing countries, the money generated from tourism is used to improve the livelihoods of local people, through investment in health care, education, water supplies and sanitation equipment. In the UK, transport, like tourism, is an important part of economic development, particularly in regions of the country that have suffered from the decline of industries such as mining, ship building and textiles.

Unit 14

(7)

Transport regulation

WEBLINK

www.caa.co.uk;
www.hse.gov.uk;
www.rail-reg.gov.uk;
www.dft.gov.uk;
www.mcga.gov.uk

Check out these websites for more information on the work of the Civil Aviation Authority, Health and Safety Executive, Office of Rail Regulation, Department for Transport and the Maritime and Coastguard Agency.

There are legal obligations on all passenger transport operators to provide safe and secure travel for their paying passengers and staff. This applies to all types of air, road, rail and sea transport:

- Air transport – the Civil Aviation Authority (CAA) is the UK's independent aviation regulator, with all civil aviation regulatory functions – economic regulation, policy on airspace, regulation of safety and consumer protection for air travellers. The Health and Safety Executive (HSE) is responsible for all aspects of safety on the ground at airports and has some responsibility for aircraft safety while airborne, for which it works in partnership with the CAA;
- Road transport – the Department for Transport (DfT) takes the lead on all matters relating to road safety. Working with other agencies, such as the HSE, it offers advice and regulates operators;
- Rail transport – the Office of Rail Regulation (ORR) is a government agency that provides economic regulation of the monopoly and dominant elements of the rail industry. This includes determining the level, structure and profile of charges levied by Network Rail and regulating its operation of the rail network. HSE is the regulatory authority for health and safety on the railways;
- Sea transport – the Maritime and Coastguard Agency (MCA) is responsible for implementing the government's maritime safety policy throughout the UK, including checks on passenger ferries and cruise ships to make sure they meet UK and international safety rules.

Unit 14

SECTION 2: MODES AND FEATURES OF PASSENGER TRANSPORT

The popularity of different modes of transport changes over time, in response to new developments in technology, government priorities and customer demand. Figure 14.1 gives an indication of how the demand for different types of transport for tourism has changed since 1951 in the UK. It shows that holiday trips by car have increased dramatically from 28 per cent in 1951 to 71 per cent in 2004. Both rail and coach/bus tourist trips have decreased over the same time period, although rail travel has begun to show an upturn in popularity in recent years.

Year	Car (%)	Train (%)	Coach/bus (%)
1951	28	48	28
1961	49	28	23
1971	63	10	17
1981	72	12	12
1991	78	6	12
1998	71	7	14
2004	71	13	6

Fig.14.1 Modes of transport used for holiday travel in the UK 1951-2004

Source: adapted from VisitBritain data

The UK government is committed to an integrated transport industry that offers a full range of reliable and efficient choices for people when making their travel decisions. In its *Future of Transport White Paper* published in 2004, the government agreed to the following objectives:

1. The road network – providing a more reliable and free-flowing service for both personal travel and freight, with people being able to make informed choices about how and when they travel;

2. The rail network – providing a fast, reliable and efficient service, particularly for inter-urban journeys and commuting into large urban areas;

3. Making walking and cycling real alternatives for local trips;

4. Providing improved international and domestic links at ports and airports.

Transport modes

In this section we look in detail at a variety of land, water-based and air travel services, starting with rail transport.

Rail transport

For one hundred years since its introduction in the mid-19th century rail transport was the most popular mode of travel for business and leisure in the UK. However, the rise in car ownership and development of air travel in the 20th century have had a marked impact on the demand for rail travel, which in 2004 accounted for just 13 per cent of all tourist travel in the UK. Train travel is, however, increasing in popularity as the government invests more than £60 billion over the next 10 years to develop a bigger, better and safer rail system.

Figures from the Association of Train Operating Companies (ATOC) indicate that around 1.05 billion passenger journeys were made on the UK rail network in 2004 – more than in any year since 1959.

As well as the network rail services there are a number of 'niche' rail products developed specifically for tourists. These include the many restored steam railways in the UK and luxury rail services such as the Orient Express.

Rail travel is increasing in popularity
(courtesy ATOC/Hull Trains)

Structure of the UK rail industry

The government, through the Department for Transport (DfT), sets the overall UK railway policy within the wider transport context, including travel by road, rail and water. The DfT works with three key public bodies in achieving its aims:

1. The Strategic Rail Authority (SRA) – is the strategic planning and co-ordinating body for the rail industry and the guardian of the interests of rail passengers. It acts as an important purchaser of train services and railway infrastructure. Its task is to provide a clear, strategic direction for rail transport in Britain, to promote rail passenger and freight transport and to encourage private investment in the rail industry;

2. The Health and Safety Executive (HSE) – is responsible for all aspects of health and safety on the railways;

3. The Office of Rail Regulation (ORR) – is independent of government and its function is to provide economic regulation of the monopoly and dominant elements of the rail industry. This includes determining the level, structure and profile of charges levied by Network Rail (which operates the infrastructure) and regulating its stewardship of the national rail network.

In Britain today, the provision of the rail network and rail services is a joint effort by several companies:

- Network Rail – is the operator of Britain's railway infrastructure, which includes 21,000 miles of track, 1,000 signal boxes, 40,000 bridges and tunnels, 9,000 level crossings and more than 2,500 stations. It operates the main passenger terminals, such as Edinburgh Waverley, London Waterloo and King's Cross. All other stations are

Unit 14

WEBLINK

www.atoc.org

Check out this website for more information on the train operating companies (TOCs) and the work of ATOC.

leased to the main train operating company using the station. Network Rail's task is to deliver a reliable and safe rail network;

- Train operating companies (TOCs) – are private companies that run the passenger train services in the UK. Currently, there are 26 TOCs, including Arriva Trains Wales, Hull Trains and Gatwick Express.

All the TOCs are members of the Association of Train Operating Companies (ATOC), which was set up by the train operators formed during the privatisation of the railways under the Railways Act of 1993. As well as being the official voice of the rail passenger industry, ATOC provides its members with a range of services that enable them to comply with conditions laid on them in their franchise agreements and operating licences.

ACTIVITY

Carry out some research into two of the train operating companies (TOCs) and find out what facilities and services they provide for their rail passengers, including regularity of services, costs of typical journeys, concessionary fares, customer service facilities, comfort and accessibility.

This activity is designed to provide evidence for P2.

Road transport

Road transport for tourism includes travel by private car, bus and coach, taxi, hired car, bicycle and even rickshaw! An increasing proportion of journeys in the UK are taken by car – up from 79 per cent of the total distance travelled in 1980 to 85 per cent in 2002. We saw earlier in this unit that travel by private car accounts for more than 70 per cent of all tourist trips taken in Britain. Cars offer a degree of flexibility, freedom, comfort and convenience that other forms of transport find hard to match. The shift towards car journeys has provided huge benefits for many people, opening up new opportunities at work and during leisure time. Part of the reason for the increase in car use in Britain is that cars are more affordable as people become better off. Improvements in production techniques and improved fuel efficiency have contributed to a fall in the relative cost of motoring and so have brought cars within reach of a far wider range of the population.

People choose their car for many tourist trips because it allows them to travel direct from one place to another in comfort. Cars can also get to places that are not always accessible by public transport services. Cars do, however, have considerable impacts on the environment and communities, leading to problems of pollution, physical erosion, loss of land to car parks and congestion in many popular tourist destinations, especially historic cities, coastal resorts and National Parks, where vehicles often spoil the very ambience that

Unit 14

WEBLINK

www.nationalexpress.com

Check out this website for more information on the National Express network and services.

attracted the tourists in the first place. Central and local governments are attempting to minimise the impact of vehicles by introducing a variety of techniques, including public transport initiatives, road pricing and pedestrianisation. The government expects to see further growth in car ownership and use over the next 30 years. The car provides many benefits, but the challenge for the government is to ensure that people have other options, including good quality public transport and the opportunity to walk or cycle.

Travel by coach is an altogether more environmentally friendly form of tourist travel than the car, transporting large numbers of tourists on scheduled services, on transfer journeys or forming the transport element of a package holiday, for example a coach holiday in the Scottish Highlands. National Express is the largest, scheduled coach service provider in Europe, with a network of services linking 1200 destinations throughout the UK and carrying 16 million passengers every year.

CASE STUDY – Stagecoach

Introduction

With its headquarters in Perth, Scotland, Stagecoach Group plc is a leading international transport group, operating bus, train, tram, express coach and ferry services in the UK, North America and New Zealand. The Group's profit in 2004 was £120 million on a turnover of more than £1.6 billion. Stagecoach employs 30,000 staff, operates 13,000 vehicles and provides services to more than 2.5 million passengers every day.

Stagecoach divisions

The Group's operations are divided into four divisions:

1. UK bus;
2. North America;
3. New Zealand;
4. Rail.

UK bus operations

Stagecoach owns 17 regional companies running more than 7,000 vehicles and covering around 100 towns and cities in the UK, including Liverpool, Manchester, Newcastle and London. The company has a 16 per cent share of the UK bus market and carries approximately 2 million passengers every day. Stagecoach also operates megabus.com, an online, inter-city coach service based on the low-cost airlines model. More than 2.6 million passengers have travelled with megabus since the first trial route was launched in August 2003 and a national network went live in March 2004.

North American operations

Stagecoach is a major provider of transport services in North America, employing around 4,400 people and operating a fleet of 2,800 coaches. Its businesses are focused on commuter services, but also include tour and charter, sightseeing and school bus operations.

New Zealand operations

Stagecoach is the largest provider of scheduled bus services in New Zealand, with a fleet of 1,000 buses based around Auckland and Wellington. The company also runs Fullers Ferries, which operates services in the Waitemata Harbour and Hauraki Gulf off Auckland.

UK rail operations

Stagecoach has two wholly-owned UK rail franchises – South West Trains (the largest franchise in the UK) and Island Line on the Isle of Wight. It also has a joint venture with the Virgin Rail Group operating two long-distance franchises – West Coast Main Line and Cross Country. Altogether, it has a 25 per cent share of the UK rail market. Stagecoach also operates the Sheffield Supertram system, comprising three light-rail routes across the city and into the suburbs.

Partnerships

Stagecoach works in partnership with a range of stakeholders at local and national levels to improve the quality of bus and coach provision. These include:

* Investors and the financial community – essential to the long-term investment in the Group's operations;
* Customers – the Group carries out extensive market research to help improve its services to the travelling public;
* Customer interest groups – the Group's businesses have a regular and ongoing dialogue with bus and rail user groups;
* Government – senior executives liaise with national and local governments on all matters relating to passenger transport operations;

- Transport authorities – Stagecoach works closely with local authorities and Passenger Transport Executives (PTEs) in the planning and delivery of bus, coach and rail services;
- Government advisory bodies and lobbying groups – the Group has constructive meetings with organisations such as the Commission for Integrated Transport, which provides advice to the UK government, and campaigning groups such as Transport 2000;
- Staff – in addition to one-to-one dialogue with its employees, Stagecoach works in partnership with trade unions on a range of issues, such as pensions, health and safety, training and pay rates;
- Suppliers – Stagecoach relies on a range of suppliers to provide products and services related to its bus, coach and rail operations.

WEBLINK

www.stagecoachgroup.com

Check out this website to help answer the questions in this case study and for more information on Stagecoach.

CASE STUDY QUESTIONS

1. What are the benefits and challenges associated with having transport operations in three different parts of the world?
2. The Group's annual report mentions 'corporate social responsibility'. What exactly is this and what activities does Stagecoach get involved with in this area?
3. What does Stagecoach do to help protect the environment?
4. How can companies such as Stagecoach help the government achieve its aim of reducing car use amongst the public?

Megabus is operated by Stagecoach

Air transport

Air transport is a major UK industry, currently carrying 200 million passengers per year. The government expects this number to double by 2020 and has outlined its plans for airport expansion to deal with this growth in the *Future of Air Transport White Paper* published in December 2003. The document includes the following key facts on the scale and importance of air transport in the UK:

- Passenger numbers – 32 million at UK airports in 1970, 189 million in 2002, and between 350 – 460 million forecast for 2020;
- Fifty per cent of the UK population flew at least once in 2001;
- Air transport movements at UK airports – 607,000 in 1970, over 2 million in 2002;
- 70 per cent of all visits made to the UK in 2002 by overseas residents were made by air, compared with 60 per cent in 1980;
- 40 percent of all passengers between Europe and North America fly to/from the UK;
- 20 per cent of international passengers start or finish their journey at UK airports;
- In 2002 there were 48 UK airlines operating a total fleet of 903 aircraft.

The White Paper also stresses the economic importance of air transport with the following facts:

- In 2001 air transport contributed £13 billion to the UK economy (2 per cent of total GDP);
- The aviation industry exported £7 billion of services in 2002;
- The UK air transport sector directly employs about 200,000 people;
- An estimated 600,000 jobs in the UK depend indirectly on the air transport industry, e.g. jobs in the energy sector generated by purchases of airline fuel, in the aerospace sector by airline purchases of equipment, in travel agencies and tour operators.

Air transport services

For statistical purposes, the International Air Transport Association (IATA) classifies air travel services into one of three categories, as follows:

- Domestic;
- International scheduled;
- International chartered;

Domestic services refer to air travel within a country, while international represents travel between different countries. Scheduled services are those that operate to a published timetable, on defined routes and under government licence. These services run regardless of the number of passengers and are used primarily by business travellers who are prepared to pay a premium for the extra convenience and flexibility offered. Many governments still fund their national airlines, for example Air France, although there is a general move away from state ownership towards private sector operation. One notable success story of recent years has been the rapid growth in one particular sector of the airline business, namely budget, low-cost or 'no frills' airlines, which sell direct to the public and offer scheduled services on domestic and international routes at low prices.

Unit **14**

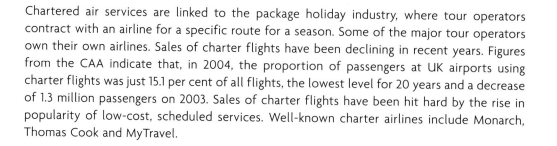

Chartered air services are linked to the package holiday industry, where tour operators contract with an airline for a specific route for a season. Some of the major tour operators own their own airlines. Sales of charter flights have been declining in recent years. Figures from the CAA indicate that, in 2004, the proportion of passengers at UK airports using charter flights was just 15.1 per cent of all flights, the lowest level for 20 years and a decrease of 1.3 million passengers on 2003. Sales of charter flights have been hit hard by the rise in popularity of low-cost, scheduled services. Well-known charter airlines include Monarch, Thomas Cook and MyTravel.

ACTIVITY

Carry out some research into a UK scheduled airline and compile a fact sheet on the company that includes details of its structure, products and services, facilities offered on board, services for passengers with special needs and different levels of service offered.

This activity is designed to provide evidence for P2.

Glasgow airport *(courtesy BAA/Glasgow Airport)*

Airports and airport infrastructure

Most airports in the UK serve local demand, generally from within their own region. However, larger airports such as Manchester, Birmingham and a number of those in the south east of England also attract passengers from a wider area. These airports provide services to more destinations, some of which would not be viable from smaller airports, and also offer more frequent services.

The major London airports (Heathrow, Gatwick, Stansted) play a dual role. Around 80 per cent of their passenger traffic has an origin or destination in London, the south east or the east of England. These regions have a very high level of demand for air travel, amounting to nearly half of total UK demand. This enables airlines to offer a very wide range of destinations from the London airports, with frequent services and one or more competing airlines on most routes. As a result, Heathrow, Gatwick and increasingly Stansted fulfil a national as well as regional role. Many travellers from other parts of the UK fly to one of these London airports in order to catch connecting flights and passengers from Wales, the midlands and parts of the south west of England travel by road or rail to the major London airports. The demand for passenger air travel is growing fastest outside the south east of England and this trend is expected to continue. As a result, airlines should be able to offer direct services to more destinations from a wider range of airports. The recent growth in popularity of the low-cost airlines has stimulated demand for air travel across the country, but has been a particularly important factor in the development of many regional airports, such as Bournemouth, Exeter and Liverpool.

As well as scheduled and charter services, air transport also includes helicopter flights and transfers, private jet hire and even flights in balloons!

Virgin balloon

Sea transport

Sea transport for tourism includes travel by ferry, cruise ship, water taxis and a variety of pleasure craft.

Ferries

In many parts of the world, ferries offer inexpensive and reliable services on short sea crossings. Places as diverse as the Greek islands, Hong Kong harbour, the Scottish Highlands and Islands, the Adriatic Sea and the Baltic coastline all rely on ferry services for everyday travel and tourist business. In places where there is strong competition between ferry operators, such as on the short sea crossings in the English Channel, there have been considerable advances in vessel technology, with the introduction of hydrofoils and jet-foils to compete with the fast, new generation of passenger ships. The opening of the Channel Tunnel in 1994 increased competition on cross-Channel services still further. In addition to operating the faster vessels, ferry companies have responded to this challenge by offering price reductions, enhanced levels of customer service and greater on-board shopping and entertainment facilities on their services. The main ferry operators in UK waters are:

- Short-sea Channel routes – P&O Ferries, Hoverspeed, Speed Ferries, Sea France and Norfolk Line;
- Western Channel – P&O Ferries, Brittany Ferries, Condor Ferries, Wightlink;
- North Sea – P&O Ferries, DFDS Seaways, Fjord Line, Superfast Ferries and Stena Line;
- Irish Sea – Stena line, Swansea Cork Ferries, Irish Ferries, SeaCat Scotland and Isle of Man Steam Packet;
- Scottish Islands – North Link Ferries and Caledonian MacBrayne.

Unit 14

ACTIVITY

Choose three of the ferry operators named above and find information on the services they operate, facilities provided on board and at terminals, costs of a typical return journey and additional products they sell, e.g. mini cruises, short breaks, holidays, etc.

This activity is designed to provide evidence for P2.

Cruise ships

The cruise sector of the travel and tourism industry is going through a period of rapid growth and change. In the past, cruising was seen as the preserve of the elderly, rich and famous. Today the number of cruise passengers is growing steadily and the sector has introduced products geared to a wide range of customers, including families, young people and groups. Prices for some cruise products have fallen as the major tour operators have entered the market. For the first time in 2003, more than one million British people took a cruise of one sort or another, according to figures from the Passenger Shipping Association (PSA), the trade body representing passenger shipping interests in the UK (see case study on page 46).

Although the UK population is ageing, with an increasing proportion of over-50s compared to under-30s, the average age of cruise passengers continues to fall. This is partly due to the increased numbers of families with children now being attracted to cruising. It is also a reflection of the younger people being attracted to the sector by the new, informal and activity-orientated brands, such as Ocean Village, Island Cruises and easyCruise, all of which are planning to expand their operations over the next two years. All of these factors combine to paint a picture of a changing profile of customers that are attracted to cruising. In short, cruise passengers are:

- Younger than in the past;
- Interested in activities while on board ship and on shore;
- Looking for short cruises as well as extended journeys;
- Interested in travelling with families and friends;
- Looking for adventure.

Cruise companies are increasingly 'segmenting the market', i.e. developing cruise products and services to meet the needs of individual segments of the market, for example families, singles and younger passengers.

Water taxis and pleasure craft

Water taxis are commonplace in the Mediterranean, especially in the Greek Islands. Their potential is yet to be fully exploited in the UK, although there are services offered on the Thames in London and in a small number of coastal locations, e.g. Falmouth in Cornwall and in the Scottish islands. Pleasure craft are not only found at sea but also on inland waterways, e.g. canals and reservoirs.

Features of passenger transport

Passengers consider a variety of features when deciding which type of transport to choose or which particular company to travel with, including:

- Regularity;
- Timetables;
- Cost;
- Level and types of services provided;
- Facilities provided (on board and at terminals);
- Accessibility and practicality;
- Speed;
- Comfort and convenience;
- Customer preferences.

Regularity

We would all like our transport services to be as regular as possible, whether on holiday or travelling closer to home. How regularly a service operates is usually related to demand – the greater the demand, the more services are provided to satisfy the demand, e.g. busy, city railway stations and airport terminals are able to offer more regular services to passengers than more remote, regional stations and airports. Transport services in rural and countryside areas are often subsidised by the government in order to be able to provide a regular service to local people and tourists to the area.

Timetables

All transport operators publish details of their services as timetables or schedules. These are available in printed form for convenience while travelling and many are also available to view online or download from the Internet. Timetables are usually drawn up to allow time for transfers between different services or between different modes of transport, e.g. an express coach operator may timetable a service to arrive at a train station in good time to

Unit 14

meet an incoming service. The government and local councils often provide finance for the production of timetables as part of their policy of encouraging greater use of public transport services.

ACTIVITY

Familiarise yourself with the National Rail Timetable and, working with another member of your group, use it to work out a selection of journeys you may be taking (or would like to take) in the coming months.

This activity is designed to provide evidence for P2.

Cost

For many people, cost is the most important consideration when using transport. People travelling on a tight budget will look for the cheapest fares possible, even if it means travelling through the night, leaving very early in the morning or arriving home from a journey very late at night. Transport operators of all kinds use variable pricing to maximise their revenue, i.e. they charge the highest prices at periods of peak demand and offer reduced off-peak rates to stimulate demand. They also offer concessionary fares to different groups of passengers, e.g. children, students, groups, over 50s, senior citizens, etc., which may be via a discount card of one sort or another. Most transport companies give discounts for tickets purchased in advance of a journey – the greater the time between booking and travel, the bigger the discount. This makes sense for the company since they receive revenue earlier than would otherwise have been the case, thereby helping their cash flow.

Level and types of services provided

All transport operators strive to provide a good standard of service to their passengers. Some offer different levels of service, which is reflected in the price paid by the customer, e.g. first or business class travel on an aircraft or train, a luxury cabin on a cruise ship or an upgraded lounge area on a ferry. Customers who are willing and able to pay extra benefit from more personal attention and extra services, such as complimentary drinks, express check-in or priority attention.

Unit 14

Facilities provided

Extra investment in transport services by the government and private sector companies is helping to improve facilities for the travelling public, both on board and at terminals. Customers' expectations are rising all the time and transport operators must respond by providing facilities that people want, whether it is 24/7 online booking, wireless Internet technology at passenger terminals or extra comfort while travelling.

Bureau de change at Stansted Airport

Accessibility and practicality

All transport operators try to provide access to their services and facilities for all sections of the community, especially people with disabilities. At the time of writing, the government is carrying out a consultation exercise on whether or not the exemption of transport operators from some of the requirements of the Disability Discrimination Act should be lifted.

WEBLINK

www.atoc.org

Check out this website for more details of facilities for disabled people on trains.

FOCUS ON INDUSTRY – Rail travel for disabled people

Special arrangements can be made for disabled people to travel by train, including those who are:

- Permanent wheelchair users;
- In need of wheelchair assistance;
- Registered blind or partially-sighted;
- Disabled Persons' Railcard holders;
- Registered deaf;
- Registered disabled.

For many years new facilities have been designed with disabled people in mind, for example level or ramped access to stations, induction loops at ticket office windows for hearing aid users, wheelchair-accessible toilets on stations and on trains, improved signage and audible messages, and spaces for wheelchairs on trains. Literature is also provided in alternative print formats for people with visual impairments. For those who need assistance during their journey, train companies can make arrangements to cover the entire journey, providing help with access to stations, wheelchair ramps for getting on and off trains or assistance in changing platforms. At stations with car parks there are designated parking spaces for disabled people close to the station entrance. Many of Britain's 2,500 railway stations have yet to be fully modernised and are, therefore, not completely accessible to wheelchair users or others who have difficulty in walking or using stairs.

Unit 14

Speed

Throughout history, developments in technology have enabled engineers to build faster means of transport to meet passengers' demands, from the earliest steam trains and ocean-going liners through to the high-speed rail services, fast ferries and jet aircraft of today. Speed must, of course, always be balanced against safety. Speed is not only important while actually travelling, but also when moving through terminals and transport interchanges, which must be designed to facilitate swift passenger flows.

Comfort and convenience

Comfort levels on board transport services and in terminals is an important consideration for all passengers, but especially older travellers and those with special needs. Increased levels of investment in public transport services and facilities in the UK are delivering enhanced levels of comfort and convenience across all modes of transport.

Customer preferences

Transport operators must respond continually to customer feedback and preferences in order to offer services and facilities that meet their needs. Regular monitoring of passengers' needs and expectations is an essential part of delivering high quality transport services.

ACTIVITY

Choose three of the different modes of transport discussed earlier in this section (rail travel, private car, coach travel, air travel, etc.) and produce a chart that gives details of the features of each mode of transport. Use the list of features discussed above on your chart – i.e. regularity, timetables, cost, level and types of services provided, facilities provided, accessibility and practicality, speed, comfort and convenience, and customer preferences.

This activity is designed to provide evidence for P2.

SECTION 3: ISSUES IN THE PASSENGER TRANSPORT ENVIRONMENT

This section explores the following key issues in passenger transport and how they impact on the UK travel and tourism industry:

- Deregulation;
- Budget airlines;
- New technology and e-tourism;
- New routes and terminals;
- Health, safety and security;
- Customer expectations.

P3 describe 2 issues
D2 Evaluate responce of industry to them.

Deregulation

Deregulation in transport is the withdrawal of government ownership or control of an enterprise or facility. It is perhaps most associated with airlines, which historically have been state-owned. Through a process of 'privatisation', many airlines and other transport companies are now operated in the private sector. Deregulation is intended to increase competition between carriers and ultimately produce better quality services and lower fares for passengers. The USA airline industry has been deregulated since 1978 and is a completely market-driven industry. Domestic traffic is almost completely deregulated, except for specific issues such as safety and security, but international traffic is governed by country-to-country agreements. Asia is the most regulated airline market in the world and is dominated by national flag carriers, i.e. state-owned or state-controlled airlines.

Historically, the European airline industry has been highly regulated. The European Union (EU) has introduced a series of measures since 1987 to allow greater freedom amongst EU airlines. This has led to a significant development in the numbers of low-cost airlines operating from regional airports across the EU. There is, however, some distortion in the European airline market since a number of state-owned airlines continue to benefit from state subsidies. Also, new airline companies sometimes find it difficult to get 'slots' at airports. Larger airlines, including British Airways, rationalise their loss-making routes by cutting destinations, using low-cost subsidiary carriers or franchising.

Deregulation of bus and coach travel, which took place in the USA in 1982 and in Britain under the Transport Act of 1985, has liberalised the market for travel and offered passengers a wide choice of operators. In the case of Europe, EU legislation allows a coach company from any member state of the EU to offer coach services in any other EU country.

Unit 14

WEBLINK

www.stagecoachgroup.com

Check out this website for more details of the Stagecoach group of companies.

FOCUS ON INDUSTRY – Stagecoach and deregulation

Stagecoach was one of the first companies to take advantage of transport deregulation in the UK in the 1980s and in the early years of the decade operated coach services in Scotland, as well as longer distance services to London. The Transport Act of 1985 deregulated bus services, which had previously been owned and operated by councils and local transport authorities. One of the early services launched by Stagecoach was Magicbus, which operated in Glasgow and offered cut-price fares to passengers. In the late 1980s, Stagecoach bought a number of former National Bus Company businesses, including Hampshire, Cumberland, United Counties, Ribble and Southdown. Stagecoach was one of the first major transport operators to expand overseas, buying the UTM bus company in Malawi.

Deregulation of the UK rail industry came with the privatisation of the railways under the Railways Act 1993. Following privatisation, the former British Rail was divided into two main elements, the first consisting of the national rail network (track, signalling, bridges, tunnels, stations and depots) with the second element being the train operating companies (TOCs) whose trains run on the network, e.g. Virgin Trains, GNER, South West Trains and First Great Western.

Budget airlines

Much of the growth in air travel discussed earlier in this unit is due in no small part to the popularity of budget, 'no frills' or low-cost airlines. There is little doubt that the introduction of low-cost airlines has revolutionised travel attitudes and habits. Research from Mintel estimated that the low-cost airline sector in Europe carried around 80 million passengers in 2004, of which over 60 million started or ended their journey at a UK airport. There are approximately 60 low-cost carriers operating within Europe, although the UK market is dominated by Ryanair and easyJet, which carried over 55 million passengers during 2004. Budget airlines currently have a 19 per cent share of the total European air travel market and this is predicted to rise to at least one-third by 2010.

New technology and e-tourism

New technology affects transport in a number of ways:

1. The means of transport itself – technology enables aircraft, trains, coaches, ferries, cruise liners, etc. to travel faster, more safely, more economically and with less harmful emissions;

Unit 14

2. The infrastructure that supports transport services – facilities such as ferry terminals, train stations and track, airport terminals, etc. benefit from new technology developments to provide a safe and efficient environment for passengers;

3. The sales and distribution of transport products – developments such as the Internet and mobile 'phone technology have revolutionised the way passengers make their travel arrangements. Low-cost airlines have led the way in doing away with paper tickets and using e-tickets instead. IATA (the International Air transport Association) has set a target of 100 per cent electronic ticketing across all airlines by the end of 2007.

New routes and terminals

We have seen earlier in this unit that the number of passengers travelling by air is predicted to double by 2020, while rail travel and cruising are steadily increasing in popularity. Transport operators respond to this increased demand by introducing new routes and working with the public sector to develop new terminals and transport infrastructure. There are often considerable objections from local people to developing new terminals. They are concerned about the impact on the environment and their quality of life. This is particularly the case with new airport developments, such as extra runways or new access roads.

ACTIVITY

Find out if there are any plans for major transport developments in your own area or at your nearest major airport. Write a newspaper article, putting the views for and against the developments.

This activity is designed to provide evidence for P3.

Health, safety and security

These are important issues for the transport sector, especially since the tragic events of September 11th 2001 and subsequent terrorist attacks around the world. Security at airports, railway stations, ferry terminals and cruise ports has increased noticeably. This sometimes results in delays for passengers, but most are happy to put up with a little inconvenience. Transport operators of all kinds must comply with stricter security guidelines when carrying out their business, which can sometimes lead to increased operating costs. Health scares and epidemics, such as foot and mouth disease, SARS and Asian bird 'flu, can also affect travel, with knock-on effects for transport providers.

[handwritten annotations in margins:]

recent examples Glasgow July 2007 – ram attack. foot n mouth 2007

D2 Response security by increased security at airports – cordons, police. hand luggage – restriction on liquids. Larger more thorough checks at security gates. increased level of x-raying: shops. cancelling flights in an emergency or re-routing. locking pilots cabin. thermal imaging to check for increased body temp (SARS). masks. announcements re unattended luggage

Unit 14

Customer expectations

The growth in the number of people using a variety of methods of transport has brought a sharper focus on passenger issues. Consumers in all sectors feel more empowered in expecting high levels of personal attention and customer service, and more confident in making complaints. Transport operators need to respond to this wider trend and with more elderly and mobility-impaired people travelling, the transport industry will need to continue to increase standards of passenger care. Training plays a vital role in helping staff to offer excellent standards of customer service to passengers.

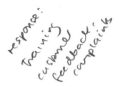

response:
Training
customer
feedback
complaints

Unit 14

SECTION 4: PASSENGER FLOWS

The growing popularity of many types of transport services means that managing passenger flows is becoming a serious issue for all transport operators, from the point of view of safety and security, as well as providing a pleasant and efficient experience for passengers.

Types of passenger flows

There are a number of locations where the flow of passengers must be managed by transport operators, including:

Passengers in the main terminal building at Glasgow airport

- To and from the terminal;
- Within and between terminals;
- Embarkation and disembarkation.

Managing traffic flows is also an important part of transport management in major facilities such as airports and ferry terminals.

Issues in passenger flows

Large numbers of passengers in confined areas highlight a number of issues, including:

- Congestion and delays – passengers waiting to buy tickets, check-in their luggage, park their cars, board an aircraft, etc. can cause delays and frustration;
- Seasonality – passenger numbers on transport services and in facilities fluctuate depending on the time of year;
- Security – is now a serious issue for transport operators and agencies such as the Immigration Service and the police;
- Special needs – elderly, disabled passengers, people with young children, etc. all need special care and attention when using transport services and facilities;
- Facilities – such as toilets, car parking, refreshment areas, retail premises, etc. must be positioned so as to facilitate smooth passenger flows;
- Major events – such as sports matches and music festivals put extra strain on transport operators and the security services.

Unit 14

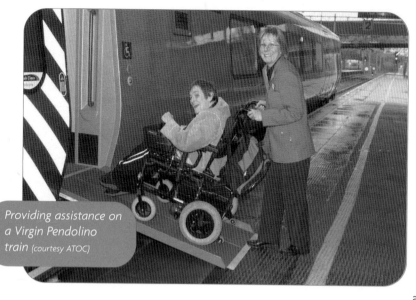

Providing assistance on a Virgin Pendolino train (courtesy ATOC)

Management of passenger flows

Transport operators have to be both proactive, i.e. making things happen, and reactive, i.e. responding to events, when managing passenger flows. Proactive management includes providing advance warning of events that could cause disruption to services or facilities, for example major engineering work on the railway or the closure of an airport terminal and transfer of passengers to another part of an airport. Charging systems, such as the Congestion Charge in London and fees for car parking, are another proactive management technique. Introducing cycle lanes, park-and-ride schemes, bus lanes and traffic-calming measures can all help to manage passenger flows effectively.

Reactive management of passenger flows involves keeping passengers informed of unforeseen events, such as a vehicle beakdown or security incident in a terminal, by making frequent announcements with news updates. In such circumstances it is usual for the transport operator to provide replacement services for passengers.

Bus lanes allow smooth passenger flows (courtesy Stagecoach)

Unit 14

WEBLINK

www.atoc.org

Check out this website for more details of information systems used by the rail industry.

FOCUS ON INDUSTRY – Keeping rail passengers informed

As more and more people are choosing to travel by train, the need for the railway industry to provide fast, accurate and impartial information is increasing. Train companies are using a range of communications technologies to provide access to information, both in advance of travel and during journeys. National Rail Enquiries handles more than 1 million telephone enquiries every week and also offers textphone and Welsh language services. Full timetable information is also provided on the Internet. Enquiries and bookings can be made from PCs and WAP-enabled mobile 'phones. Train operators are improving static information facilities at stations by providing new customer information systems and 'help points', which either generate information electronically or connect passengers directly to train control staff. Many stations benefit from 'real time' information and, on trains, the staff pass on the information they receive (via mobile 'phone, radio or pager) from signalling centres and control offices. New trains introduced onto the network have passenger information screens on board and audio messages to tell passengers which train they are on and to inform them as they approach each stop.

UNIT SUMMARY

This unit has examined the passenger transport sector and in particular its links with travel and tourism. This has involved exploring how different modes of transport have developed, the geographical dimensions of transport, economic issues and the role of regulatory bodies. You have investigated the structure of various modes of transport – land-based, sea and air – and found that factors such as new technology and increasing customer expectations are influencing how the transport industry is developing. You have found that travel by car is the most popular type of travel for tourism in the UK, but it does bring with it environmental and social impacts. A range of issues concerned with transport have been considered in details, for example deregulation, the growth of low-cost airlines, technology and health, safety and security. Finally, you have been introduced to the concept of passenger flows in transport, the major issues to do with flows and how they are managed by transport operators and facility managers. Throughout the unit you have been shown many industry examples, while the case study on the Stagecoach Group plc highlights key issues facing a company with interests in different types of travel in different parts of the world.

If you have worked methodically, by the end of this unit you should have:

- Examined the passenger transport environment;
- Investigated the features of different modes of passenger transport;

Unit 14

- Explored current issues affecting passenger transport operations;
- Examined how organisations manage passenger flows.

You are now in a position to complete the assignment for the unit, under the direction of your tutor. Before you tackle the assignment you may like to have a go at the following questions to help build your knowledge of passenger transport operations.

Test your knowledge

1. How has the development of the private car influenced travel for holidays and day visits?
2. What effect did the introduction of jet aircraft have on the development of international tourism?
3. Explain the relationship between transport and tourism.
4. Name three organisations that have responsibility for the regulation of transport in the UK.
5. Why do you think that rail travel for tourist trips is growing in popularity?
6. What is a train operating company (TOC) and which TOCs operate in your local area?
7. Explain the role of Network Rail in the UK rail industry.
8. What factors are contributing to the rapid growth in air travel in the UK?
9. Why is there increased demand for regional airports in the UK?
10. List five features that passengers consider when deciding which type of transport to choose.
11. How has deregulation affected different sectors of the transport industry?
12. Explain how new technology affects the transport sector.
13. What are the implications for transport operators of the increased measures needed to ensure health, safety and security in transport?
14. List and describe three key issues concerning passenger flows.
15. Giving examples, explain the difference between proactive and reactive management of passenger flows.

UNIT 14 ASSIGNMENT: Passenger transport operations

Introduction

This assignment is made up of a number of tasks which, when successfully completed, are designed to give you sufficient evidence to meet the Pass (P), Merit (M) and Distinction (D) grading criteria for the unit. If you have carried out the activities and read the case study in this unit, you will already have done a lot of work towards completing the tasks for this assignment.

Unit 14

Scenario

You have been lucky in finding a summer placement job working for one of the top travel trade newspapers in the country. You will be reporting to Mary Wright, the newspaper's transport correspondent. Mary is working on a feature on passenger transport for the next edition of the newspaper.

The feature is divided into four main areas:

1. The passenger transport environment;
2. Features of different modes of passenger transport;
3. Issues affecting the passenger transport environment;
4. Managing passenger flows.

Mary wants you to carry out some research for the feature and present the information to her as a series of Word documents that she can edit and incorporate into the feature, plus a presentation. She has asked you to complete the following four tasks.

Task 1

Your first document is a report in which you should:

(a) Describe the passenger transport environment;

(b) Analyse the effect of two specific issues concerned with the passenger transport environment.

These tasks are designed to produce evidence for P1 and M1.

Task 2

The document for this task should be presented as three case studies, in which you should:

(a) Describe the features of three different modes of passenger transport;

(b) Explain how the features of the three different modes of passenger transport selected for task 2 (a) affect their appeal;

(c) Analyse how passenger transport organisations have adapted features to meet passenger needs.

These tasks are designed to produce evidence for P2, M2 and D1.

Unit 14

Task 3

Produce a written report in which you should:

(a) Describe two issues affecting passenger transport operations;

(b) Evaluate the effectiveness of measures taken by passenger transport organisations to respond to issues that affect them.

These tasks are designed to produce evidence for P3 and D2.

Task 4

Prepare and deliver an illustrated presentation in which you should:

(a) Describe how passenger transport organisations manage passenger flows;

(b) Describe two issues affecting passenger flows, explaining how organisations respond to them.

These tasks are designed to produce evidence for P4 and M3.

Incoming and Domestic Tourism

INTRODUCTION TO THE UNIT

Much of the focus of the travel and tourism industry and media in the UK is about taking holidays abroad. However, incoming tourism (visitors coming to this country from abroad) and domestic tourism (British people taking holidays in their own country) are very important sectors of the travel and tourism industry. The 27.5 million overseas visitors who came to Britain in 2004 spent £13 billion, while British people taking holidays, day visits and short breaks at home contribute greatly to the economy by creating jobs and generating wealth.

In this unit you will learn about the needs and expectations of incoming and domestic tourists, highlighting the similarities and differences of each. You will also examine the popularity and appeal of the UK to both incoming and domestic tourists. In order to understand how tourism is managed, you will investigate the roles played by a range of organisations involved with UK incoming and domestic tourism, including government departments and agencies, voluntary bodies and the commercial sector. The unit concludes with an examination of heritage tourism in the UK, looking at different heritage attractions, their themes and status.

WHAT YOU WILL STUDY

During the course of this unit you will:

1. Differentiate between the **needs and expectations** of incoming and domestic tourists;
2. Examine the **popularity and appeal** of the UK to both incoming and domestic tourists;
3. Examine the role played by different **types of organisations** involved in incoming and domestic tourism;
4. Investigate **heritage tourism** within the UK.

You will be guided through the main topics in this unit with the help of the latest statistics, industry examples and case studies. You should also check out the weblinks throughout the unit for extra information on particular organisations or topic areas and use the activities to help you learn more.

ASSESSMENT FOR THIS UNIT

This unit is internally assessed, meaning that you will be given an assignment (or series of assignments) to complete by your tutor(s) to show that you have fully understood the content of the unit. A grading scale of pass, merit or distinction is used for all internally assessed units, with higher grades awarded to students who show greater depth in analysis and evaluation in their assignments. An assignment for this unit, which covers all the grading criteria, can be found on page 254. Don't forget to visit www.tandtONLine.co.uk for all the latest industry news, developments, statistics and tips to help you with your assignments.

Unit 15

SECTION 1: NEEDS AND EXPECTATIONS OF TOURISTS

This section concentrates on the needs and expectations of both domestic and incoming tourists, but begins by examining some key definitions of 'tourism', 'incoming tourism', 'domestic tourism' and 'outbound tourism'.

Definitions

The World Tourism Organisation (WTO), a specialist agency of the United Nations and recognised as the leading international body in international tourism, states that tourism comprises:

'...the activities of persons travelling to and staying in places outside their usual environment for not more than one consecutive year for leisure, business and other purposes'.

Probably the most widely accepted definition of tourism in use in the UK today is:

'Tourism is the temporary, short-term movement of people to destinations outside the places where they normally live and work, and activities during their stay at these destinations; it includes movement for all purposes, as well as day visits or excursions' (Tourism Society 1976).

WEBLINK

www.world-tourism.org
and
www.tourismsociety.org

Check out these websites for information on the work of the World Tourism Organisation and the Tourism Society.

Types of tourism

There are three main types of tourism:

1. Domestic tourism – this is when people take holidays, short breaks and day trips in their own country;
2. Incoming/inbound tourism – this is when people enter a country from their own country or another country which is not their home;
3. Outbound tourism – this is when people travel away from the country where they normally live.

Some examples illustrating the differences between the different types of tourism are given in Figure 15.1.

ACTIVITY

Working with a partner, list the particular needs of each of the tourists in the nine examples given in Figure 15.1. Discuss and record the major differences that you find between incoming and domestic tourists.

This activity is designed to provide evidence for P1.

Unit 15

TYPE OF TOURISM			
Reason for travel	Domestic	Incoming	Outbound
Leisure	A couple from Sheffield taking a short break in the Peak District	A family from France visiting the Edinburgh International Festival	A student from Macclesfield taking the Eurostar to Lille
VFR	A family from Hull on a day trip to visit relatives in Bridlington	A brother and sister from Taiwan visiting their friends in London	A student visiting her father in Belgium
Business	A salesman from Manchester making sales calls throughout Wales	An aircraft engineer from Toulouse visiting the BA offices in west London	Two researchers from Belfast flying to Tokyo for a conference

Fig. 15.1 Examples of incoming, domestic and outbound tourism

Fig. 15.2 Examples of visitor needs

WEBLINK

www.foodfestival.co.uk

Check out this website for more information on the Ludlow Food and Drink Festival.

Needs of the visitor

The following sections of this unit look in detail at visitor needs (shown in Figure 15.2), highlighting the special requirements of both domestic and incoming tourists.

Food and drink

As well as meeting tourists' basic needs for sustenance, food and drink plays an important role in a tourist's holiday experience – eating pasta while in Italy, paella in Spain or drinking whisky in Scotland or freshly-squeezed orange juice in Florida are examples of the important links between food and tourism. Countries and regions increasingly use images of food and drink to promote their destinations to visitors, as well as encouraging tourist businesses to offer local produce to their guests. Britain, for example, has a growing number of food festivals and farmers' markets that are not only popular with local people, but also domestic and incoming tourists, who appreciate the chance to sample local cuisine.

FOCUS ON INDUSTRY – The Ludlow Food and Drink Festival

The town of Ludlow in Shropshire was one of the first places in Britain to stage a food and drink festival back in 1995. The original twin aims of the festival were to promote the area's small food and drink producers, and encourage visitors to explore the town's shops, restaurants and pubs, thereby encouraging tourism and contributing to the local economy. The festival has grown into the UK's foremost event of its kind and visitor numbers have grown steadily since the first festival, reaching an all-time record in 2003 when 17,050 people entered Ludlow Castle during the three days. The festival is organised and operated almost entirely by volunteers, with any surplus funds being re-invested into the following year's event.

Unit 15

Transport

Tourists, whether domestic or incoming, need transport services and facilities that are convenient, safe, frequent, reliable and offer good value for money. This holds true whether visitors are on business, travelling for leisure or visiting friends and relatives. Figures from the Office of National Statistics indicate that incoming tourists to the UK in 2004 used the following types of transport to reach this country:

- Air   20 million visits;
- Sea   4.7 million visits;
- Channel Tunnel   2.99 million visits.

These figures indicate that nearly three-quarters of all overseas visitors to Britain arrive by air. Clearly, these travellers need a good network of routes and gateway airports, plus efficient transit arrangements to be able to move through airports speedily and make onward connections by air, road, rail or sea. Tourists coming to the UK from abroad may be less familiar than British people with our travel systems and ticketing arrangements, so staff need to be well-trained and systems need to be as user-friendly as possible for people whose first language may not be English.

The majority of British people travelling in this country on day visits, short breaks and long holidays use their cars rather than take public transport. Nearly three-quarters of all tourist trips are taken by car, while train travel and journeys by coach account for 12 per cent and 6 per cent respectively. Domestic air travel currently accounts for just 5 per cent of all tourist trips within the UK, but is the fastest-growing public transport sector, with low-cost airlines in particular offering new routes to more regional airports.

Travel by coach appeals to both incoming and domestic tourists

ACTIVITY

Log on to the following VisitBritain website and locate and name the airports on an outline map of the UK that you can download from www.tandtONLine.co.uk
www.visitbritain.com/VB3-fr-FR/Images/VB3%20Airports_tcm162-69924.pdf

Information

Access to information prior to taking a trip and while in a destination is vital to encourage incoming and domestic tourists to visit an area and to get the most out of their stay. The supply of tourist information on Britain for overseas visitors is co-ordinated by VisitBritain, the government-funded body responsible for marketing Britain to the rest of the world (and England to the British). It operates 23 information offices in 35 overseas markets around the world, distributing brochures and other publicity materials, maintaining websites and answering enquiries from potential travellers to Britain (see case study on page 237). The National Tourist Boards covering Wales, Scotland and Northern Ireland also promote their respective countries to incoming and domestic tourists.

Tourist information centres play a key role in servicing the needs of tourists while in their destination. Staff offer invaluable local advice on attractions, accommodation, events and transport services, as well as carrying out a range of revenue-earning activities such as selling guide books and making bookings on behalf of customers.

Quality assurance

Tourists, whether from the UK or overseas, expect high standards of service and excellent tourism facilities that are independently checked for quality. Up to now, there has been considerable confusion amongst domestic and incoming tourists about accommodation grading standards in the UK, since the National Tourist Boards have devised different schemes based on a variety of symbols, including diamonds, stars, keys and rosettes. There are also schemes offered by motoring organisations such as the AA and RAC to add to the confusion. From 2005-2006, however, VisitBritain is co-ordinating the use of common standards across all the systems currently used by the National Tourist Boards of England, Scotland and Wales, the AA and the RAC. This should result in a more user-friendly way for incoming and domestic tourists to gauge standards in serviced accommodation establishments.

In England, VisitBritain and its partners operate quality assurance schemes in a number of tourism sectors, including:

* Accommodation – hotels, guest accommodation, self-catering (including agencies), hostels, campus accommodation, camping and caravan parks, holiday centres, boats (broad and narrow) and hotel boats;
* Attractions – the Visitor Attraction Quality Assurance Service (VAQAS), operating in England and Wales, monitors factors at attractions that affect overall quality, and recommends improvements;
* Tourist information centres – those centres that wish to join the England TIC network must meet the network criteria;

WEBLINK

www.wtbonline.gov.uk

Check out this website for the latest information on compulsory registration of accommodation in Wales and quality issues generally.

- Walkers and Cyclists Welcome schemes – introduced in 2004 to advise accommodation providers on how to meet the particular needs of these visitors;
- Accessibility – the national scheme was re-launched in 2003, revised in 2004 and a caravan parks' version launched in 2005.

Most UK tourism quality systems are voluntary, but the Wales Tourist Board is presently consulting on the feasibility of introducing compulsory registration of tourist accommodation.

Health, safety and security

Quality assurance at a visitor attraction

Britain is one of the safest countries in the world for tourists to visit and explore, but recent terrorist events around the world, and the London bombings of 7/7 2005 in particular, have made safety and security a key issue for tourists and those involved in managing the travel and tourism industry in the UK. Following 9/11, extra security measures were introduced at airports across the world, while the London bombings led to heightened security at railway stations across the country. Although such measures can cause extra delays, most travellers are willing to sacrifice a little time in return for a safer journey.

Domestic and incoming tourists tend to react differently to health, safety and security concerns. British people generally take a pragmatic approach to travel and tend not to cancel holiday bookings or change their plans to any great extent. Some overseas visitors, however, react quickly to security incidents and cancel bookings immediately. VisitBritain, using research commissioned by its Tourism Industry Emergency Response Group (TIER), estimates that the 7/7 2005 London bombings will result in a 2 per cent fall in overseas visitor numbers for 2005, representing a loss to the UK economy of at least £300 million. As 50 per cent of all overseas visitors travel to London, this equates to a fall in revenue of £150 million to the capital.

Cultural awareness

We saw in Unit 10 that tourism can have both negative and positive impacts on the culture and traditions of tourist destinations (see page 98). For many tourists, learning about an area's culture is an essential feature of their holiday experience. For example, the art galleries in major European cities and the sites of ancient civilisations in South American countries are magnets for international tourists. In the UK, incoming tourists are particularly

Unit 15

keen to explore our heritage and culture, learning about our language and traditions. As people become better educated and more discerning, the travel and tourism industry must respond by offering both domestic and incoming tourists products that meet their needs for a more culturally-enriching experience.

Language interpretation

For more than half of all overseas visitors to Britain, English is not their first language, making language interpretation a particular need for many incoming tourists to the UK. Before they travel, information in a person's own language makes travel planning much easier. This is why tourist boards produce brochures, advertising and websites in the home language of overseas visitors, particularly targeting countries with the greatest number of visitors to the UK. When in Britain, a person's stay can be made much more enjoyable by offering a range of facilities, for example:

- Signposting in many languages;
- Multilingual menus;
- Tour guides who can speak more than one language;
- Multilingual audio guides at attractions;
- Leaflets and brochures in a range of languages.

An understanding of other languages, no matter how limited, can often make overseas visitors to the UK feel more welcome and comfortable. Welcome, bienvenue, wilkommen or bienvenido, said in a warm and friendly manner in any language makes a visitor to a foreign country feel special and wanted. Staff working in travel and tourism can take advantage of training courses to improve their language skills, such as the following example available via the regional tourist organisations in the UK.

WEBLINK

www.welcometo
excellence.co.uk

Check out this website for more information on the Welcome International training programme.

FOCUS ON INDUSTRY – Welcome International

Welcome International (formerly Welcome Host International) is a one-day customer service training course designed to give people working in the travel and tourism industry greater confidence when meeting and greeting international visitors in another language. Part of the Welcome to Excellence series of training programmes, Welcome International aims to meet, greet and inform visitors in two languages from the following: Arabic, Chinese (Mandarin), Dutch, French, German, Italian, Japanese, Norwegian and Spanish. Organisations whose staff complete Welcome International benefit from the improved quality of customer service and personal touch extended to visitors in this highly competitive industry. Course content includes language practice, cultural aspects and national country facts.

Unit 15

Visitor expectations

We all have different expectations about our holidays, business trips and visits to friends and relatives. Expectations and anticipation are very important in travel and tourism, because people often don't know what their accommodation or destination will be like until they arrive. The industry is very much about 'selling dreams' and everybody hopes that their expectations will be met, or even exceeded, but this isn't always the case!

ACTIVITY

Carry out a small-scale survey of a selection of friends and relatives to find out if the expectations they had about a recent holiday or day trip were met or not, giving reasons.

This activity is designed to provide evidence for P1.

Customer service

The standard of service that tourists receive is perhaps the single most important factor that affects their holiday or travel experience. Poor service can ruin a holiday, whereas friendly, attentive and efficient staff can make a trip all the more memorable.

Visitors expect high quality customer service standards

Visitors from overseas may be used to different standards of service from staff working in travel and tourism. The travel and tourism industry must continue to train staff in the importance of high quality customer service, which benefits not only visitors but also individual businesses and the industry itself.

Cost

Everybody looks for good value for money when they are travelling, whether on a trip to Paris with a budget airline or an expensive cruise across the Atlantic aboard Cunard's Queen Mary 2. For business people, who often have to travel at short notice using premium services, cost is not always their main consideration. Research carried out by VisitBritain indicates that the UK is considered to be an expensive place to visit by many incoming tourists, particularly those from Europe's emerging economies, for example the Czech Republic, Latvia and Estonia. The cost of food, drink and public transport are singled out as being especially high, particularly in major

Unit 15

cities around the UK. Fluctuations in exchange rates can affect the cost of visiting a country; for example, a rise in the value of the pound against the Euro will make it more expensive for visitors to Britain from countries such as France, Spain and Germany. Many domestic and incoming tourists use the Internet to find the best prices for travel, holidays and accommodation, hoping to pick up a good-value deal at short notice.

Facilities, products and services

Just as tourists expect high standards of customer service, they also expect their travel and tourism facilities, products and services to meet their needs fully. For incoming tourists, this begins from the moment the visitor researches their trip, through making a booking and finally arriving at their destination, for example:

1. Pre-visit planning – visitors need access to informative brochures, websites and staff to enable them to plan a successful trip to the UK;
2. Making bookings – incoming tourists may use the services of a travel agent, tour operator or book direct with transport and accommodation providers. Whichever method is used, the process must be reliable and efficient;
3. Travel to the destination – facilities such as airports, ferry terminals and train stations, plus the transport services they support, should be as simple as possible to pass through, with minimum disruption and effort;
4. Staying in the destination – accommodation, tourist information, attractions, transport and events should all be of a standard that meets, or exceeds, the visitors' needs and expectations;
5. Return travel – as with their journey to the UK, returning to their own country should be as stress-free as possible for overseas visitors.

Domestic tourists have similar needs that are met by companies and organisations working within the UK. It is the job of the many elements of the travel and tourism industry – private, public and voluntary sector – to supply both domestic and incoming tourists with high quality tourism facilities, products and services.

Interaction with visitors and the host community

A pleasurable part of visiting different parts of your own country or an overseas destination is the chance to mix with other visitors and the 'host community', i.e. the people who live in the destinations visited. It is always interesting to learn about other people's ways of life and make new friends. Farm tourism is an excellent way to get to know the way of life of country people and is very popular with both British people and visitors from overseas.

Unit 15

WEBLINK

www.farmstayuk.co.uk

Check out this website for more information on farm holidays in the UK.

FOCUS ON INDUSTRY – Farm Stay UK

Farm Stay UK was established in 1983 as the Farm Holiday Bureau with 23 local groups. Today, the organisation has more than 1000 members co-ordinated in 94 groups across the UK. Its regions are similar to those of the Regional Development Agencies (RDAs) in England, plus one each for Scotland, Wales and Northern Ireland. Farm Stay UK is a farmer-owned consortium whose primary functions are to:

1. Promote the concept of farm tourism in the UK;
2. Help members expand their businesses through pro-active marketing and sales support;
3. Assist farmers in broadening their income base through diversification.

The consortium markets farm-based bed & breakfast, self-catering and camping accommodation via its main annual publication *Stay on a Farm* and its interactive website. The organisation finances its entire operation through membership fees boosted, wherever possible, by income from sponsorship or advertising.

Purpose of visit

Visitor needs and expectations vary according to why people are travelling. Business travellers often have specific needs, for example express check-in and check-out at hotels, and electronic ticketing at airports to save time. A young person travelling around Europe using an Inter-Rail pass will have very different needs, for example budget accommodation, good-value places to eat and cheap entertainment.

SECTION 2: POPULARITY AND APPEAL OF THE UK

Since the early days of travel and tourism, Britain has been one of the world's most popular tourist destinations for British people and visitors from overseas. This section examines the reasons for this popularity and explores the appeal of the UK.

Popularity of the UK

According to data from the World Tourism Organisation (WTO), Britain was ranked sixth in the league table of popular tourist destinations in 2004, behind France, Spain, USA, China and Italy (see Figure 15.3). International tourism is a very competitive business, so Britain will need to continue to offer high standards of service and excellent tourist facilities if it is to retain its position in the table and compete in the global tourism marketplace.

Country	2003	2004
1. France	75.0	75.1
2. Spain	51.8	53.6
3. United States	41.2	46.1
4. China	33.0	41.8
5. Italy	39.6	37.1
6. United Kingdom	24.7	27.7
7. Hong Kong (China)	15.5	21.8
8. Mexico	18.7	20.6
9. Germany	18.4	20.1
10. Austria	19.1	19.4

Fig. 15.3 World's most popular tourist destinations (millions of arrivals)

Incoming and outbound visitor flows

You learned in Unit 10 that, every year since the mid-1980s, Britain has had a deficit (negative position) on its 'travel balance', i.e. more has been spent by British people travelling abroad than by overseas visitors coming to the UK. Figures from the International Passenger Survey (IPS) indicate that the deficit in 2004 amounted to minus £17.2 billion, made up of £12.8 billion earned from overseas visitors to the UK, less expenditure of £30 billion by British people making visits abroad.

Britain not only has a deficit on *earnings* on the travel balance, but also on the actual number of incoming and outbound visits, as shown in Figure 15.4.

Figure 15.4 demonstrates that the number of visits abroad by British people has been growing steadily since 1999, while overseas visits to the UK over the same period have declined slightly (although recent figures show that 2004 was a record year for incoming tourism with 27.5 million visitors).

Unit 15

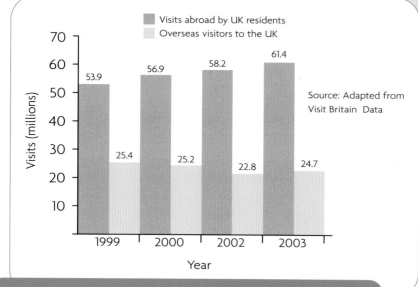

Visits abroad by UK residents
Overseas visitors to the UK

70
60 — 61.4
58.2
56.9
53.9
50
25.4 25.2
40   22.8 24.7

Source: Adapted from
Visit Britain Data

Visits (millions)

1999   2000   2002   2003
Year

Fig. 15.4 Trends in incoming and outbound UK tourism 1999-2003

ACTIVITY

Study the figures given in Figure 15.4 and list some reasons for (1) the steady growth in outbound tourism from the UK, and (2) the 'static' picture concerning the number of overseas visitors to Britain. What more do you think could be done by the travel and tourism industry to increase incoming tourism to the UK?

This activity is designed to provide evidence for P2.

In terms of holidays (rather than visits), 1998 saw a milestone in UK tourism, since it was the first year that the number of long (4+ nights) holidays taken by the British abroad was greater than long holidays taken in the UK. Since that date, the difference between the two has continued to grow.

Visitor flows within the UK to key destination regions

All parts of the UK benefit from tourism to a greater or lesser extent. More than half of all overseas visitors to Britain visit London, while both domestic and incoming tourists explore all corners of the country. Figures from VisitBritain indicate that domestic tourists made a total of 151 million trips in the UK in 2003, 121 million of which were in England and 11.6 million in Wales. In 2002, 18.5 million domestic tourism trips were made to Scotland and 1.74 million to Northern Ireland.

The south west of England was the most popular region with domestic tourists in 2003, closely followed by the south east.

ACTIVITY

Visit the StarUK website (www.staruk.org.uk) and find information on the regional breakdown of domestic visitors to the different regions in England. Mark the numbers of visitors to each region on a blank map of the UK, after having drawn on the regional boundaries (see page 239 in this book for a map of the regions). Remember that you can download a blank map of the UK from www.tandtONLine.co.uk.

This activity is designed to provide evidence for P2.

Unit 15

Average length of stay

Data from the United Kingdom Tourism Survey (UKTS) indicates that over 70 per cent of tourism trips taken by British people in the UK last between 1-3 nights, with an overall average length of 3.25 across all trips. This highlights the importance of short breaks to the UK tourism industry and the relative drop in popularity of 7 and 14-night holidays. The average length of stay of overseas visitors to Britain tends to be longer than for domestic tourists, reflecting the extra time needed to travel to and within this country. In 2003, the average length of stay in the UK by overseas residents was 8 nights (business trips 4 nights, visits to friends and relatives 11 nights and holidays 7 nights).

Generating countries for inbound tourism to Britain

Data from VisitBritain indicates that the number of visits from the top 5 generating countries for inbound tourism to Britain in 2004 were:

1. USA — 3.62 million;
2. France — 3.25 million;
3. Germany — 2.97 million;
4. Irish Republic — 2.58 million;
5. Netherlands — 1.62 million.

Visitors from the USA are attracted by Britain's culture, heritage and history. First-time visitors tend to visit London and nearby towns and cities such as Bath, Cambridge, Oxford and Stratford-upon-Avon, whereas those who have been to Britain before explore more widely throughout the country. Visitors from France, Germany, the Irish Republic and the Netherlands can arrive in the UK relatively quickly, using air services, rail travel, ferry services or the Channel Tunnel.

Visits to UK tourist attractions

Britain has a wealth of natural and built attractions that cater for the needs of both incoming and domestic tourists. Figure 15.5 shows the 20 most popular UK attractions for 2002.

Attraction	Visitors 2002
Blackpool Pleasure Beach	6,200,000
Tate Modern	4,618,632
British Museum	4,607,311
National Gallery	4,130,973e
London Eye	4,090,000
Natural History Museum	2,957,501
Victoria and Albert Museum	2,661,338
Science Museum	2,628,374
Pleasureland Southport	2,000,000e
Tower of London	1,940,856
Eastbourne Pier	1,900,000e
Eden Project	1,832,482e
York Minster	1,570,500e
Please Beach Great Yarmouth	1,500,000e
National Portrait Gallery	1,484,331
Legoland Windsor	1,453,000
Flamingo Land	1,393,300
Windermere Lake Cruises	1,266.027
Drayton Manor	1,200,000e
Tate Britain	1,178,235
Source: VisitBritain	e = estimate

Fig. 15.5 Visits to the top 20 UK attractions 2002

Unit 15

Trends and influences affecting incoming and domestic tourism

There are many factors that have an influence on tourism to and within Britain, including:

- The Internet – growth in its use is having a dramatic effect on how tourists of all kinds collect information and make their travel arrangements;
- Development of low-cost airlines – companies such as Ryanair and easyJet are opening up new destinations in Europe, stimulating inbound tourism to Britain and fuelling a dramatic rise in domestic air travel within the UK;
- Higher expectations among tourists – domestic and incoming tourists are demanding higher customer service levels and high quality tourist facilities in all sectors of the UK travel and tourism industry;
- Health, safety and security – 9/11 and other global terrorist attacks, plus the London bombings of 7/7/2005, have short-term effects on incoming and domestic tourism;
- Political and economic factors – such as 'approved destination status' (see page 78 in Unit 10), the emerging economies of Europe and the Far East, interest rates and fluctuations in exchange rates, can influence trends in travel and tourism.

Low-cost airlines are having a dramatic impact on incoming and domestic tourism

The challenge for public and private sector tourism organisations is to be able to respond to these factors and provide visitors with products and services that meet their needs in a fast-moving and highly competitive global industry.

Appeal of the UK

The appeal of the UK to domestic and incoming tourists is made up of many interrelated factors, which are discussed in the following sections of this unit.

Features and attractions

Although the UK is relatively small in comparison to many other countries of the world, it has an abundance of fine landscapes, from Land's End in Cornwall to John O' Groats on the northern tip of Scotland. Domestic and overseas visitors are attracted to its rugged

Unit 15

mountains, beautiful coastline, picturesque dales, desolate moorlands, woodlands, lakes, rivers, estuaries and many other features that complete the scene. The landscape in the UK is a major selling point for travel and tourism. As well as natural attractions, Britain offers tourists a host of built attractions of all kinds, from castles and ancient monuments to theme parks and museums.

Special events

Many UK tourist destinations stage events, of national, regional or local significance, as a way of boosting visitor numbers to an area. Themes vary from celebrations of anniversaries and carnivals to sporting events and musical extravaganzas.

ACTIVITY

Working in a small group, carry out some research to find out what events are being staged in your own area for visitors and local people in the near future. Choose a selection of events that have different themes, e.g. sporting, food and drink, heritage, gardening, music, etc., and make a display of publicity materials for the events.

This activity is designed to provide evidence for P3.

Facilities and services

Britain has a very wide variety of accommodation and attractions that appeal to visitors of all types. Destinations that have invested in new facilities and services for visitors have a distinct advantage over those that have not. Seaside resorts such as Brighton, Scarborough and Bournemouth have successfully diversified into business tourism by developing conference facilities and associated accommodation. 'Wet weather facilities', such as undercover swimming and leisure domes, extend the tourist season and are not affected by poor weather conditions, for example Center Parcs.

Image

Britain has a clear image with many overseas visitors as a welcoming destination with strong historical and cultural traditions. At the same time, it is a very contemporary and cosmopolitan place to visit, with some of the most dynamic cities in the world. VisitBritain is responsible for co-ordinating the marketing of Britain abroad and for projecting a positive image to the rest of the world (see case study on page 237).

Unit 15

Needs and expectations

Every person is unique and has different needs and expectations from a trip to a destination. Those responsible for planning and managing tourism in the many areas of Britain must be able to identify visitor needs through regular market research exercises and use the data gathered to provide facilities and services that tourists want, thereby meeting, or even exceeding, visitor expectations.

Climate

Britain has a temperate climate, with warm, wet summers and cool, wet winters – so it is clear that most overseas tourists visit Britain for something other than its climate! It does, however, produce the lush, green landscapes that are so popular with visitors to the countryside.

Accessibility

Britain is very accessible via a range of transport services and gateways, making it one of the most popular tourist destinations in Europe. New air routes are being introduced regularly and the high-speed rail link to the Channel Tunnel is due to be completed by 2007. In years to come, the UK is likely to see increased numbers of tourists from the emerging economies of the former Soviet states and the Far East, including China and South Korea.

Cost

We saw earlier in this unit that Britain is considered to be an expensive destination by many overseas visitors, particularly in relation to food and drink prices. Commercial travel and tourism operators must ensure that they don't 'kill the goose that lays the golden egg', by charging high prices and alienating visitors to the UK.

Unit 15

SECTION 3: ORGANISATIONS INVOLVED WITH INCOMING AND DOMESTIC TOURISM

You have learned in other units on your course that travel and tourism is a very complex industry made up of many different organisations. In the following sections of this unit we examine the organisations particularly involved with incoming and domestic tourism in the UK.

Types of organisations

The organisations involved with incoming and domestic tourism fall into one of three types:

- Public sector – organisations that are funded from public money, e.g. the National Tourist Boards (NTBs), Regional Tourist Boards (RTBs), Regional Development Agencies (RDAs), local authorities, government departments and English Heritage;
- Private sector – these are the commercial businesses that provide the majority of facilities and services for visitors, e.g. transport operators, accommodation providers, incoming tour operators, attractions, etc. It also includes trade bodies such as the British Hospitality Association and UKinbound;
- Voluntary sector – these include membership organisations such as the National Trust and Youth Hostels Association (YHA), plus lobbying groups such as the Tourism Alliance.

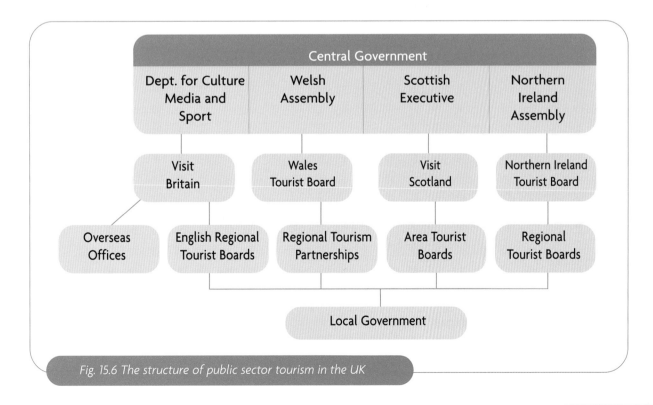

Fig. 15.6 The structure of public sector tourism in the UK

Unit 15

Public sector organisations

The public sector plays a major role in UK incoming and domestic tourism, as you can see from Figure 15.6, which shows the relationships between the various public sector bodies.

WEBLINK

www.culture.gov.uk

Check out this website for the latest information on the work of DCMS in UK tourism.

The Department for Culture, Media and Sport (DCMS) is responsible for UK tourism policy. It sets the agenda for tourism, supports the industry to improve what it has to offer, provides funding and helps to promote a positive image of Britain abroad. In 1999, it published the national tourism strategy *Tomorrow's Tourism*, which was concerned with the framework for UK tourism, achieving quality, developing sustainable tourism and monitoring progress. This was updated in July 2004 when DCMS launched *Tomorrow's Tourism Today*, an action plan setting out the responsibilities of public and private sector organisations in the key areas of marketing, quality, skills and data collection.

Other government departments that have an indirect involvement with aspects of tourism include the Department for Transport (aviation, roads, railways, London Underground), Department for Environment, Food and Rural Affairs (food industry, forestry, sustainable development, climate change, environmental protection, water issues, wildlife and conservation, energy efficiency, rural affairs, countryside issues, inland waterways), Department for Education and Skills (Sector Skills Councils), the Home Office (liquor licensing), the Treasury (direct and indirect taxation) and the Foreign and Commonwealth Office (advice to travellers).

National Tourist Boards

The UK has four National Tourist Boards:

- VisitBritain – responsible for promoting the whole of Britain abroad and England to the British;
- Wales Tourist Board – concerned with improving the economic and social prosperity of Wales through effective marketing and development of tourism;
- VisitScotland – exists to support the development of the tourism industry in Scotland and to market Scotland as a quality destination;
- Northern Ireland Tourist Board – responsible for the development, promotion and marketing of Northern Ireland as a tourist destination.

The national boards are funded mainly from central government sources, channelled through the DCMS, Welsh Assembly Government, Scottish Executive and Northern Ireland Office/Assembly.

Unit 15

Introduction

VisitBritain is the UK's National Tourism Organisation (NTO) responsible for marketing Britain to the rest of the world and England to the British. Its mission is to:

'build the value of tourism by creating world-class destination brands and marketing campaigns and also build partnerships with – and provide insights into – other organisations which have a stake in British and English tourism.'

VisitBritain has its headquarters in west London and employs approximately 450 staff, 60 per cent of whom are based overseas in Britain's key tourism markets.

VisitBritain's goals

The organisation has specific goals for each of its five key stakeholders:

1. Overseas customer – to promote Britain overseas as a tourist destination, generating additional tourism revenue throughout Britain and throughout the year;
2. Domestic customer – to grow the value of the domestic market by encouraging key audiences to take additional and/or longer breaks in England;
3. Governments – to provide advice to government on matters affecting tourism and contribute to wider government objectives;
4. Strategic tourist board partners – to work in partnership with the devolved administrations and the National and Regional Tourist Boards to build the British tourism industry;
5. Staff – to achieve all goals by making efficient and effective use of resources and by being open, accessible, professional, accountable and responsive.

VisitBritain works in partnership with Wales Tourist Board, VisitScotland and the Northern Ireland Tourist Board to promote an attractive image of Britain. It provides tourist information and gathers essential market intelligence for the UK tourism industry.

Funding

VisitBritain is funded from the public purse by the Department for Culture, Media and Sport (DCMS) to promote Britain overseas as a tourist destination and to lead and co-ordinate England's tourism marketing. Its government grant to fund the promotion of Britain overseas in 2004-2005 was £35.5 million. The total funding available for marketing England in the same year was £14 million, of which £3.6 million was deployed directly through the Regional

Unit 15

Development Agencies (RDAs). A further £1.5 million 'challenge fund' was available for domestic marketing subject to VisitBritain raising £3.5 million in partnership funding. VisitBritain also raised around £17 million of non-government funding in 2004-2005 through partnerships and other income-generating activities.

Overseas operations

VisitBritain has a network of 23 overseas offices covering 35 key markets around the world. The overseas offices work closely with British diplomatic and cultural staff, the local travel trade and media to stimulate interest in Britain. In the UK, it has strategic partnerships with many other organisations with an interest in tourism, including the British Council, UKinbound, the British Hospitality Association, the UK Immigration Service and the Tourism Alliance.

The British Tourism Development Committee (BTDC)

The BTDC is VisitBritain's main mechanism for consulting with the UK tourism industry. The Committee acts as a forum for discussion between VisitBritain and other statutory tourist boards, as well as other public and private sector travel and tourism organisations. It advises government on a range of issues, including the European Union, product development, environmental, transport and tourism issues, plus strategic aspects of marketing policy. The BTDC has 50 members, including all the key trade associations, but also organisations such as the YHA and Farm Stay UK, which represent small and medium-sized enterprises. It is chaired by the Chief Executive of VisitBritain.

WEBLINK

www.visitbritain.com

Check out this website to help answer the questions in this case study and for more information on the work of VisitBritain.

CASE STUDY QUESTIONS

1. What is the 'market intelligence' that VisitBritain gathers on behalf of the UK tourism industry?
2. What impact is new technology likely to have on VisitBritain's work in the future?
3. Mark the position of VisitBritain's overseas offices on a blank map of the world (you can download this from www.tandtONLine.co.uk)
4. Carry out some research into VisitBritain's current level of funding from the DCMS.

Unit 15

Regional tourism structure in the UK

Up to 1999, regional tourism matters in England were the responsibility of Regional Tourist Boards (RTBs), but the launch of Regional Development Agencies (RDAs) in England in that year marked a change in government support for regional tourism. RDAs are funded from central government to promote economic development, including tourism, in their areas. In most regions, the RDAs work with the RTBs to develop future plans for tourism development and marketing. There are currently 9 Regional Tourist Boards in England and 4 Regional Tourism Partnerships (RTPs) in Wales, as shown in Figure 15.7.

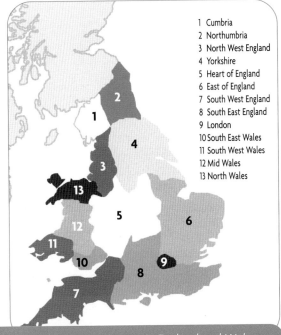

1 Cumbria
2 Northumbria
3 North West England
4 Yorkshire
5 Heart of England
6 East of England
7 South West England
8 South East England
9 London
10 South East Wales
11 South West Wales
12 Mid Wales
13 North Wales

Fig. 15.7 Regional tourism structure in England and Wales

Public sector tourism at local level

Today, there are few local councils in the UK that are not actively involved in some way with promoting their areas to incoming and domestic tourists. Tourism is seen as an excellent way of generating revenue, creating jobs and helping economic development in urban and rural areas of the UK. Local authorities use their resources to provide as wide a range of tourism facilities and services that finances will allow. In a typical area, this might include:

- Promotional leaflets, brochures and websites;
- Parks and gardens;
- Theatres;
- Museums;
- Tourist information centres (TICs);
- Accommodation booking services;
- Sports and leisure centres;
- Outdoor activity centres;
- Art and craft galleries.

Many local authorities support the establishment of local tourism groups and associations that promote partnership between the private, public and voluntary sectors of the industry.

Unit **15**

ACTIVITY

Carry out some research to find out what activities your local authority (or one nearby that is involved with tourism) undertakes to encourage visits by incoming and domestic tourists.

This activity is designed to provide evidence for P4.

Private sector organisations

Private sector organisations of all sizes provide the majority of facilities and services for incoming and domestic tourists. These organisations include:

- Transport operators – specialise in a range of air, land and sea services to get visitors to the UK from abroad and meet the travel needs of domestic and incoming tourists while in Britain;
- Accommodation providers – supply a full range of hotels, guesthouses, inns, B & Bs, camping, caravanning and other self-catering accommodation to suit the needs of a wide variety of leisure and business travellers;
- Tour operators – specialise in 'packaging' travel and tourism products and services, such as accommodation, transport, tickets for attractions and events, etc. Many incoming tour operators, i.e. those that sell packages and tours to overseas visitors to the UK, are members of the trade association UKinbound.

WEBLINK

www.bitoa.co.uk

Check out this website for more information on the work of UKinbound.

FOCUS ON INDUSTRY – UKinbound

UKinbound was founded in 1977 as BITOA to represent the commercial interests of British tour operators specialising in providing tours and tourism services to overseas visitors to Britain. The primary aim of the association is to help its members manage successful, profitable businesses that are part of a vibrant and sustainable inbound tourism industry. It does this by focusing on three key areas:

- Advocacy – to champion the interests of UKinbound members with government;
- Professionalism – to promote best practice and encourage lifelong learning through training and staff development;
- Networking – to provide opportunities for its members to develop relationships with suppliers, buyers and partners in the UK and overseas.

Unit 15

Voluntary sector organisations

The voluntary sector provides many of the attractions that are so popular with incoming and domestic tourists in Britain, such as stately homes, gardens, protected coastlines, heritage attractions, nature reserves, museums and galleries. Key organisations in voluntary sector tourism in the UK include the YHA (see page 86), English Heritage and the National Trust.

WEBLINK

www.english-heritage.org.uk

Check out this website for more information on English Heritage.

FOCUS ON INDUSTRY – English Heritage

English Heritage is a public agency that advises the government on all matters concerning the historic environment. It is probably best known for the 400+ historic sites that is manages and makes available to the public, including Barnard Castle, Stonehenge and Dover Castle. It is funded through the Department for Culture, Media and Sport (DCMS) and also works closely with the Office of the Deputy Prime Minister on planning, housing and transport issues, plus the Department for Environment, Food and Rural Affairs (defra) on countryside matters. English Heritage employs approximately 1,650 staff in total, around its 9 regions throughout England and in its head office in London. It works with central government departments, local authorities, voluntary bodies and the private sector to:

1. Conserve and enhance the historic environment;
2. Broaden public access to the heritage;
3. Increase people's understanding of the past.

English Heritage has a travel trade team that specialises in meeting the needs of incoming and domestic tour operators. It offers familiarisation visits to its properties, the supply of images for use in tour operators' brochures and information on itineraries for groups and individual visitors.

WEBLINK

www.nationaltrust.org.uk

Check out this website for more information on the work of the National Trust and a full listing of its properties and protected areas.

FOCUS ON INDUSTRY – The National Trust

The National Trust is the country's largest private landowner and a registered charity that works to preserve and protect the coastline, countryside and buildings of England, Wales and Northern Ireland (the National Trust for Scotland is a separate organisation). It is completely independent of government and relies on membership fees, donations, legacies and revenue raised from its commercial operations for its income. The Trust currently has 3.4 million members and 43,000 volunteers. It welcomed more than 12 million people to its pay-for-entry properties in 2004, while an estimated 50 million people visited its open-air properties. The Trust protects and opens to the public more than 300 historic houses and gardens, including Tatton Park in Cheshire, Lanhydrock in Cornwall and Sissinghurst Castle Garden in Kent.

Unit 15

Interaction between organisations

So far in this section we have investigated individual organisations and agencies that work in different sectors of incoming and domestic tourism. However, in reality, interaction between organisations takes place on a regular basis and working in partnership is seen as essential to providing products and services that meet the needs and expectations of incoming and domestic tourists.

WEBLINK

www.hadrians-wall.org

Check out this website for more information on the Hadrian's Wall Tourism Partnership and its current activities.

An excellent example of interaction between different sectors of the tourism industry is the Hadrian's Wall Tourism Partnership, established in the mid-1990s to encourage sustainable development of this World Heritage Site and maximise the benefits of tourism to the area. Public agencies involved in the partnership include the Countryside Agency, ONE NorthEast (the Regional Development Agency for the area), English Heritage, Northumberland National Park and a variety of local councils. The voluntary sector is represented by the Vindolanda and Senhouse Trusts, the YHA and the National Trust. Private sector enterprises include hotels, guesthouses, attractions, activity centres and tour operators.

The role of organisations

The primary role of all organisations and individuals involved with incoming and domestic tourism in the UK is to maximise visitor numbers, so as to gain economic and social benefits, while minimising negative tourism impacts on destinations and host communities. This is achieved through a variety of activities, as shown in Figure 15.8.

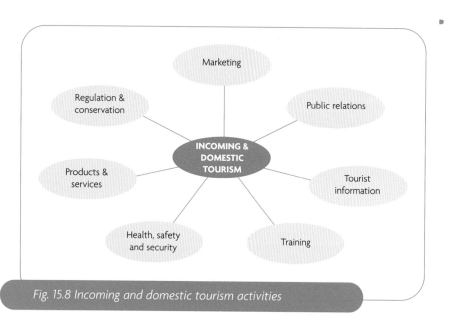

Fig. 15.8 Incoming and domestic tourism activities

- Marketing – this is a key activity of all organisations working in incoming and domestic tourism, and includes market research, advertising, direct marketing, sales promotions and public relations (PR). Tourist boards promote their particular part of the UK, while individual businesses market to their own customers;

Unit 15

- Public relations – activities such as press launches, distributing press releases and hosting familiarisation trips for journalists, are excellent ways of promoting destinations to incoming and domestic tourists;
- Tourist information – tourist boards and local authorities supply information on destinations and tourist facilities to visitors before they travel and while in destinations;
- Training – in order to provide visitors with high standards of service and excellent tourist facilities, tourist boards and other public agencies encourage tourism businesses to invest in staff training on a regular basis;
- Health, safety and security – this is a major issue for all organisations involved in incoming and domestic tourism. Visitors have a right to expect that their journeys to destinations and time spent in the UK is as safe and secure as possible;
- Products and services – the wide range of organisations working in incoming and domestic tourism work hard to offer tourism products and services that meet the needs of a wide variety of tourists, from the UK and overseas;
- Regulation and conservation – public sector agencies implement a range of regulations concerning tourism products and services, including consumer protection, transport regulations, planning laws, etc. As we saw earlier in this unit, there are many public and voluntary sector organisations involved in conservation of land and buildings in the UK.

ACTIVITY

Visit the marketing section of the Wales Tourist Board trade website www.wtbonline.gov.uk and gather information on the Board's 'Big Country' UK marketing campaign to attract visitors (or another recent campaign). Working with a partner, devise and deliver a presentation that explains key features of the campaign, e.g. aims, target markets, marketing activities and costs.

This activity is designed to provide evidence for P4.

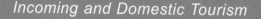

Unit 15

SECTION 4: HERITAGE TOURISM

Edinburgh's Whisky Heritage Centre

'Heritage tourism' is a wide-ranging term covering all types of tourist activity that has a connection with the past and which is of interest to visitors. Britain's heritage is a magnet for overseas visitors, but is also popular with people from the UK. Visitors are drawn to Britain's unique heritage, in particular its historic towns, landscapes, castles, stately homes, gardens, royalty and ancient monuments, in order to learn more about the traditions of a specific site or tourist destination. Heritage tourism is also used in urban regeneration schemes, for example by attracting visitors to Wigan Pier, Beamish Open Air Museum and Big Pit Mining Museum (see case study on page 248). Using the word 'heritage' in the names of attractions helps to convey a sense of the past and to attract more visitors.

WEBLINK

www.hlf.org.uk

Check out this website for more information on the Heritage Lottery Fund and recent projects that it has funded.

FOCUS ON INDUSTRY – The Heritage Lottery Fund (HLF)

One of the biggest sources of investment in Britain's heritage over the past decade has been money from the National Lottery, in particular the Heritage Lottery Fund (HLF). In 1994, heritage was identified as one of the 'good causes' that Lottery money would be used to benefit. Since 1995, the HLF has given over £3 billion to 15,000 projects, including:

- £1.17 billion to more than 2,000 projects involving museums and libraries (many in historic buildings);
- £1 billion to over 4,000 projects whose main purpose is historic buildings and monuments;
- £604 million to projects supporting landscape and biodiversity;
- £222 million to industrial, maritime and transport heritage projects;
- £13 million to over 900 community projects designed to celebrate local heritage.

Projects funded by the HLF range from small grants to community groups to help look after local heritage that matters to them, to awards for projects in many of the UK's most prestigious World Heritage sites. While the HLF supports major projects such as Hadrian's Wall, the British Museum and Stonehenge, over two-thirds of its awards have gone to projects of less than £50,000.

Unit 15

Heritage attractions

It is difficult to underestimate the importance of heritage attractions to the UK tourism industry. As many as 80 per cent of all attractions in the UK can be classified as 'heritage', including:

- Rural activities;
- Monuments, ruins and historic sites;
- Historic cities and towns;
- Castles and palaces;
- Churches and cathedrals;
- Museums and galleries;
- Visitor centres;
- Gardens and parks;
- Festivals and events.

ACTIVITY

Using this list of types of heritage attractions as a guide, find out which types of attractions can be found in your local area. Gather information on one local attraction from each type and make an information booklet giving details that would be useful to incoming and domestic tourists.

This activity is designed to provide evidence for P5.

Rural activities

The ways of the countryside and farming practices have long fascinated visitors to rural areas. Attractions such as farming museums, farm parks, farm open days and self-guided trails, add to the rich cultural heritage that is so popular with incoming and domestic tourists.

Monuments, ruins and historic sites

Many of the UK's ancient monuments, ruins and historic sites are managed and made available to visitors by public agencies such as English Heritage and CADW in Wales. Voluntary sector bodies, including the National Trust and local archaeological trusts, conserve historic sites and carry out important research.

Unit 15

Cities and towns

The majority of first-time visitors to the UK visit London as part of their stay, attracted in the main by its associations with history, tradition, royalty and heritage. They often follow a set itinerary that takes in many of Britain's historic cities and towns. This round trip, sometimes known as the 'milk run', often follows this route: London – Oxford – Bath – Cardiff – Chester – the Lake District – Edinburgh – York – Cambridge – London. Returning visitors often seek out more remote areas 'off the beaten track' to experience traditional British customs and hospitality. Historic towns and cities benefit greatly from the revenue generated by incoming and domestic tourists.

Castles and palaces

WEBLINK

www.cadw.wales.gov.uk;
www.historic-scotland.gov.uk

Check out these websites for more information on castles and other historic properties in Wales and Scotland.

Castles are major heritage attractions for tourists, particularly in Wales and Scotland. In Wales, many castles have been awarded World Heritage Site status, including those at Caernarvon, Harlech and Conwy. North of the border, Edinburgh Castle is the best-known and most-visited of all heritage properties in Scotland.

The Royal Palaces in Britain, owned by The Queen as Sovereign and held in trust for the nation, contribute greatly to this country's appeal as a tourist destination. The Historic Royal Palaces (HRP) Agency is funded by the Department for Culture, Media and Sport (DCMS) to preserve and present to the public a selection of the Royal Palaces that are no longer used by The Queen or members of the Royal Family. These properties include the Tower of London, Hampton Court Palace, the State Apartments at Kensington Palace, the Banqueting House, Whitehall and Kew Palace with Queen Charlotte's Cottage.

Churches and cathedrals

As well as fulfilling an important religious function, many British churches and

Edinburgh Castle is very popular with incoming and domestic tourists

cathedrals are important attractions in their own right. Many overseas tourists and visitors from the UK like to explore country churches and visit the magnificent cathedrals that are found in cities such as Winchester, York, Durham and Canterbury. Revenue from tourists is often ploughed back into the upkeep of the buildings so as to make them available for future generations.

FOCUS ON INDUSTRY – Economic and social impact of cathedrals in England

Recent research published in Heritage Counts examined the economic and social value to local communities of the 42 Anglican cathedrals in England. There were 8.8 million visits to these cathedrals in 2003, although separate research by the Church of England, which included Westminster Abbey, indicated that the number of visits was as high as 12.5 million. Spending by visitors attracted to the local area by the presence of a cathedral was estimated at £91 million per year to the local economy, while the total economic impact was estimated to be £150 million, supporting some 5,500 jobs.

Museums and galleries

Britain has an abundance of museums and galleries of all sizes and types, operated by public, private and voluntary organisations. The Department for Culture, Media and Sport (DCMS) sponsors some of England's finest museums and galleries, including the Natural History Museum, the Tate Galleries in London, Liverpool and St. Ives, the National Maritime Museum in Greenwich and the National Railway Museum in York, enabling them to offer free entry to all visitors. Since it was introduced in 2001, this free admission policy has been a great success – visits to museums have increased by 75 per cent nationally. In 2004, there were 34 million visits to all the museums and galleries sponsored by the DCMS.

CASE STUDY – Big Pit Mining Museum

Introduction

Big Pit National Mining Museum of Wales, based around a real coal mine in the South Wales valleys, is one of the UK's leading industrial heritage museums. It is located close to the town of Blaenavon, which was awarded World Heritage status in 2000. Big Pit welcomes incoming tourists from all over the world and domestic visitors from across the UK.

Development of the museum

The museum was established in 1983 after closure of the working mine in 1980. However, until 2001, lack of funding meant that many of the buildings on the surface were left untouched and out of bounds to the public. A period of closure followed, during which a £7 million redevelopment was carried out, and the museum was fully re-opened in February 2004. Since 2001, Big Pit has been part of the National Museums and Galleries of Wales (NMGW) group. It benefits, like all NMGW sites, from free access for visitors funded by the Welsh Assembly Government. Big Pit has welcomed nearly 2.4 million visitors in its 22-year history and the introduction of free entry to the museum has boosted visitor numbers considerably in recent years. In 2004, the museum had a record 141,000 visitors, made up of individuals, parties and education groups. In 2005, Big Pit won the prestigious £100,000 Gulbenkian Prize for Museum of the Year and is on target to beat its previous record visitor numbers for the year.

Facilities for visitors

The highlight of a visit to Big Pit is the hour-long underground tour which is led by ex-miners. Visitors descend 300 feet in the original pit cage and are guided along underground roadways, through air doors and past engine houses, all built by generations of miners. On the surface, there are colliery buildings of all types open to visitors, including the winding engine-house, blacksmiths' workshops and the original pithead baths. The baths were the first to be installed at the site and date back to 1939. They currently house Big Pit's main exhibition space where the history of the coal mines of South Wales is explored and the stories of the communities that grew up around them are told, from the earliest days to the miners' strikes and pit closures of the 1980s. Big Pit also has multimedia displays of modern mining. Although the museum is on the side of a steep hill, much of it is accessible to those with mobility problems and visually/hearing-impaired visitors are catered for. A maximum of four wheelchair users are allowed underground at any one time for safety reasons and the site welcomes assistance dogs, although they cannot be taken on the underground tour. The museum has two catering outlets and a gift shop

Unit 15

Educational visits

Big Pit hosts educational visits from primary school children to university groups. It offers a resource room for teachers, group leaders, students and other specialists who wish to carry out research work at the museum. The room contains reference books, maps, original documents and has Internet access. The museum's Education Officer handles all education enquiries and provides teaching resources for schools.

CASE STUDY QUESTIONS

1. What different types of 'interpretation' does Big Pit offer to its visitors?
2. Why is it important for heritage attractions like Big Pit to offer facilities for education visits?
3. In what ways has Big Pit benefited from being a member of the National Museums and Galleries of Wales (NMGW) group?
4. Which other attractions are part of the NMGW group?

WEBLINK

http://www.nmgw.ac.uk/www.php/bigpit/

Check out this website to help answer the questions in this case study and for more information on Big Pit National Mining Museum of Wales.

Visitor centres

Visitor centres are found in natural and built environments, and are designed to provide information and advice for visitors to a tourist area or facility. They often include a variety of interpretation methods, i.e. ways to educate and inform visitors. These include guided walks, audio-visual displays, exhibition panels and self-guided walks from the centre. Visitor centres are popular in National Parks and other areas with protected status, where they are often part of an overall plan to manage the flow of visitors and their cars, thereby contributing to sustainable tourism development.

Gardens and parks

Gardens and parks give visitors the chance to unwind and enjoy Britain's natural beauty. Organisations such as the National Trust, the Royal Horticultural Society (RHS) and National Gardens Scheme, offer incoming and domestic tourists the chance to explore some of the finest gardens to be found anywhere in the world, e.g. Powys Castle Gardens, the RHS at Wisley and Stourhead.

Festivals and events

Festivals and events are an excellent way of boosting the numbers of tourists to an area. They may be based on a particular theme, such as sport, music, food and pageantry, or

Unit 15

Henley regatta

staged to celebrate the anniversary of a particular event or person, e.g. 2005 is the 200th anniversary of the Battle of Trafalgar and has been marked by a series of special events. Events take place in both urban and rural areas, helping to spread the benefits of tourism right across the country.

WEBLINK

www.heritageopendays.org.uk

Check out this website to find out more about Heritage Open Days.

FOCUS ON INDUSTRY – Heritage Open Days

Heritage Open Days celebrate England's architecture and culture by offering free access to properties that are usually closed to the public or normally charge for admission. Every year on four days in September, buildings of every age, style and function open their doors to the public, ranging from castles to factories, town halls to tithe barns, parish churches to Buddhist temples. Co-ordinated by the Civic Trust in partnership with English Heritage, the event relies on the enthusiasm and expertise of local people. Thousands of volunteers from all walks of life share their knowledge with some 800,000 visitors every year, making Heritage Open Days the largest voluntary cultural event held in England.

Heritage themes

So far in this section we have seen that heritage tourism covers a very wide range of activities, facilities and events for tourists. Heritage attractions sometimes focus on a particular theme to make them stand out from the competition and develop a USP (unique selling proposition – something that sets them apart from other attractions). Common themes are:

- Industry – areas of the UK that were once important for industry often turn to heritage tourism as a way of regenerating their economies, e.g. shipbuilding areas like Tyneside, coal mining regions (see the case study on Big Pit on page 248) and textile towns such as Bradford;
- Literature – associations with characters from books and writers can be put to good

advantage in attracting tourists to an area, e.g. Shakespeare's birthplace in Stratford-upon-Avon, Catherine Cookson Country in the north-east of England, Thomas Hardy's links with Dorset and the many places associated with Dylan Thomas in South Wales. Hay-on-Wye, on the English-Welsh border, markets itself as 'the town of books' and holds a world-famous literary festival every summer;

- Society – heritage attractions often show the way of life of people from the past and how societies develop, e.g. the Weald and Downland Open Air Museum in Sussex and the Museum of Welsh Life at St. Fagans in Cardiff. Actors in period dress are sometimes used to create an authentic experience for visitors;

- Agriculture – the development of farming is a popular theme for heritage attractions right across the UK. Many members of the National Farm Attractions Network, a national organisation providing advice on setting up a farm attraction, are based on heritage, e.g. rare breeds, historic machinery, traditional farming methods, etc;

- Military – attractions such as the Cabinet War Rooms, the Fleet Air Arm Museum in Somerset and the Royal Armouries in Leeds are popular with people who have an interest in the military and armed forces;

- Royalty and tradition – overseas visitors are especially attracted to all aspects of Britain's Royal Family, from visiting Buckingham Palace to watching the changing of the guard or Trooping the Colour, the historic military parade which takes place in London every year to mark the Sovereign's birthday;

- Education – universities in historic cities, including Oxford, Cambridge, Durham and Bath, attract visitors as well as students;

- Religion – we saw earlier in this section that churches and cathedrals are major attractions for incoming and domestic tourists.

Protected status

Destinations and attractions are given 'protected status' to conserve their special qualities for future generations to enjoy. This protection comes in many forms, including:

1. National Parks;
2. Areas of Outstanding Natural Beauty (AONBs);
3. World Heritage Sites;
4. Conservation zones;
5. Heritage Coasts.

National Parks

'National Park' is a status given to areas that have some of the UK's finest scenery and landscapes. To date, twelve National Parks have been designated in England and Wales since the 1949 National Parks and Access to the Countryside Act. This includes the Broads, which was set up under a special Act of Parliament in 1988, and the New Forest, designated a National Park in March 2005. The Countryside Agency is currently consulting on establishing

Unit 15

a new South Downs National Park. The word 'national' does not mean that the Parks are owned by the government; most of the land within National Park boundaries is privately owned and often under severe pressure from visitors and their vehicles.

ACTIVITY

t and t ONLine

Find out the locations of all the National Parks in England, Wales and Scotland, plus the proposed Mourne National Park in Northern Ireland. Mark them on a blank map of the UK (you can download one from www.tandtONLine.co.uk).

This activity is designed to provide evidence for P5.

Areas of Outstanding Natural Beauty (AONBs)

There are currently 41 AONBs in England and Wales. They range from the wild open moorlands of the North Pennines to the green belt countryside of the Surrey Hills and the intimate valley of the Wye, which straddles the border with Wales. AONBs can be popular destinations for travel and tourism, although, unlike National Parks, they are not designated for their recreational value. The Countryside Agency has proposed stronger measures for their management and more funding for their upkeep. In total, AONBs in England cover around 15 per cent of the landscape

World Heritage Sites

UNESCO established the World Heritage Committee to compile a list of properties and sites around the world considered to be of outstanding universal value. The list includes some of the most famous attractions in the world, for example the Great Barrier Reef in Australia, the Great Wall of China, the Acropolis in Athens and the Taj Mahal in India. The UK currently has 26 World Heritage Sites, which include Ironbridge Gorge, the Tower of London, the Royal Botanic Gardens at Kew and Hadrian's Wall.

ACTIVITY

t and t ONLine

Visit the World Heritage Sites section of the DCMS website (www.culture.gov.uk) and mark the locations of the UK's sites on a blank map (you can download one from www.tandtONLine.co.uk). Choose one of the sites and compile a fact sheet of useful information on the site for incoming and domestic tourists.

This activity is designed to provide evidence for P5.

Unit 15

WEBLINK

www.civictrust.org.uk

Check out this website to learn more about the Civic Trust.

Conservation zones

Conservation zones are established in urban and rural areas to protect areas from development that is considered to be out of keeping with the locality. Planning authorities are responsible for deciding which areas should be designated as conservation zones. The Civic Trust is a voluntary organisation that works with people to promote thriving towns and villages, developing partnerships between communities, government and businesses to help regeneration and local improvement.

Heritage Coasts

There are 46 Heritage Coasts in England and Wales. They are among the most precious assets for wildlife and landscape, as well as for tourism. Concern over the harmful impact of increasing numbers of visitors led to their designation and a plan of action which includes creating and repairing footpaths, cleaning up bathing water and removing litter. Currently, 32 per cent of England's scenic coastline is conserved as Heritage Coasts.

UNIT SUMMARY

This unit has investigated the important categories of incoming and domestic tourism. You have examined the needs and expectations of both overseas visitors and UK tourists, highlighting the particular needs of incoming tourists. You have spent time considering the popularity and appeal of the UK, examining statistics on incoming and outbound visitor flows, visitor flows within the UK and key generating countries for UK tourism, including the USA, France and Spain. You have found that there are many organisations involved in incoming and domestic tourism, operating in the public, private and voluntary sectors, each with different roles. Your investigation of heritage tourism has shown that it is extremely important to the UK tourism industry, particularly incoming tourism. You have examined various themes in heritage tourism and considered a range of 'protected' areas. Throughout the unit you have been shown many industry examples, while the case studies on VisitBritain and Big Pit highlight key issues in the development of incoming and domestic tourism.

If you have worked methodically, by the end of this unit you should have:

- Differentiated between the needs and expectations of incoming and domestic tourists;
- Examined the popularity and appeal of the UK to both incoming and domestic tourists;
- Examined the role played by different types of organisations involved in incoming and domestic tourism;
- Investigated heritage tourism within the UK.

Unit 15

You are now in a position to complete the assignment for the unit, under the direction of your tutor. Before you tackle the assignment you may like to have a go at the following questions to help build your knowledge of incoming and domestic tourism.

Test your knowledge

1   Define 'incoming tourism' and 'domestic tourism', giving one example of each.
2. List the different types of transport used by incoming tourists to the UK, giving their relative popularity.
3. Why is the Wales Tourist Board considering introducing compulsory registration of tourist accommodation?
4. What is Farm Stay UK?
5. Explain what is meant by a 'deficit on Britain's travel balance'.
6. What is the average length of stay in Britain of overseas visitors?
7. Which is the top generating country for incoming tourism to the UK?
8. List and explain three factors that have an influence on tourism to and within Britain.
9. List and explain the roles of three public sector organisations involved in incoming and domestic tourism in the UK.
10. What is the primary role of VisitBritain?
11. What is the British Tourism Development Committee (BTDC)?
12. Give an example of interaction between different organisations involved in incoming and domestic tourism in the UK.
13. What is 'heritage tourism'?
14. What are Heritage Open Days?
15. List and explain three common themes found in heritage tourism.

UNIT 15 ASSIGNMENT: Incoming and domestic tourism

Introduction

This assignment is made up of a number of tasks which, when successfully completed, are designed to give you sufficient evidence to meet the Pass (P), Merit (M) and Distinction (D) grading criteria for the unit. If you have carried out the activities and read the case studies throughout this unit, you will already have done a lot of work towards completing the tasks for this assignment.

Unit 15

SCENARIO

As part of your course, you have secured a placement with the Regional Development Agency (RDA) for your area, to work with Tom Singleton, the Agency's Senior Tourism Business Development Executive. Tom has been asked to make a presentation at a national seminar for all RDA Tourism Business Executives and produce a booklet that his colleagues can take away from the seminar and use in the course of their work. The subject of the presentation and the booklet is incoming and domestic tourism, and Tom would like you to complete the following tasks.

Task 1

Tom is going to start his presentation by examining the needs and expectations of both incoming and domestic tourists. He would like you to gather information on this topic and make a presentation, in which you should:

(a) Describe the needs and expectations of incoming and domestic tourists;

(b) Compare and contrast the needs and expectations of incoming and domestic tourists;

(c) Analyse the interaction of different types of organisations involved in incoming and domestic tourism to meet the needs of incoming and domestic tourists.

These tasks are designed to produce evidence for P1, M1 and D1.

Task 2

The first section of the booklet that Tom needs to produce focuses on the popularity and appeal of the UK to incoming and domestic tourists. He would like you to produce this section of the booklet, in which you should:

(a) Assess the popularity of the UK to incoming and domestic tourists;

(b) Describe the factors which give the UK appeal to both incoming and domestic tourists;

(c) Explain how different types of organisations involved in incoming and domestic tourism are able to increase the appeal and popularity of the UK to incoming and domestic tourists.

These tasks are designed to produce evidence for P2, P3 and M2.

Unit 15

Task 3

Tom is going to finish his presentation by looking at the different types of organisations involved in incoming and domestic tourism. He would like you to research this topic and make a presentation, in which you should:

Describe the role of different types of organisations involved in incoming and domestic tourism.

This task is designed to produce evidence for P4.

Task 4

Heritage tourism is a major growth area in the region and nationally, due in no small part to the extra funding from the Heritage Lottery Fund (HLF). The second section of the booklet that Tom needs to produce concentrates on various aspects of heritage tourism in the UK. He would like you to produce this section of the booklet, in which you should:

(a) Describe the different types of heritage attractions in the UK, giving a specific example of each;

(b) Explain how the travel and tourism industry use heritage themes to increase the popularity and appeal of the UK to incoming and domestic tourists;

(c) Analyse the significance of heritage tourism to incoming and domestic tourists.

These tasks are designed to produce evidence for P5, M3 and D2.

Unit 18
Visitor Attractions

INTRODUCTION TO THE UNIT

Visitor attractions play a vital role in the travel and tourism industry, offering excitement, fun, education and activities for all types of people from the UK and overseas. It is often an attraction that tempts people to visit a tourist destination in the first place. Attractions can be purpose-built, such as a theme park or family entertainment complex, or naturally-occurring, for example National Parks, forests and lakes.

In this unit you will learn about different types of visitor attractions and the products and service they offer. You will investigate the positive and negative impacts of attractions, focusing on how positive impacts can be maximised and negative aspects minimised. You will discover how attractions use different kinds of interpretation to inform and entertain visitors, including displays, leaflets and costumed guides. Finally, you will investigate the appeal of attractions to various types of visitors and the key features that affect the decision to visit, such as pricing, access, location and products. Supervised visits to local and national attractions and talks by people working in the attractions sector will help you to understand how attractions operate and the techniques used to attract and retain visitors.

WHAT YOU WILL STUDY

During the course of this unit you will:

1. Examine the range of **products and services** provided by visitor attractions;
2. Explore the **impact** of visitor attractions;
3. Examine a range of techniques used for visitor **interpretation;**
4. Investigate the **appeal of** visitor attractions to different types of visitor.

You will be guided through the main topics in this unit with the help of the latest statistics, examples and industry case studies. You should also check out the weblinks throughout the unit for extra information on particular organisations or topic areas and use the activities to help you learn more.

ASSESSMENT FOR THIS UNIT

This unit is internally assessed, meaning that you will be given an assignment (or series of assignments) to complete by your tutor(s) to show that you have fully understood the content of the unit. A grading scale of pass, merit or distinction is used for all internally assessed units, with higher grades awarded to students who show greater depth in analysis and evaluation in their assignments. An assignment for this unit, which covers all the grading criteria, can be found on page 300. Don't forget to visit www.tandtONLine.co.uk for all the latest industry news, developments, statistics and tips to help you with your assignments.

t and t ONLine

Unit 18

SECTION 1: PRODUCTS AND SERVICES AT VISITOR ATTRACTIONS

Introduction

Visitor attractions are at the heart of the UK travel and tourism industry, with the top 20 major charging attractions alone accounting for 45 million visits in 2003, according to data from the DCMS (Department for Culture, Media and Sport). The UK has almost 6,500 visitor attractions, including country parks, historic properties, theme parks, zoos, gardens, farm parks, places of worship, museums and galleries. Together they offer a wealth of unique experiences for international and domestic visitors alike. Attractions act as a major draw for visitors, generating income and jobs for local and regional economies. They also stimulate business activity in other sectors of the travel and tourism industry, such as tour operators, accommodation providers and transport operators (see Figure 18.1).

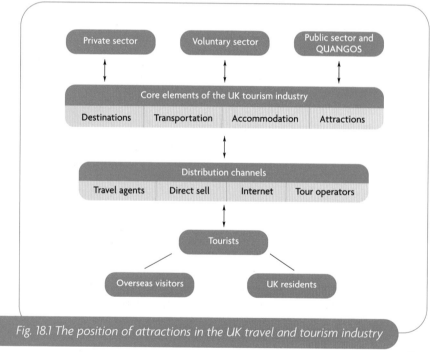

Fig. 18.1 The position of attractions in the UK travel and tourism industry

Figure 18.1 shows us that attractions are one of the 'core elements' of the UK travel and tourism industry, together with destinations, transportation and accommodation. Visitors to an attraction spend money in the destination where it is located by, for example, staying in local tourist accommodation, using transport services, eating out in a variety of catering establishments and visiting entertainment venues. Visitor attractions are operated by a range of private, voluntary and public sector organisations, as you can see from the examples of some of the UK's most popular attractions shown in Figure 18.2. Private sector attractions are first and foremost in business to make a profit, whereas attractions operated by the voluntary and public sectors have broader social and community objectives, such as conservation of buildings and the landscape. They too, however, must be run in a business-like manner and earn as much revenue as possible.

Unit **18**

PRIVATE SECTOR	VOLUNTARY SECTOR	PUBLIC SECTOR
Alton Towers	York Minster	Buckingham Palace
Chatsworth House	Jorvik Viking Centre	Big Pit Mining Museum
London Eye	Ironbridge Gorge	Edinburgh Castle
Drayton Manor	Salisbury Cathedral	British Museum
Legoland Windsor	White Cliffs of Dover (NT)	Science Museum

Fig. 18.2 Private, voluntary and public sector attractions

ACTIVITY

Carry out some research into three visitor attractions in your own area, or one nearby that caters for tourists. Find out if each attraction is operated by a private, public or voluntary sector organisation. Present your findings as a chart. Describe the products and services for visitors provided by each attraction.

This activity is designed to provide evidence for P1.

What is a 'visitor attraction'?

We all have our own ideas of what we think is a visitor attraction – if you live in the north of England, you might consider Albert Dock in Liverpool, the Lowry Art Gallery in Salford Quays, Manchester or Cadbury World in Birmingham as examples of visitor attractions. People living in the south of England might mention The British Airways London Eye, Thorpe Park or Chessington World of Adventures. Welsh people may include Snowdon, Techniquest in Cardiff or Caernarvon Castle on their list of attractions, while residents of Scotland may well mention the Scott Monument in Edinburgh, the Isle of Skye or the Burrell Collection in Glasgow. The people of Northern Ireland would surely put the Giant's Causeway, the mountains of Mourne or the Waterfront Hall in Belfast towards the top of their list of visitor attractions. These examples make it clear that both natural and built attractions appeal to visitors.

The National Tourist Boards of England, Northern Ireland, Wales and Scotland each carry out an Annual Survey of Visits to Visitor Attractions. Up to 2002, VisitBritain (and its predecessors the English Tourist Board/English Tourism Council) produced two UK-wide reports based on the results of these surveys. Since 2003, only separate reports for each country have been produced. The formal definition of a 'visitor attraction' used in these surveys is:

'An attraction where it is feasible to charge admission for the sole purpose of sightseeing. The attraction must be a permanently established excursion destination, a primary purpose of which is to allow public access for entertainment, interest or education; rather than being a primary retail outlet or a venue for sporting, theatrical, or film performances. It must be open to the public, without prior booking, for published periods each year, and should be capable of attracting day visitors or tourists, as well as local residents'.

It is important to remember that this definition has been agreed just for the purposes of the surveys carried out by the tourist boards – attractions such as one-off events and shopping centres are not covered by this definition, but are clearly important in attracting visitors.

The results of the 2002 VisitBritain UK-wide survey showed that the five most popular charging attractions were:

1. British Airways' London Eye;
2. Tower of London;
3. Eden Project, Cornwall;
4. Legoland Windsor;
5. Flamingo Land Theme Park and Zoo, North Yorkshire.

The most popular free attractions in the same year were:

1. Blackpool Pleasure Beach;
2. Tate Modern, London;
3. British Museum, London;
4. National Gallery, London;
5. Natural History Museum, London.

WEBLINK

www.visitbritain.com;
www.wtbonline.gov.uk;
www.scotexchange.net;
www.nitb.com

Check out these websites for the latest details of visits to attractions in England, Wales, Scotland and Northern Ireland.

Primary and ancillary products and services

Managers of visitor attractions aim to maximise the revenue from their customers in order to make a profit and re-invest money into new facilities for visitors. They do this by offering a variety of 'primary' and 'ancillary' products and services. The main facility, and principal reason for visiting the attraction, is known as the 'primary product'. If you visit a theme park, for example, the primary product is made up of the rides that provide excitement and fun. The primary product at a museum are the artefacts on display, while the prime reason for visiting a stately home is to see the architecture and furniture in the building, and learn about the way of life of the people who lived there in the past. The primary product doesn't change a great deal over time, but attraction operators have to regularly update their 'product' to give people a reason to visit again; if a theme park, for example, did nothing to introduce new rides and facilities on a regular basis, it would soon lose its customers and become unprofitable. Attractions often stage events that appeal to different types of visitors as a way of revitalising their primary product and generating extra income.

Unit 18

www.chatsworth-house.co.uk

*Check out this website
for more information on
events and facilities at
Chatsworth House.*

FOCUS ON INDUSTRY – Events at Chatsworth House

As well as welcoming visitors to the stately home and gardens, Chatsworth House in Derbyshire runs a series of special events that appeal to a wide variety of visitors, for example:

- Horse trials;
- An angling fair;
- A country fair;
- Concerts;
- Behind-the-scenes days;
- Farm shop events and demonstrations;
- Garden events;
- Sewing school courses;
- Vintage car rallies;
- Farmyard and woodland walks.

Offering such a wide variety of events helps to the keep the primary product refreshed and gives visitors who have been before a good reason for making a return visit.

Ancillary products and services are very important to visitor attractions, since they enhance the 'visitor experience' and generate revenue from additional sales. They include:

- Shops – selling gifts, souvenirs and products linked to the attraction, e.g. knitwear at a woollen mill and wine at a vineyard;
- Food and drink – for sale in restaurants, cafés, fast-food outlets, ice cream parlours, etc. The larger attractions feature well-known brands, such as McDonalds, Burger King and KFC;
- Children's play areas – often provided at no extra charge to provide somewhere for youngsters to let off steam and for parents to have a break;
- Picnic areas – places for individuals and groups to eat their own food. Picnic areas increase a person's 'dwell time' at an attraction, i.e. the total amount of time spent on site;
- Toilets – the availability and cleanliness of toilets is very important to visitors. Poor facilities create a bad impression with visitors and affect the number of repeat visits;
- Parking – visitors may have to pay to park their cars or the facility may be provided for free. Depending on the size of the attraction, there may be transport from the car parks to the main entrance, e.g. by land train, monorail or coaches.
- Services for visitors with special needs – providing accessible attractions is now a legal requirement under the Disability Discrimination Act and makes good business sense as well;

- Corporate hospitality and room hire – hosting business functions, meetings and even weddings is an excellent way for attractions to increase their income, particularly out of season when visitor numbers may be low;
- Photography – another income-earning activity, especially in theme parks, where visitors are given the chance to buy a photo of themselves while on a ride;
- Education services – school, college and university groups make up a sizeable proportion of the visitors to many attractions, so providing facilities such as a classroom, guided walks, illustrated talks and fact sheets adds to the visitors' experience, as well as making good business sense.

Visitors usually have to pay an extra charge for most ancillary products and services, thereby generating extra revenue for the attraction. This 'secondary spend' as it is sometimes known, can be very profitable for the attraction – profit margins on, for example, selling gifts, food and drink, can be far higher than margins on entrance fees to the attraction.

WEBLINK

www.at-bristol.org.uk/corporate

Check out this website for more information on At-Bristol and its corporate events.

FOCUS ON INDUSTRY – At-Bristol's corporate events

At-Bristol is home to three visitor attractions in the regenerated harbour side area of Bristol. Explore At-Bristol is a hands-on science and discovery centre that uses the latest multimedia equipment; Wildwalk At-Bristol is 'a living rainforest in the heart of the city', exploring the diversity of the natural world, with animals, plants and a variety of sound and vision technologies; IMAX At-Bristol offers film entertainment on a giant scale and houses one of only three IMAX cinema screens in the UK. Using the many different parts of the three attractions, At-Bristol offers a wide variety of corporate events, including:

- Banquets and receptions;
- Conferences, meetings and presentations;
- Product launches, trade fairs, location shoots and concerts;
- Incentive outings, team-building activities and debate forums;
- Wedding receptions, family functions, wedding and naming ceremonies.

At-Bristol also has access to public areas surrounding the attractions that can be used for corporate events. Millennium Square can seat up to 4,500 people or accommodate 7,500 standing, while the smaller Anchor Square is designed to seat 1,000 people or accommodate 2,000 standing. Both squares are used for large events such as open-air concerts and exhibitions of public art.

ACTIVITY

Choose five visitor attractions spread across the country and find out what facilities and services they offer for corporate events. Make a fact sheet on each of the attractions giving full details of the corporate facilities on offer.

This activity is designed to provide evidence for P1.

Types of visitor attractions

The following sections of this unit look in detail at the many different types of attractions available in the UK, which can be grouped under the following headings:

1. Heritage attractions;
2. Historic monuments and properties;
3. Cultural attractions;
4. Gardens, wildlife and environmental attractions;
5. Natural attractions;
6. Theme parks;
7. Entertainment facilities;
8. Events.

We are all familiar with large, well-known attractions across the UK, but it is important to remember that the majority of visitor attractions throughout Britain are not household names. Small museums, craft galleries, shops, leisure facilities and farm attractions, to name but a few, are crucial to the economic well-being of many areas of the country. Together, they form the 'critical mass' of attractions in a locality that forms the basis for encouraging tourists to explore and perhaps stay overnight, thereby contributing valuable revenue to the local economy.

Heritage attractions

Britain has a rich and varied heritage that appeals to many visitors from home and abroad. Right across the country there are large and small attractions that celebrate past events, industrial processes, traditions and landscapes, for example:

- Ironbridge Gorge Museum in Shropshire;
- Jorvik Viking Centre in York;
- Welsh Slate Museum in Llanberis, north Wales;
- Beamish Open Air Museum in County Durham;

Unit 18

- Quarry Bank Mill in Cheshire;
- National Maritime Museum at Greenwich, London;
- Lulworth Cove Heritage Centre, Dorset;
- New Lanark World Heritage Village, Scotland;
- Giant's Causeway Visitor Centre, Northern Ireland.

Jorvik Viking Centre in York

Heritage attractions tend to focus on a particular theme or activity and use a variety of interpretation techniques to tell a story or explain a process (you will learn more about interpretation later in this unit). English Heritage is the publicly-funded agency that advises the government on all matters concerning heritage and the historic environment. It also manages, and makes available to the public, more than 400 historic sites in England, including Barnard Castle, Stonehenge and Dover Castle. CADW does a similar job in Wales.

Some of Britain's finest heritage attractions have been awarded UNESCO World Heritage Site status in recognition of their unique contribution to the world's natural and built heritage. The UK currently has 26 World Heritage Sites, which include Ironbridge Gorge, the Tower of London, the Royal Botanic Gardens at Kew and Hadrian's Wall. The Cornwall and West Devon mining landscape has recently been chosen as the UK's 2005 nomination for becoming a World Heritage Site. The final decision as to whether it has been successful will be made by the World Heritage Committee at its annual meeting in the summer of 2006.

Historic monuments and properties

Britain's historic monuments and properties are amongst the finest in the world and are a major draw for tourists from the UK and overseas. Most are in public ownership or are owned by the National Trust, a registered charity and the country's biggest landowner. Some are in private ownership, including Chatsworth House and Blenheim Palace. The following are some of the UK's most popular historic monuments and properties:

- Tower of London;
- Edinburgh Castle;
- Windsor Castle;

Unit 18

- Roman Baths at Bath;
- Stonehenge, Wiltshire;
- Chatsworth House, Derbyshire;
- Tatton Park, Cheshire;
- Blenheim Palace, Oxfordshire.

Churches, cathedrals, ancient monuments and sites are also important attractions for visitors, for example St Paul's Cathedral in London, Glastonbury Tor in Somerset and the sites of past battles.

St Paul's Cathedral (courtesy Sampson Lloyd/St Paul's Cathedral)

Cultural attractions

Museums and art galleries are amongst the most popular cultural attractions with visitors. They display ancient and modern artefacts in a variety of settings, using a variety of techniques to inform, educate and entertain visitors. The following are amongst Britain's most popular cultural attractions:

- Tate Modern;
- British Museum;
- Science Museum;
- National Gallery;
- Natural History Museum;
- The Lowry, Salford Quays, Manchester;
- Museum of Welsh Life at St Fagan's, Cardiff;
- Ulster Folk and Transport Museum, Northern Ireland.

Some destinations attract visitors because of their associations with music, the arts or famous people. Shakespeare's birthplace in Stratford-upon-Avon is a magnet for UK and overseas visitors alike, while many tourists visit the haunts of Dylan Thomas in Wales and Thomas Hardy in Dorset. The cultural diversity in cities such as Leeds, Manchester, Cardiff, London and Bradford is used as a springboard for themed events and short breaks, e.g. curry weekends in Bradford and visits to the Chinatown areas of London and Manchester.

Unit 18

The Science Museum in London *(courtesy of SSPL/Science Museum)*

ACTIVITY

Carry out some research into three cultural attractions in the UK. For each attraction, produce an illustrated fact sheet that describes (1) the primary and ancillary products on offer to visitors; (2) corporate hospitality facilities; (3) services and facilities for visitors with special needs.

This activity is designed to provide evidence for P1.

Gardens, wildlife and environmental attractions

Gardens, wildlife and the environmental attractions are growing in popularity as people become more interested in the world around them and the impact that modern life has on the planet. Gardens range from the large-scale attractions such as Kew Gardens and the National Trust's Stourhead Garden in Wiltshire to the many, small gardens open to the public as part of the National Gardens Scheme. Zoos have long been popular with visitors, but have changed their emphasis over the years to reflect the public's desire to see animals in a more natural setting. The following are some of Britain's most popular gardens, wildlife and environmental attractions:

- Eden Project in Cornwall;
- Chester Zoo;
- Kew Gardens in Surrey;
- London Zoo;
- The Deep in Hull;
- The Royal Horticultural Society (RHS) gardens at Wisley in Surrey;
- Royal Botanic Gardens in Edinburgh;
- The Botanic Gardens in Belfast;
- Stourhead Garden in Wiltshire;
- Glasgow Botanic Gardens.

Unit 18

Environmental attractions combine a fun day out with the chance to learn about issues such as conservation, energy use and sustainability. Examples of these types of attractions include the Centre for Alternative Technology (CAT) in Machynlleth, west Wales and the Eden Project in Cornwall, the subject of the next case study.

CASE STUDY – The Eden Project

Introduction

The Eden Project is one of the UK's most popular tourist attractions, welcoming more than 5 million visitors since it opened in March 2001. Built on the site of a former China clay works near St Austell in Cornwall, Eden was part-funded by a grant of £43 million of National Lottery money from the Millennium Commission. The attraction's centrepieces are the largest two conservatories in the world, known as 'biomes', that recreate different climates from around the world and house a variety of exotic plant species. Visitors can wander around the site or join one of the guided tours. As well as being a visitor attraction, Eden is also an educational resource in the widest sense of the word and a living exhibition of sustainable development.

Eden's organisation and mission

Eden promotes itself as *'a global garden for the 21st century, a gateway to a sustainable future and a dramatic setting in which to tell the fascinating story of mankind's dependence on plants'*. Its primary message is:

'Eden explores the human dependence on plants, and in doing so reveals our global interdependence. This in turn leads us to interpret economic, social and environmental impacts on a wider stage, not only out of curiosity and a shared humanity, but also because these factors affect us all'.

The Eden Project is the home of the Eden Trust, a UK-registered charitable trust – the Trustees are ultimately responsible for Eden's actions and its sustainable future. The project was the brainchild of Tim Smit, now Eden's Chief Executive, who had previously put his energies into developing the Lost Gardens of Heligan, also located in Cornwall, into a leading garden attraction. The Eden Trust has recently established the Eden Foundation, which will be the focus for all future activities at the attraction, working with a range of partner organisations to explore new approaches to sustainable living.

Products and services at Eden

The biomes are undoubtedly the most recognisable feature of the Eden Project and the primary product that attracts visitors. At 50 metres high, the hot tropics biome houses plants from South America, West Africa, Malaysia and the Tropical Islands, including bananas, coffee, balsa, mahogany, orchids, spices and tropical ferns. The smaller, warm temperate biome showcases the cradle of civilisation around the Mediterranean, with citrus, olives, herbs and vines, a rich variety of plants from the South African regions, drifts of colourful Californian annual plants and also banks of fruits, vegetables, pulses and grains. Each plant has its own story and the attraction uses a wide variety of interpretation techniques to inform visitors to the full.

The biomes at the Eden Project

Visitors approach the attraction via the visitor centre, which includes the Eden Shop – already one of the site's most successful and highly-regarded ventures. The shop offers a combination of environmentally-friendly products from around the world, local produce and Eden-branded merchandise. Also within the visitor centre is the ticketing hall, plant areas, a coffee shop and the Gallery Restaurant offering panoramic views of the biomes below. Further refreshment facilities are located in the building that links the two biomes, including Morocco Red – a restaurant serving tastes from around the world, but using local produce – and café Zzubb Zzubb, offering a range of light meals and snacks. Other catering points can be found outdoors, with the emphasis on quality, 'Cornishness', freshness and value for money. Extensive toilet and baby changing facilities are available in the visitor centre and elsewhere in the attraction. More than half of the attraction's staff are first aid trained and there are also fully-qualified paramedics on site at all times.

Eden's education programme

Approximately 250 schoolchildren visit the Eden Project every day, from Cornwall, across the UK and even from overseas. The aims of the attraction's formal education programme are to:

Unit 18

1. Link the National Curriculum with the real world, real issues and current stories;
2. Run enrichment programmes for teachers;
3. Explore the ways people learn and develop effective learning and communication;
4. Motivate and engage people of all ages, abilities, ethnicity and background.

In addition to science education programmes, Eden covers a number of other areas of the curriculum, including art, history, numeracy, literacy, design and technology.

WEBLINK

www.edenproject.com

Check out this website to help answer the questions in this case study and for more information on the Eden Project.

CASE STUDY QUESTIONS

1. What facilities and services does Eden offer visitors with special needs?
2. What interpretation techniques does Eden offer its visitors to make their visit as enjoyable and instructive as possible?
3. What activities does Eden carry out to minimise its impact on the local environment and community?
4. Describe the different categories of visitors that you think are likely to be attracted to the Eden Project, explaining precisely what appeals to each category.

Natural attractions

The great outdoors is a major attraction for visitors who want to escape from the pressures of modern life and enjoy fresh air, exercise and beautiful landscapes. Many of Britain's natural areas are protected against overdevelopment, so that future generations can enjoy what many people treasure today. These 'protected areas' include:

- National Parks – to date, twelve National Parks have been designated in England and Wales since the 1949 National Parks and Access to the Countryside Act. This includes the Broads, which was set up under a special Act of Parliament in 1988, and the New Forest, designated a National Park in March 2005. The Countryside Agency is currently consulting on establishing a new South Downs National Park. The word 'national' does not mean that the Parks are owned by the government; most of the land within National Park boundaries is privately owned and often under severe pressure from visitors and their vehicles;
- Areas of Outstanding Natural Beauty (AONBs) – there are currently 41 AONBs in England and Wales. They range from the wild open moorlands of the North Pennines to the green belt countryside of the Surrey Hills and the intimate valley of the Wye, which straddles the border with Wales. AONBs are popular with visitors, although, unlike National Parks, they are designated more for their wildlife than recreational value;

WEBLINK

www.countryside.gov.uk;

www.ccw.gov.uk;

www.snh.org.uk;

www.ehsni.gov.uk

Check out these websites for more information on National Parks and other protected areas in England, Wales, Scotland and Northern Ireland.

▪ Heritage Coasts – there are 46 Heritage Coasts in England and Wales. They are among the most precious assets for wildlife and landscape, as well as for tourism. Concern over the harmful impact of increasing numbers of visitors led to their designation and a plan of action which includes creating and repairing footpaths, cleaning up bathing water and removing litter. Currently, 32 per cent of England's scenic coastline is conserved as Heritage Coasts.

Theme parks

A theme park is a visitor attraction offering permanent rides and entertainment in a themed setting or range of settings, providing something for the whole family. Most theme parks charge one price for unlimited access to all rides and attractions in a fun environment. Since the first UK theme park opened at Thorpe Park in 1979, there has been a rapid rise in the number of attractions and volume of visitors. Figures from Euromonitor show that visitor umbers to UK theme parks grew to nearly 50 million in 2003, with Blackpool Pleasure Beach being the most popular UK leisure park accounting for nearly 7 million visitors.

Although each UK theme park has its own particular attractions, there are certain common characteristics that theme parks exhibit, for example:

▪ Parks offer a mix of facilities and activities, e.g. 'white knuckle' rides, live entertainment, animals, gardens, events, children's play areas, education centres, corporate hospitality, retail and catering;
▪ Most parks operate on a seasonal basis between Easter and the end of October;
▪ Most visitors are family groups from the C1/C2 social classes;
▪ Group bookings account for between 10-25 per cent of all visitors;
▪ Typically, parking for 3000-4000 cars is provided;
▪ Site areas range from as little as 12 acres to 800 acres plus, with 130-140 acres being a typical size;
▪ Parks are generally close to the motorway network, ensuring very large two-hour catchment populations (up to 15 million);
▪ Length of stay on site averages between 6 and 7 hours, presenting park operators with ample opportunities for generating secondary spend, e.g. at catering and retail outlets.

In addition to Blackpool Pleasure Beach, other popular UK theme parks include:

▪ Alton Towers, Staffordshire;
▪ Thorpe Park, Surrey;
▪ Chessington World of Adventures, Surrey;
▪ Oakwood Leisure Park, Pembrokeshire;

Unit 18

- Pleasureland Theme Park, Southport;
- Pleasure Beach, Great Yarmouth;
- Drayton Manor, Staffordshire;
- Legoland Windsor.

Legoland Windsor

ACTIVITY

The Tussauds Group is one of the world's leading visitor attraction companies. Carry out some research into the Group and use your findings to write a 1,000-word newspaper article, which should include information on its history, structure, financial performance, plus details of the attractions it operates in the UK.

This activity is designed to provide evidence for P1.

CASE STUDY – Chessington World of Adventures

Introduction

Chessington World of Adventures is part of the Tussauds Group of visitor attractions. The attraction started life as Chessington Zoo, which was opened in July 1931 as a private venture by Reginald Goddard who invited the public to view his private animal collection. After the War Chessington soon became known for the different types of entertainment it could offer, including a circus, a funfair and a miniature railway as well as the zoo. Despite these developments, the attendance figures of over 800,000 began to decline in the early 1970s and the Zoo was in need of further investment.

In 1978 the Pearson Group bought Chessington and when they later bought Madame Tussauds, they put all their leisure interests together to form the Tussauds Group. Planning for the redevelopment of Chessington began in 1981 and six years later the £12 million upgrade was completed and officially opened by HRH Prince Edward. The opening coincided with the opening of the M25 motorway, which gives easy access to the attraction from various parts of the country. Approximately 18 million people live within a 2-hour drive of the site. Every year the attraction welcomes more than 1 million visitors and employs at least 1,000 members of staff.

Location and access

Chessington is located 12 miles from London, two miles from the A3 and M25 motorway. The attraction offers free parking for visitors. The park is accessible by public transport – regular South West Trains services run from Waterloo, Clapham Junction and Wimbledon to Chessington South Station, a 10-minute walk from the attraction. Chessington is served by regular bus services from nearby Kingston and Epsom. The attraction welcomes disabled guests and provides a range of services to make their time at Chessington as enjoyable as possible. Full details are given in the attraction's detailed guide for disabled visitors.

Products and services at Chessington

The primary product at Chessington consists of the various rides, events and entertainments aimed at the family market; these include Dragon's Fury, Dragon Falls, Vampire, Bubbleworks, Rameses Revenge and Tomb Blaster. The park has categorised its rides and attractions according to an 'adventure rating'. The four levels of adventure are:

1. Mini adventurer (for tiny tots);
2. Junior adventurer (for younger adventurers);
3. Family adventurers (for all the family – height and size restrictions may apply);
4. Experienced adventurers (for the older adventurer).

The managers of the attraction aim to launch a new attraction every year in order to refresh the product and give people a reason for making a return visit. Once the type of ride has been agreed, it can take as long as three years for the project to be completed, so careful long-term planning is crucial. Ancillary products and services at Chessington include places to eat, games, photography, corporate hospitality and services for visitors with special needs. The attraction offers the opportunity for students studying travel and tourism, business or animal husbandry to visit the site and take advantage of an educational talk as part of their trip.

Facilities for corporate events

Chessington offers tailor-made packages for corporate visitors, including team building/activity days, day delegate packages and fun days. Groups of all sizes can be catered for, including major events involving up to 10,000 visitors.

Unit 18

WEBLINK

www.chessington.co.uk

Check out this website to help answer the questions in this case study and for more information on Chessington World of Adventures.

CASE STUDY QUESTIONS

1. Describe the target markets that Chessington World of Adventures is aiming to attract and explain how the facilities are geared to meet the needs of each target market.
2. List the specific facilities and services the attraction offers visitors with special needs.
3. Carry out some further research on Chessington's facilities for corporate customers and prepare detailed lists of what is available.
4. Describe the impacts that Chessington has on the local environment and community, and explain how it tries to minimise its negative and maximise its positive impacts on both.

Entertainment facilities

Entertainment facilities, such as nightclubs, casinos, discos, theatres, concert halls, arenas and opera houses, are important attractions that provide entertainment opportunities for visitors to an area and local residents. Indoor arenas, such as the NIA in Birmingham, the ExCel Arena in London's Docklands and Sheffield Arena, are major venues for concerts, attracting people from a wide catchment area. Much of the appeal of UK tourist destinations is the wide range of entertainment facilities they offer visitors. Seaside resorts such as Scarborough, Blackpool and Brighton, for example, attract tourists with a variety of live shows, concert events and 'night life' opportunities. Smaller towns and cities also attract day visitors from their immediate area to enjoy the entertainment at nearby cinemas, theatres, night clubs and arts centres.

WEBLINK

www.culture.gov.uk

Check out this DCMS website for the latest information on the development of 'super casinos' in the UK.

FOCUS ON INDUSTRY – New 'super casinos' for the UK

The government proposed the introduction of eight new, regional 'super casinos' in the UK as part of the 2005 Gambling Act. These new casinos would be allowed to open 24 hours a day, with unlimited jackpots. The Act will also introduce compulsory checks on gambling websites, set up a new Gambling Commission to 'police' the industry and create a new offence of permitting a child to gamble. Following pressure from Members of Parliament and charities concerned about the possible harmful effects of gambling, the government agreed to recommend the opening of just one 'super casino' in the UK. The exact location of the facility has yet to be decided, but at the time of writing, Blackpool Borough Council had submitted a bid to build the casino and had secured the backing of the North West Regional Development Agency.

Unit 18

Events

Staging events is an excellent way of attracting visitors to an area and gaining significant revenue from entrance fees and secondary spending opportunities, such as car parking fees and the sale of food, drink and a variety of merchandise. Events are particularly useful for destinations that don't have extensive built and natural attractions to tempt visitors or are located in remote areas away from major centres of population. Events cater for an extremely wide variety of visitor interests – everything from sport, music and food to history, gardens and books. Britain has music events that appeal to all tastes, from the Cardiff Singer of the World Competition to the Glastonbury and V music festivals. Sporting events such as the British Grand Prix at Silverstone, football and rugby matches at the Millennium Stadium in Cardiff and the tennis championships at Wimledon, attract thousands of visitors from the UK and overseas. Major cultural events such as the Edinburgh Festivals and Notting Hill Carnival have international reputations.

Jousting at Warwick Castle

Health, safety and security at visitor attractions

Health, safety and security are very important considerations for the attractions sector of the travel and tourism industry, with the requirements of the 1974 Health and Safety at Work, etc. Act being the main UK legislation at present. This Act places a number of important responsibilities on attraction operators, such as:

1. Providing safe and healthy working conditions for employees;
2. Making available safe devices and protective equipment;
3. The company consulting its own employees to ensure that safe and healthy work practices continue to be used.

Health and safety is a particular issue for theme park operators, most of which have a health and safety committee to make sure the company's responsibilities are carried out. Day-to-day responsibility is delegated to individual managers and supervisors.

Other health and safety legislation and regulations that can affect visitor attractions includes:

- Fairgrounds and Amusement Parks Guidance on Safe Practice;
- The Health and Safety at Work, etc. Act 1974;
- The Management of Health and Safety at Work Regulations 1999;
- The Provision and Use of Work Equipment Regulations 1998;
- The Disability Discrimination Act 1995;
- Control of Substances Hazardous to Health (COSHH) Regulations 1999;
- Manual Handling regulations 1992.

Under the Management of Health and Safety at Work Regulations 1999, employers have a duty to carry out risk assessments that should highlight potential health and safety risks and lead to positive action being taken to put matters right. Even the smallest attraction needs to give attention to the health and safety needs of staff and visitors. Bad publicity given to poor health and safety procedures leading to accidents involving members of the public, can have disastrous effects on attractions, e.g. a serious accident on a theme park ride can reduce visitor numbers overnight.

Potential hazards for visitors to attractions include:

- Unguarded or unsupervised machinery and equipment;
- Fast-moving rides and monorails;
- Accidents involving animals;
- Slippery or broken walkways;
- Loose or broken wiring;
- Poor lighting indoors and outside;
- Leaks of steam, water, gas or oil;
- Blocked aisles and walkways;
- Fire hazards;
- Water hazards;
- Poor signposting.

Another important part of the Management of Health and Safety at Work Regulations 1999 that has implications for attractions is a section that places a duty on employers to take account of the lack of experience of young people in the workplace. All members of staff who are 18 years of age and under must be given an individual risk assessment before they start work.

Unit 18

WEBLINK

www.warwick-castle.com

*Check out this website
for more information on
Warwick Castle.*

FOCUS ON INDUSTRY – Health and safety at Warwick Castle

Warwick Castle, part of the Tussauds Group, has a Health and Safety Committee, which is a forum for discussing any issues members of staff wish to raise, via their representative. The committee is chaired by the attraction's Head of Operations, with each department represented by a member of staff and the Health and Safety Officer acting as an adviser. The committee discusses all health and safety issues and minutes of their meetings are distributed to all members of staff at the attraction. To ensure that the attraction's health and safety procedures are correctly implemented, the Health and Safety Officer may seek external advice from a number of sources, including:

- Architects;
- Police;
- Fire service;
- Ambulance service;
- Health and Safety Executive (HSE);
- Environmental Health Officer;
- Specialist health and safety external bodies.

Access to visitor attractions

In the case of visitor attractions, 'access' is an all-embracing term covering:

- Geographical access – transport routes and parking;
- Physical access to the attraction – particularly for people with mobility problems and other special needs;
- Access for all sectors of the community – regardless of, for example, their age, gender, race or income level. This is often reflected in the attraction's pricing policy, e.g. reduced prices for certain categories of visitors.

Warwick Castle

Access to an attraction can have negative impacts on the local community and environment. Attractions need to implement measures to make sure that their operations impact as little as possible on local communities.

Unit 18

WEBLINK

www.tourismforall.info

Check out this website for more information on Tourism for All.

FOCUS ON INDUSTRY – Tourism for All

Tourism for All is a national registered charity which provides information to people with disabilities and older people in relation to accessible accommodation and other tourism facilities, including visitor attractions. It provides expertise and support to the tourism and hospitality sector in order to provide accessible services for all people. Tourism for All works with a very wide network of organisations and individuals who support its objectives, including VisitBritain, the Disability Rights Commission and the British Resorts Association, plus a large number of local authorities.

Security at visitor attractions

Attraction operators are legally responsible for providing a safe and secure environment for their staff and visitors, plus any other people who visit the site. Security is a particular issue in relation to the following:

- Visitors and their possessions;
- Money taken for admission and in retail/food outlets;
- Artefacts and equipment in the attraction;
- Information relating to the business and its customers;
- Staff and their possessions.

Many attractions now employ security firms to patrol on-site and to work with the emergency services in the event of security breaches.

WEBLINK

www.chessington.co.uk

Check out this website for more information on Chessington World of Adventures.

FOCUS ON INDUSTRY – Security at Chessington World of Adventures

Security is taken very seriously at Chessington, as the following extract from its website explains:

'Security is important for the enjoyment and the safety of our guests and cast (members of staff). It is the job of security hosts in the Park to ensure that it is possible for all our guests to enjoy all the facilities offered by Chessington World of Adventures. Security cameras now monitor all areas of the Park and CCTV cameras are fitted in the shops, rides and the Park in general, and merchandising goods are security tagged'.

Unit 18

Managing visitor and traffic flows

Regardless of the size of an attraction, attention will need to be given to how visitors and their vehicles will be controlled on-site and in the immediate vicinity of the attraction in order to ensure maximum safety and convenience for visitors. Operators can introduce visitor and traffic management by, for example:

- Controlling the number of visitors – e.g. timed ticketing, peak and off-peak pricing to encourage/discourage visitors at particular times, restricted marketing to do the same, etc;
- Modifying the behaviour of visitors – e.g. zoning particular activities, channelling visitor flows, queue control with entertainment to keep visitors occupied while queuing, offering pre-booked tickets, etc;
- Adapting the attraction to meet visitor use – e.g. new features to diffuse visitor flows, protection of vulnerable objects from damage, amended facilities for visitors with specific needs, etc;
- Techniques used to control traffic flow to and from the attraction – e.g. size and location of car parks, park-and-ride facilities, traffic calming measures (humps on roads, bollards), encouraging the use of public transport, etc.

Customer care and services

Attractions are no different to any other sector of the travel and tourism industry in needing to provide customers with excellent standards of customer care and service if they are to be successful. You have learned elsewhere in your course that looking after customers well leads to repeat business, increased revenue, a good company image and staff who enjoy their work.

Signposting on the Cornwall coast path

Unit 18

WEBLINK

www.nmm.ac.uk

*Check out this website
for more information on
the National Maritime
Museum.*

FOCUS ON INDUSTRY – Customer care at the National Maritime Museum, Greenwich

The National Maritime Museum (NMM) in Greenwich is the largest maritime museum in the world and is rated in the top ten places to visit by the UK's Association of Leading Visitor Attractions (ALVA). Excellent customer service is part of the museum's responsibilities, objectives and values, and is provided in a variety of ways:

1. Meeting and greeting customers as they enter the museum sites;
2. Value-added interpretation;
3. Written information;
4. Education services;
5. Retailing products;
6. Hospitality and catering;
7. Targeted products and services;
8. Virtual access to the museum and its collections via its websites;
9. Providing an information and pre-booking service.

The basic customer service that the NMM provides is access for everyone to its historical buildings and collections. In the year March 2003 to March 2004, the museum recorded over 1.35 million visitors through its three sites – the National Maritime Museum, the Queen's House and the Royal Observatory, Greenwich.

Signage

Good signage is often taken for granted by visitors to attractions – it's only when signs are wrong or non-existent that you realise how important they are to ensuring a good day out. Signs are needed to direct people to the attraction, show them where to park and point out key areas of the attraction, including toilets, first aid points and catering outlets. Signs should be made of materials that reflect the attraction's environment, e.g. wooden signs in forest attractions and visitor centres, steel and plastic in hi-tech attractions and industrial heritage museums.

Visitor satisfaction

All attractions, whatever their size, need regular feedback from visitors on their levels of satisfaction with the attraction and its facilities. This is collected using a variety of techniques, such as:

1. On-site visitor surveys – either carried out by interviewers or using self-completed questionnaires;
2. Focus groups – where small numbers of visitors are asked in-depth questions about their experiences at the attraction;
3. Observation – staff observing visitors' reactions while at the attraction and reporting back to management.

The feedback from these activities enables attraction operators to change aspects of their 'product' to improve the visitors' experience. Attractions can also take part in assessments of their quality, as the next example explains.

WEBLINK

www.vaqas.org.uk

Check out this website for more information on VAQAS.

FOCUS ON INDUSTRY – Visitor Attraction Quality Assurance Service (VAQAS)

VisitBritain's VAQAS offers a quality assessment service for visitor attractions. It helps to identify strengths of an attraction and highlights areas for development. The service is available to attractions of all types and sizes. The assessment takes the form of an annual visit to the attraction at any time when it is open to the public. The visit, by an experienced assessor, is unannounced, although one key contact at the attraction will be advised beforehand. All areas that impact on the quality of the visitor experience are included in the assessment, ranging from the initial enquiry to departure from the attraction. The assessment is followed by a one-to-one debrief with the attraction's operators. Each visit is followed by an assessment report and, if successful, the accreditation 'Quality Assured Visitor Attraction'. VAQAS was launched nationally in 2001 and, to date, more than 600 attractions have been accredited, including the British Airways' London Eye, Kew Gardens, the National Railway Museum and Castle Howard.

Queuing

It is a fact of life that nobody likes to queue! Having to queue at attractions can sometimes be frustrating for visitors, who don't want to waste time when they really want to be enjoying their day out. Queuing is a particular problem at theme parks, since the capacity of the rides is limited. Theme parks, and other attractions, use a number of techniques to help keep queuing to a minimum, such as:

- Timed ticketing – this controls visitor flows and reduces queuing. Tickets can normally be ordered in advance by telephone and online using the Internet, or bought on-site;
- Displays showing the maximum queuing times on rides;

Unit 18

- Virtual queuing' – this is a system that allows visitors to reserve their place in a 'virtual queue', thereby allowing them to spend time enjoying other rides rather than standing in line. Some systems use a pager that visitors carry around with them;
- Information leaflets that suggest the quietest times to visit the attraction to avoid queuing.

Some of the UK's most popular attractions use these sorts of techniques to reduce queuing times, for example the British Airways' London Eye, Alton Towers, the National Maritime Museum in Greenwich and Thorpe Park in Surrey.

Dealing with complaints

You have learned about the skills and techniques for dealing with complaints in other units on your course – in short, staff must stay calm, listen to what the visitor has to say, agree a plan of action with the visitor and make sure that it is carried out. Many attractions record the number of complaints received and use this as a tool to measure how well the attraction is doing over a period of time.

Data protection

Visitor attractions are legally bound to protect any information about visitors held as part of their business activity. Under the requirements of the Data Protection Act, such information must be held securely, not passed to third parties and only used for the purpose that it was originally collected.

Staffing and staff training

WEBLINK

www.welcometoexcellence.com

Check out this website for more information on the Welcome to Excellence series of training courses.

Staff working in visitor attractions must be trained in a number of areas, such as customer service, first aid, ride operations and retail. Training brings benefits to the attractions, with higher visitor satisfaction levels, increased sales, more repeat business, less staff turnover and improved recruitment. Some attractions send their staff on courses offered under the Welcome to Excellence series of training programmes run in conjunction with the Regional Tourist Boards.

Unit 18

Information

High quality information, both before they visit and while on-site, helps visitors to plan their visit to an attraction and make informed decisions about what to do while they are there. Visitors need certain basic information – opening times, prices, location, refreshment facilities – as well as more specific information on what the attraction has to offer visitors. Much of this information is made available on attractions' websites and in printed leaflets and guides. Websites have the advantage of publishing changes to basic information at short notice and can be used as a publicity tool to encourage people to visit an attraction. As well as providing information to the general public, attractions may have to supply other travel trade companies, including coach companies and tour operators, with details to incorporate into their tour programmes. Members of the press will also request information from time to time.

Unit 18

You have learned in other units on your course that the travel and tourism industry has a number of impacts, both positive and negative, on destinations and the people who live there. The same is true of visitor attractions – the bigger the attraction the greater the impacts are likely to be and the more measures needed to reduce the negative effects.

Impacts of visitor attractions can be classified as:

1. Socio-cultural – these are the effects that attractions have on people, their culture and quality of life;
2. Economic – these include creating jobs, generating incomes and helping to regenerate derelict areas;
3. Environmental – include issues such as pollution, erosion and congestion associated with attractions;
4. Political – factors such as legislation, regulations and government policies that affect visitor attractions.

The following sections of this unit examine each of these in detail, in relation to impacts on:

- The local environment;
- Local communities;
- Visitors;
- Wider issues concerning society in general.

In each of the sections there are examples of how attractions can maximise their positive impacts on local communities and the environment, while at the same time minimising negative effects.

Socio-cultural impacts

Broadening and revival of culture

Attractions give visitors the chance to experience past and present-day cultures, through viewing artefacts and objects, taking part in activities and using 'hands on', interactive exhibits. Cultural attractions, such as museums and art galleries, have a twin role of conserving items of value and making them available to the general public. The government encourages visits to attractions by 'sponsoring' some of the UK's most popular cultural attractions, i.e. the Department for Culture, Media and Sport (DCMS) provides funding to the attraction so that it can offer everybody free access. Since it was introduced in 2001, this free admission policy has been a great success – visits to museums have increased by 75 per cent nationally. In 2004, there were 34 million visits to all the museums and galleries sponsored by the DCMS and in the same year nearly 6 million more visits were made to England's formerly charging museums and galleries than in the year before the charges were dropped. Visits to museums that have always been free, such as the National Gallery, the Tate and the British Museum, rose by 9 per cent over the same period.

The British Museum in London (courtesy and copyright British Museum)

Visitor attractions can have positive cultural impacts by stimulating the revival of traditional activities in local communities, for example arts, crafts and customs. In the Peak District of Derbyshire, the ancient custom of 'well dressing' dates back hundreds of years and is a major attraction for visitors and local people. Wells are decorated with flower petals, berries, moss, cones and seeds, which are pressed into clay held in a wooden framework. Well dressing is celebrated in more than 60 towns and villages throughout Derbyshire, including Hope, Eyam and Tideswell. Many attractions that celebrate our industrial heritage, for example Ironbridge Gorge, sell traditional items that are made locally, thereby continuing past skills and practices. The positive cultural impacts of attractions need to be maximised by effective marketing of activities and by staging exhibitions and events that appeal to as wide a cross-section of society as possible. Reducing or even scrapping admission prices for certain categories of visitors will also have a positive effect.

Dilution of culture

Visitor attractions can sometimes have negative cultural impacts on local communities and environments. Attractions can sometimes feel rather artificial and come across as not being authentic. For example, when local people put on displays of traditional dancing at attractions and events, it can sometimes feel as if the dancing is taking place just to entertain the tourists and is not a true reflection of how it is normally performed. Attractions can try to minimise their negative cultural impacts by only staging truly authentic activities and displaying them in a professional manner. They can also use a variety of interpretation techniques to better inform and educate their visitors about local customs, cultures and traditions.

Unit 18

Economic impacts

As well as providing excitement, fun and education for millions of domestic and overseas tourists every year, the 6,500 visitor attractions found in the UK generate significant economic benefits for local communities, including employment, generating revenue, investment and regeneration.

Employment in visitor attractions

Providing jobs is one of the key positive impacts of the UK attractions sector. Precise figures on the numbers employed in visitor attractions are very difficult to gauge, since there is no category for jobs in attractions in government figures. However, 2003 data indicates that there were 86,700 people employed in libraries, museums and other cultural facilities. Most of these jobs are full-time, but many attractions, including theme parks and water parks, employ mostly seasonal staff. This often leads to a high turnover of staff and sometimes makes it difficult for attraction operators to persuade their employees to commit to training courses on a regular basis.

There is a trend in UK tourism towards all-year-round tourism, particularly associated with the growth in short breaks and additional holidays. It is not uncommon now for British people to take a holiday abroad plus two, three or even four short beaks in the UK every year, either to the countryside or in cities (or a mixture of the two). This helps create more permanent employment in visitor attractions, since the operators can be sure of revenue outside the traditional peak season. This is particularly true for attractions that include activities that are not weather-dependent, e.g. mountain biking, canoeing, white-water rafting and orienteering. The same applies to attractions that cater for the schools market – schoolchildren visit during term time when visitor numbers tend to be lower, thereby helping to spread revenue and jobs throughout the year.

Revenue, investment and regeneration

WEBLINK

www.national-lottery.co.uk

Check out this website for more information on the National Lottery and the 'good causes' it supports.

As well as providing jobs, another important positive economic impact of visitor attractions is the revenue generated from visitors and investors. The money spent by visitors at an attraction and in the surrounding area is re-circulated in the local economy via the 'multiplier effect', for example when people employed in attractions spend their wages in local shops and on local services (see page 77 in Unit 10 for more information on the multiplier effect).

Attractions have benefited enormously from the National Lottery. To date, some £17 billion has been awarded to 'good causes', which has included investment in many visitor attraction projects in sport, the arts, heritage and the environment.

Unit 18

Attractions often feature in multi-use regeneration projects, particularly in urban areas of the country. They are built alongside new entertainment venues, eating places, shopping outlets and sports facilities as part of urban regeneration projects, e.g. at Cardiff Bay, Bristol Harbourside, the Don Valley in Sheffield and Albert Dock in Liverpool.

WEBLINK

www.edenproject.com

Check out this website for more information on the economic impact of the Eden Project.

FOCUS ON INDUSTRY – Economic impact of the Eden Project

Research results released in 2004 show that the Eden Project (see case study on page 267) has injected nearly half a billion pounds worth of business back into the economy of Cornwall and the south west region of England. Eden has received £55.4 million of funding from the National Lottery via the Millennium Commission since it was built in 2001, but is estimated to have generated more than £460 million in economic impact on the local economy. Eden's operators estimate that, if visitors numbers remain as they have been since opening, the attraction's first 10 years of full operation should generate over £2 billion in economic output.

Eden has contributed to the economy in many ways. The attraction pays out £8 million in wages to local people every year, employing 600 temporary staff in the peak season and 380 people full-time all year round. Eden also uses local suppliers wherever possible, with knock-on effects to other businesses. The project has been responsible for attracting thousands of visitors to Cornwall. In 2003 there were 1.4 million visitors to the attraction, 90 per cent of whom had travelled into the county and more than half of the 90 per cent said that Eden had influenced their choice of holiday.

Environmental impacts

Visitor attractions can have considerable negative impacts on the environment and local communities, including congestion, noise and pollution. All new, large visitor attraction projects must carry out an environmental impact assessment (EIA) to indicate the likely environmental impacts and how these will be minimised or eliminated altogether. Attractions can also have a positive environmental impact, by being operated in a sustainable way that makes best use of the earth's resources. Certain attractions use the theme of the environment to inform visitors about current issues, such as the greenhouse effect, energy use and global warming.

Congestion and noise

People living close to attractions may have to put up with traffic congestion and extra noise generated by visitors. Where this becomes a serious problem, attraction operators often work in conjunction with local councils to agree solutions to the problems, which could include reserved parking spaces for residents only, restrictions on levels of noise and traffic diversions. Operators of the Alton Towers theme park in Staffordshire have worked with local people to install CCTV security cameras in Alton village and a number of other locations close to the attraction to improve security for local residents. In an effort to be seen as 'good neighbours', many attractions offer free or reduced price admission to people living nearby.

Pollution

Pollution associated with visitor attractions could involve noise, litter, vehicle emissions, chemical/oil spills, waste discharges, etc. The environmental impact assessments mentioned previously must include details of possible pollution and what measures will be put in place to deal with the problem.

Sustainability

Operating visitor attractions in a sustainable way is becoming an important consideration in the UK, as people become more concerned about environmental issues and the government introduces the concept of 'sustainability' into more of its policies, including those to do with tourism. Sustainability is all about using resources wisely so that future generations can enjoy what we have today.

A key objective of government is to reduce people's dependency on the car and to encourage travellers to use more public transport services. Figures show that it is having some success in this area, particularly in cities. Public transport services in rural areas, however, are often not able to offer the frequency and coverage of service that people want. Many visitor attractions play their part in encouraging people to leave their cars at home by promoting access by public transport. Many UK National Parks operate bus and train services that allow visitors to travel to and within the park without the need for a car.

WEBLINK

www.pembrokeshire
greenways.co.uk

*Check out this website
for more information on
Pembrokeshire
Greenways.*

FOCUS ON INDUSTRY – Pembrokeshire Greenways

Pembrokeshire Greenways is an initiative to encourage local residents and visitors, of all abilities, to access the countryside by sustainable means of transport, through walking, cycling, bus and train travel. The project covers the whole of Pembrokeshire, including the area covered by the Pembrokeshire Coast National Park, and is managed by a partnership of organisations that includes Pembrokeshire County Council, the National Park, the National Trust and Pembrokeshire Access Group. The project's website has details of a variety of walking and cycling routes, plus details of inter-connecting bus and train services. The Pembrokeshire 'Puffin' is a coastal bus service that is designed to help people walk the coast path without having to use a car.

WEBLINK

www.greenauditkit.org;
www.greendragonems.com.

*Check out these websites
for more information on
the Green Audit Kit and
Green Dragon
environmental schemes*

The government, via Regional Tourist Boards (RTBs) and Regional Development Agencies (RDAs), encourages all tourism businesses, including attractions, to operate in a more environmentally-friendly manner, through training and business advice. In England, attractions can follow the guidelines in the Green Audit Kit, while those in Wales can apply for Green Dragon accreditation. Both schemes offer practical solutions to saving energy, reducing waste, promoting public transport, recycling, saving water and protecting the environment.

ACTIVITY

Describe the impacts of three visitor attractions in your local area, or an area nearby that caters for tourists, on the local environment and community. Explain how the three attractions have minimised negative impacts and maximised positive impacts.

This activity is designed to provide evidence for P2 and D1.

Political impacts

UK and EU policy

The Department for Culture, Media and Sport (DCMS) is the government department responsible for setting tourism policy (although the Welsh Assembly Government, Scottish Executive and Northern Ireland Assembly have powers in their respective areas). DCMS works in partnership with the attractions sector to:

1. Improve and enhance the quality of its product;
2. Develop the skills of those working in the sector;
3. Generate better data for analysis;
4. Promote and market attractions in the UK and internationally.

Tourism policy in the European Union (EU) is the responsibility of a department known as DG Enterprise, which encourages high quality, sustainable attractions across all member states of the EU. Some UK attractions have benefited from EU funding for new buildings and equipment, particularly in parts of the UK that are considered to be in need of extra investment, e.g. the Eden Project in Cornwall, The Deep in Hull and the National Waterfront Museum in Swansea. We saw earlier in this unit that the National Lottery has provided funding for a number of new attractions in recent years.

There are a number of interest groups representing visitor attractions that try to influence tourism policy in the UK and Europe, by lobbying officials to get their message heard. These include the Tourism Alliance, Association of Leading Visitor Attractions (ALVA), Museums Association and the Historic Houses Association (HHA).

Legislation and regulations

We saw earlier in this unit that visitor attractions have to comply with many laws and regulations, not least in terms of health and safety requirements. Other legislation that is of particular relevance to attractions includes the Disability Discrimination Act, the Data Protection Act, the Licensing Act and Food Safety Regulations

Maximising the positives and minimising the negatives

In this section of the unit we have considered the socio-cultural, economic, environmental and political impacts concerning visitor attractions. The key to developing a sustainable attractions sector is to maximise its positive impacts and minimise its negative effects. We have seen that this can be achieved in a number of ways, for example:

1. Using a range of education and interpretation techniques to inform visitors;
2. Developing all-year-round attractions;
3. Promoting public transport services;
4. Using local products and services;
5. Carrying out environmental impact assessments;
6. Lobbying the UK government and EU officials;
7. Promoting sustainable business schemes.

ACTIVITY

Using this list of seven examples as a starting point, produce a chart showing the techniques that attractions can use to maximise positive impacts and minimise negative impacts. Remember to include all types of impacts – socio-cultural, economic, environmental and political.

This activity is designed to provide evidence for P2 and D1.

Unit 18

SECTION 3: INTERPRETATION AT VISITOR ATTRACTIONS

The Association for Heritage Interpretation (AHI) defines interpretation as *'the art of helping people explore and appreciate our world'*. Interpretation is all about giving visitors to all types of attractions not just an enjoyable experience, but one that will help them understand better the place they are visiting. It can be thought of as the many techniques used to 'tell a story' at an attraction. Visitor attractions as diverse as farms, ancient monuments, gardens, museums, wildlife reserves, stately homes, National Parks, forest areas and theme parks, all offer interpretation facilities for visitors using a variety of techniques, including:

- Displays;
- Guided tours;
- Audio-visual facilities;
- Signposting;
- Visitor centres.

There are many factors that need to be taken into consideration when choosing which interpretive techniques to use in an attraction, for example:

1. Location – facilities inside an attraction may not work in a countryside setting;
2. Cost – the budget that the attraction has to work within;
3. Target audience – design and content will differ from one type of visitor to another;
4. Longevity – deciding how the long the interpretation will be in place;
5. Reliability and maintenance – making sure that breakdowns are kept to a minimum;
6. Degree of interaction required – whether active of passive interpretation is needed;
7. Security – issues such as theft of equipment and vandalism.

As well as adding to the visitor experience, interpretation can also be used to manage visitors at an attraction. For example, guides can control where, when and for how long visitors dwell at a site. This is particularly important in the case of small attractions with limited space for large numbers of visitors. Visitors to Anne Hathaway's cottage in Stratford-upon-Avon are escorted around the property by fully-trained guides to enhance their experience and to control visitor numbers and throughput. Self-guided trails can be planned so as to divert visitors away from environmentally sensitive areas of an attraction.

Unit 18

WEBLINK

www.english-heritage.org.uk

Check out this website for more information on English Heritage.

FOCUS ON INDUSTRY – Interpretation at English Heritage

English Heritage is a public body, funded by the Department for Culture, Media and Sport (DCMS), and is responsible for over 400 historic properties in England (CADW: Welsh Historic Monuments does a similar job in Wales). English Heritage has developed a wide range of visitor services, including site interpretation and publications, in order to enhance visitor satisfaction and increase the likelihood of repeat visits. There are:

- Defined minimum standards of presentation for all properties;
- Explanatory graphic displays, audio tours, audio-visual presentations and exhibitions;
- Colour guidebooks and souvenir guides, many of which have been revised to be more attractive and readable;
- Children's activity sheets at some sites;
- Guided walks at many sites;
- Brief, plastic-covered guides are provided at some sites where entry is free, designed to be used on site and left for the next visitor.

English Heritage is the largest developer and user of audio tours for interpretation of historic properties, with more than 50 sites now offering this service. At Battle Abbey, Stonehenge, Framlingham Castle, Down House and Eltham Palace, there are interactive audio tours using the hand-held 'wand' system, which gives visitors the flexibility to choose which information they want to listen to, accessed by a numbered keypad. In addition, English Heritage is working to provide audio tours created specially for visitors with visual impairments, thereby increasing access to its sites.

ACTIVITY

Log on to the English Heritage website (www.english-heritage.org.uk) and choose six properties/sites for some further research. Make a chart showing the different interpretation facilities that each property/site offers, including facilities for people with special needs. Use the *Accessibility Guide* on the website to help you with this task.

This activity is designed to provide evidence for P3.

Unit 18

Displays

Displays at attractions can be either active or passive. Active displays allow people to interact with exhibits or artefacts to learn more about them. This is particularly appealing to children and young people who often have very enquiring minds! Passive displays tend to be associated with museums and art galleries. The main types of displays found in attractions include:

> *Displays in the 'Making the modern world' gallery at the Science Museum*
> *(courtesy of SSPL/Science Museum)*

- Interactive displays – 'hands on' facilities that allow visitors to touch and interact with exhibits to learn more;
- Static boards – provide information in text and graphic form for visitors;
- Virtual displays – using 3-D computer technology to simulate an event or setting, for example a virtual tour of a house or castle ruins showing how it would have looked in days gone by;
- Auditory – defined points at which to listen to information or sound guides (sometimes in different languages) that can be carried by the visitor while they are at the attraction;
- Animateurs – actors and costumed guides playing the part of people from the past and interacting with visitors in the attraction;
- Electronic – using computer-generated images, audio-visual displays or animatronics, i.e. moving models of past and present animals, for example dinosaurs.

> *An interactive display at the Wales Millennium Centre, Cardiff*

Unit 18

Guiding

Guiding is a type of interpretation that gives visitors the chance to delve more deeply into an attraction and its facilities. Guides can take a number of forms, including:

- Printed guides – such as leaflets, maps, books, brochures, etc. These are relatively cheap to produce, but may not have a great deal of visual impact when compared to other types of interpretative techniques;
- Audio guides – provide a commentary while visitors are moving around an attraction. They are quite expensive initially, but do offer the visitor a very comprehensive experience;
- Guided tours – group activities where a guide leads visitors on a tour of an attraction. These person-to-person tours are one of the best ways of interpreting an attraction, but guides need to be well-trained;
- Self-guided tours – when visitors use a leaflet or series of signposts to take themselves on a tour of an attraction. Self-guided tours are particularly popular at countryside attractions and give people the chance to walk at their own pace.

Special needs

Visitors with special needs may need particular interpretation facilities if they are to get the most out of their visit to an attraction. Depending on the nature of their special needs, these facilities could include:

Interpretation at the Jorvik Viking Centre in York

- Large print information leaflets and displays;
- Braille information and magnifiers;
- Tactile maps and exhibits;
- Audio guides and hearing loop systems;
- Sensory exhibits;
- A MiniCom telephone number for bookings.

Under the terms of the Disability Discrimination Act, attractions must make their facilities accessible to all visitors, regardless of their circumstances. Providing specialist interpretation facilities for these customers, although not a legal requirement for attraction operators, is seen as an important part of their work.

SECTION 4: APPEAL OF VISITOR ATTRACTIONS

It is clear that not all visitor attractions will appeal to every type of person in the UK or tourist from overseas. Some people will look for thrills, fun and excitement by visiting theme parks and entertainment venues, while others will prefer the peace and quiet of trips to the countryside, stately homes and gardens. To be successful, any attraction must be clear on precisely which type or types of visitors it is targeting and provide the right facilities and amenities to meet their target markets' needs. Market research is used to gather information on existing and potential visitors to attractions, and is an essential first step in identifying customers' needs.

Having established its target market(s), a visitor attraction must develop a 'product' that its customers will appreciate and enjoy. It will need to give attention to a number of considerations, including:

- The main features offered by the attraction;
- Extra features aimed at particular types of visitors, e.g. coach parties, school visits, visitors from abroad, conferences and corporate hospitality;
- Special events and activities, e.g. historic car rallies, balloon festivals, music concerts, etc;
- Catering facilities, e.g. restaurants, pizza parlours, ice cream outlets, cafés, etc;
- Other facilities, e.g. baby changing, wheelchairs, buggies, car parking, transport links, etc.

Types of attractions

The many types of visitor attractions found in the UK were discussed in detail at the beginning of this unit (see pages 263 to 274). You will need to refer to these pages when completing this part of the unit. We saw that attractions can be categorised into:

1. Heritage attractions;
2. Historic monuments and properties;
3. Cultural attractions;
4. Gardens, wildlife and environmental attractions;
5. Natural attractions;
6. Theme parks;
7. Entertainment facilities;
8. Events.

These attractions clearly appeal to different types of visitors, as the next section of this unit explains.

Unit 18

Types of visitor

Visitor attractions appeal to different people for different reasons; one family may enjoy a day out at London Zoo, for example, while another might prefer a trip to the nearby Natural History Museum; yet another family may choose somewhere else entirely, perhaps a trip on the London Eye. Whatever the reasons behind the choice of an attraction, all sites have a wide range of types of visitors, each with different characteristics. For a typical visitor attraction, these could be:

The British Museum appeals to a variety of visitors (courtesy and copyright British Museum)

- Incoming tourists to the UK – overseas visitors tend to be attracted by Britain's natural and built heritage and often use London as a convenient starting point for their holiday;
- Educational parties – are important sources of revenue for attractions, particularly outside the peak season. Many attractions offer an education service to school and college groups, which includes fact sheets on the attraction, illustrated talks by members of staff and reduced price entry;
- Groups with special interests – these may be on an organised event or travelling independently. Examples include members of gardening clubs visiting stately homes and car enthusiasts going to a vintage car rally at an attraction;
- Families – are a key market for many attractions, particularly theme parks and other entertainment venues. Attractions must offer a range of facilities to appeal to all members of the party;
- Different age groups – from the youngest baby to senior citizens, visitor attractions must cater for a wide age range in their visitors;
- Visitors with special needs – must be provided with a range of facilities to make their visit as enjoyable as possible;
- Corporate customers – are a very good source of revenue for many attractions, which provide facilities for training days, product launches, team-building events and staff incentives.

This list gives an indication of the difficult task of satisfying the needs of each of these different types of visitor, often referred to as 'markets', and stresses the importance of precise market research to identify exactly who visits an attraction and whether they are happy with the 'product'.

WEBLINK

www.alton-towers.co.uk

Check out this website for more information on Alton Towers.

FOCUS ON INDUSTRY – Visitors to Alton Towers

Alton Towers in Staffordshire is one of the UK's most popular paying attractions. The types of visitors to the attraction can be broken down as follows:

- Individuals;
- Coach groups;
- Companies for corporate events;
- School parties;
- Group organisers.

The age profile of visitors to Alton Towers is as follows:

Age (yrs)	Percentage
Under 7	4.8
8-12	4.0
13-17	19.2
18-24	28.9
25-34	21.1
35-44	14.3
45-54	5.9
Over 55	1.9

Alton Towers attracts people from all over the UK and has extensive facilities and services for visitors with special needs.

ACTIVITY

Choose a local visitor attraction and find out what particular markets it is trying to attract and whether the type of visitors has changed in the last five years. Describe the appeal of the attraction to each of the visitor types that you have identified.

This activity is designed to provide evidence for P4.

Features

It is the features of a visitor attraction that make it appeal (or not) to visitors. An attraction that has few features and whose operators have not invested in new facilities and services will struggle to survive. Key features that influence the appeal of a destination include:

- Location;
- Price;
- Transport;
- Seasonality;
- Access;
- Products and services;
- Interpretation.

Location

The location of natural attractions and many cultural sites is pre-determined, but developers can choose where to build new visitor attractions, subject to planning regulations. An attraction that is located close to a large urban area will have a large population on which to draw, but will also be in competition with many other attractions. Visitors look for attractions that are conveniently located and have good car and public transport access. Good signposting to and within the attraction is also important.

Price

The cost of visiting an attraction is an important consideration that will affect its appeal to visitors. Most attractions operate a variable pricing policy, offering different entry prices depending on when a person is visiting, e.g. peak season and off season rates, discounts for early evening and mid-week visits, etc. Attractions also charge different prices according to the type of visitor, as the following example from the Eden Project illustrates (2005 prices):

	Individuals	Groups (10+)
Adults	£12.50	£10.00
Children under 5 years	free	free
Children 5 – 15 years	£5.00	£4.00
Full-time students	£6.00	£5.00
Seniors (60 + years)	£9.50	£7.00
Family	£30.00	-

Attractions in the public sector, such as leisure centres and museums, sometimes offer concessionary rates for local people, including lone parents and unemployed people.

Transport

Most visits to attractions in the UK are made using a car or coach. Car drivers look for plenty of space for parking and easy access to and from the site. This is particularly true for visitors with special needs, who require parking facilities close to the attraction entrance. Coach companies that transport schools and other groups to attractions expect good access and parking facilities as well, plus some facilities for their drivers to take a break in comfort.

Seasonality

Not all visitor attractions are open all year round. Their operators consider that it is not economic to open for the small numbers of visitors who may visit in the winter. The types of visitors who come to attractions vary according to the time of year. Families come at weekends and during school holidays, whereas school groups visit during term time. Retired people have more flexibility in when they can visit and often take advantage of off-peak discounts to make their trip during quiet mid-week periods. Events for corporate guests take place throughout the time an attraction is open to the public.

Access

Visitors look for speedy access arrangements when visiting an attraction so as not to waste time. Any 'shuttle' transport that is provided must run at frequent intervals and facilities for buying entrance tickets must be well staffed in order to keep queuing time to a minimum. Larger attractions give visitors the chance to pre-book by telephone of on the Internet so as to save time queuing when they arrive. Access to attractions is an important issue for visitors with special needs – many attractions now offer comprehensive services for these visitors to comply with the Disability Discrimination Act.

Products and services

Different customers make use of the different products and services on offer at attractions. Families, for example, tend to make use of a wide range of facilities, such as baby changing, toilets, places to eat and lost children points. Visitors from overseas may need to use an attraction's interpretation facilities if they are provided in their own language, e.g. an audio tour. Enthusiasts of one kind or another make a beeline for the main facility at attractions, e.g. 'white knuckle' rides, traction engines at a steam rally or the paintings at an art gallery.

Unit 18

Interpretation

We saw earlier in this unit that there are many types of interpretation available at visitor attractions. Individuals and groups who really want to get an educational experience out of their visit to an attraction will look for comprehensive guide books, guided tours and static displays. Children are drawn to 'hands on' exhibits and artefacts that they can touch. Overseas visitors may need interpretative materials to be available in different languages.

UNIT SUMMARY

This unit has explored the visitor attractions sector and recognised the important role that attractions play in the economic and cultural life of the country. You have examined the primary and ancillary products and services offered by attractions, and considered important aspects of health, safety and security at attractions. Socio-cultural, economic, environmental and political impacts of attractions have been studied in detail and you have learned how attractions can maximise their positive impacts while keeping their negative impacts to a minimum. You have learned the difference between information and interpretation at attractions, and have examined the various interpretation techniques that can be used in natural and built attractions to enhance visitors' understanding and enjoyment. You have considered the appeal of attractions to different types of visitors, including incoming tourists, educational groups and visitors with special needs. Finally, different features that affect the appeal of attractions have been investigated. Throughout the unit you have been shown many industry examples, while the case studies on the Eden Project and Chessington World of Adventures, highlight key issues in the operation and impact of visitor attractions.

If you have worked methodically, by the end of this unit you should have:

- Examined the products and services provided by visitor attractions;
- Explored the impact of visitor attractions;
- Examined a range of techniques used for visitor interpretation;
- Investigated the appeal of visitor attractions to different types of visitor.

You are now in a position to complete the assignment for the unit, under the direction of your tutor. Before you tackle the assignment you may like to have a go at the following questions to help build your knowledge of visitor attractions.

Unit 18

Test your knowledge

1. List the five most popular charging attractions in the UK in 2002.
2. What is the difference between a 'primary' and 'ancillary' product and service at a visitor attraction?
3. What types of corporate hospitality events are staged at visitor attractions?
4. List five popular UK heritage attractions.
5. What is a World Heritage Site?
6. Name five popular UK cultural attractions.
7. Why do you think the Eden Project has been so successful since it opened in 2001?
8. What aspects of security must attraction operators pay particular attention to?
9. What is a 'virtual queue'?.
10. List the four main categories of impacts of visitor attractions and give one positive and one negative example of each.
11. Describe three ways in which a visitor attraction can minimise its negative impacts on the local environment and community.
12. What are the key points to bear in mind when deciding which interpretation techniques to select for a visitor attraction?
13. What interpretation techniques are particularly suitable for visitors with special needs?
14. What are the key features of an attraction that make it appealing to visitors?
15. How does seasonality affect the type of visitors to an attraction?

UNIT 18 ASSIGNMENT: Visitor attractions

Introduction

This assignment is made up of a number of tasks which, when successfully completed, are designed to give you sufficient evidence to meet the Pass (P), Merit (M) and Distinction (D) grading criteria for the unit. If you have carried out the activities and read the case studies throughout this unit, you will already have done a lot of work towards completing the tasks for this assignment.

Scenario

Your uncle Jim works for a consultancy firm that specialises in advising governments in the new European Union (EU) member states on tourism projects. Three of the Baltic countries that have recently joined the EU – Latvia, Lithuania and Estonia – are planning to join forces to develop and promote new tourist attractions in their countries. Your uncle is heading the project to advise the countries and has invited you to help him over the summer.

Unit 18

The project focuses on four main areas:

1. The products and services provided by visitor attractions;
2. Impacts of visitor attractions;
3. Interpretation techniques used by visitor attractions;
4. The appeal of visitor attractions to different types of visitors.

He wants you to complete the following four tasks. You can use the same three examples of visitor attractions in different tasks or choose different examples each time.

Task 1

Produce three case studies that describe the products and services provided by three different visitor attractions.

This task is designed to produce evidence for P1.

Task 2

Produce a written report in which you should:

(a) Describe the impacts of a visitor attraction on the local environment and community;

(b) Explain how three different visitor attractions have minimised negative impacts and maximised positive impacts on a local community and environment;

(c) Suggest strategies to maximise positive and minimise negative impacts of a visitor attraction, justifying suggestions.

These tasks are designed to produce evidence for P2, M1 and D1.

Task 3

Prepare and deliver an illustrated presentation in which you should:

(a) Describe interpretation techniques used by three different visitor attractions;

(b) Compare and contrast a range of interpretation techniques used by three different visitor attractions.

These tasks are designed to produce evidence for P3 and M2.

Task 4

Produce a written report in which you should:

(a) Explain the appeal of three different visitor attractions to different types of visitor;

(b) Compare and contrast the appeal of three different visitor attractions to different types of visitor;

(c) Suggest how three different visitor attractions could increase their appeal to different types of visitor, justifying suggestions.

These tasks are designed to produce evidence for P4, M3 and D2.

Index

Index

Index

Index

Index